To my friends from Eric look forward to working with you — Allen Stewart

Windows Server® 2008

Hyper-V™

Windows Server® 2008 Hyper-V™
Insider's Guide to Microsoft's Hypervisor

John Kelbley

Mike Sterling

Allen Stewart

Wiley Publishing, Inc.

Acquisitions Editor: Agatha Kim

Development Editor: Stephanie Barton

Technical Editor: Arno Mihm

Production Editor: Eric Charbonneau

Copy Editor: Tiffany Taylor

Production Manager: Tim Tate

Vice President and Executive Group Publisher: Richard Swadley

Vice President and Publisher: Neil Edde

Book Designer: Judy Fung

Compositor: Craig Johnson, Happenstance Type-O-Rama

Proofreader: Kim Wimpsett

Indexer: Ted Laux

Project Coordinator, Cover: Lynsey Stanford

Cover Designer: Ryan Sneed

Cover Image: Ryan Sneed

Library of Congress Cataloging-in-Publication Data

Kelbley, John, 1967-
  Windows server 2008 Hyper-V : insiders guide to Microsoft's Hypervisor / John Kelbley, Mike Sterling, Allen Stewart. — 1st ed.
    p. cm.
  ISBN 978-0-470-44096-4 (paper/website)
  1. Microsoft Windows server Hyper-V. 2. Virtual computer systems. I. Sterling, Mike, 1977- II. Stewart, Allen, 1969- III. Title.
  QA76.9.V5K45 2009
  005.4'476—dc22
                      2009005639

10 9 8 7 6 5 4 3 2

Dear Reader,

Thank you for choosing *Windows Server 2008 Hyper-V: Insider's Guide to Microsoft's Hypervisor*. This book is part of a family of premium-quality Sybex books, all of which are written by outstanding authors who combine practical experience with a gift for teaching.

Sybex was founded in 1976. More than thirty years later, we're still committed to producing consistently exceptional books. With each of our titles we're working hard to set a new standard for the industry. From the paper we print on to the authors we work with, our goal is to bring you the best books available.

I hope you see all that reflected in these pages. I'd be very interested to hear your comments and get your feedback on how we're doing. Feel free to let me know what you think about this or any other Sybex book by sending me an email at nedde@wiley.com, or if you think you've found a technical error in this book, please visit http://sybex.custhelp.com. Customer feedback is critical to our efforts at Sybex.

Best regards,

Neil Edde
Vice President and Publisher
Sybex, an Imprint of Wiley

Acknowledgments

Writing a book about a new technology is a complex task, and like most such labors, it has been a team effort. As the front cover notes, this book has (at least) three authors, with contributions from many others. Sincere thanks go out to my co-writers and their families (who suffered much like mine!). Dividing the book into separate sections allowed us to, we hope, produce a better book more quickly than any one of us could have on our own. Writing a book sounds like a great idea before you start (and it is), but it takes far longer to complete and requires a great deal more effort than I ever would have imagined. My wife, Sylvia, and my sons, Andrew and Alexander, have been more than patient with me this last year while I put off other commitments and borrowed computer capacity from the infrastructure at home.

Many co-workers and friends helped out (including many members of the Virtualization Nation), but I am most grateful for the feedback from the technical titans who were willing to read, critique, or contribute to my chapters (Arno Mihm, Alexander Lash, James O'Neill, Ben Herman, Alex Kibkalo, and Matt Lavallee). The dialogues with James and Ben in particular on the scripting chapters were great for the book (and for me), with my regret being that we didn't write an entire book about Hyper-V scripting. There just isn't enough space in two chapters for all the suggestions from James, Ben, and Alex.

Thanks to the patient, professional editors (Agatha Kim, Stephanie Barton, and Eric Charbonneau) and others at Wiley who turned our ideas, sentences, and cocktail-napkin class diagrams into things more intelligible. The editorial process is still largely a mystery to me—a testament to the quality of their work!

—*John Kelbley*

When I sat down with John for dinner in Houston, I had no idea what I was getting myself into. "Hey Mike, want to help me write a book?" After a couple glasses of wine, he had convinced me that writing a book was a great idea. Now that the book is complete, I can heartily agree.

Having worked with virtualization since the beginnings of Virtual PC for the Macintosh, I've seen huge advancements made with the usage of virtualization. No longer is it just a fun tool for your friends on your Mac—we've moved on to server virtualization and even more wide-scale adoption of what was previously a niche technology. This book is a way for me to try to get some of the information that has sat in my head for the last 10 years onto paper.

No acknowledgments section would be complete without a list of people I need to thank. First and foremost, I need to thank my wife, Nancy, and my son, Maxwell—the reason I had enough time to write my portions of the book. Thank you for supporting me through the late nights that were necessary to get this done. My co-authors, John and Allen, were immensely helpful in making sure we covered everything. Our technical reviewers, Arno and James, did a great job of keeping us honest. Last, I need to thank the editorial staff—Agatha, Stephanie, and Eric—who have done an exceptional job of taking our words and crafting them into something that people want to read.

—*Mike Sterling*

Hmm, what did I get myself into? I thought, as I was writing at 3 a.m. on a cold wintery morning. Just kidding. I am super-excited to write about virtualization technology, a disruptive technology that will affect information technology for years to come. We have only started to scratch the surface and discover the many ways we'll use virtualization technology. This is the first salvo into what is and will become a common technology in any company's IT infrastructure. The more I work with enterprise customers that are pushing the scenarios and use cases for virtualization, the more the virtualization vision expands.

I would like to thank my parents—most of all my mother, Bernice, for instilling in me the importance of hard work, an anything-is-possible approach to life, and a glass-is-always-half-full attitude. To my little girl, Allana, thanks for giving Daddy the extra push I need: thanks, Bear. To my sisters Joyce, Brenda and my nieces, thanks for not bothering me when I had to write (just kidding—love you guys). To my brother Dwayne, thanks for putting up with an absent brother—love you, man. To my other family members—Les, Cheryl, and Donna—thanks for the support. My co-authors, John and Mike: you guys rock!! Jason Buffington, DPM expert: thanks for the DPM chapter; you're the man. Thanks for the technical review, Arno. Thanks to Iain, Ram, and Chris for making working in the Windows Server Group the best job a guy could have. The editorial staff has super-human patience and skill; I would like to thank Agatha, Stephanie, and Eric, who've done an exceptional job, and we could not have done it without them.

—*Allen Stewart*

About the Authors

John Kelbley is a senior technical product manager with Microsoft's Platform Tech Strategy team based in the Northeastern United States. He joined Microsoft in 2002 after working at a number of large enterprises as a management consultant, IT manager, and infrastructure architect. John has more than 20 years of computing industry experience with a focus on infrastructure architecture. This is the first book he has authored since leaving grade school.

Mike Sterling is a program manager in the Windows Server team at Microsoft, focused exclusively on virtualization. Prior to this role, Mike spent 10 years in software testing, working on products such as Virtual PC, Virtual Server, and Hyper-V. When he's not working, he can be found playing World of Warcraft or out taking photographs.

Allen Stewart is a principal program manager lead in the Windows Server group at Microsoft. Allen focuses on virtualization technologies such as hardware virtualization, virtualization management, and application virtualization. Allen has more than 15 years of IT experience in the transportation, financial services, and software industries. He has held various positions as a senior systems programmer, systems architect, and systems consultant. Allen is a Microsoft certified architect, and he is on the board of directors of the Microsoft Certified Architect Program. When not playing with his little girl, Allana, or exploring new technology on his home systems, he loves to play basketball (he could probably beat President Obama in a pickup game...you hear that, Mr. President?).

Jason Buffington has been working in the networking industry since 1989, with a majority of that time being focused on data protection. He has spoken around the world at large technology events and been published in several periodicals. With more than 18 years of storage/backup experience, Jason is currently the senior technical product manager for Microsoft Storage Solutions, with a special focus on Data Protection Manager. He has previously held roles with Double-Take, Cheyenne (CA) ARCserve, and various systems integrators. Jason telecommutes from Dallas, Texas, where he is happily married to Anita for 16 years and is the proud father of three great kids—Joshua, Jaden and Jordan. He can be reached at JasonBuffington.com.

Contents at a Glance

Contents

Foreword

What's old is new again. In the case of virtualization, truer words have never been spoken. In the past few years, virtualization—a technology commonplace for decades on mainframe systems—has made its way to commodity x86/x64 systems, and its renaissance is changing the way companies do business. Virtualization is a hot technology for many reasons; and if you haven't considered virtualization, there's no better time than the present. As is the case with most burgeoning technologies, a lot of confusion exists in the marketplace, starting with the term itself.

Virtualization is one of the most overloaded terms in the recent past. In the most generic sense, it simply means the abstraction of resources. The most popular type of virtualization is machine virtualization, where a virtual machine is presented in software with its own virtual hardware and abstracted from the underlying physical hardware. This allows most x86 workloads to run unmodified within virtual machines, isolated from other workloads, and opens up new ways to deploy and manage software.

Adoption of virtualization is accelerating due to the confluence of three main factors:

♦ The mainstream adoption of 64-bit (x64) hardware that provides the memory capabilities needed to run multiple workloads concurrently

♦ The rise of multi-core processors with built-in virtualization hardware assists

♦ Increased competition, resulting in prices that are dramatically lower (if not free) for high performance, hypervisor-based virtualization

From a benefits standpoint, virtualization offers significant advantages in terms of greater system utilization, lower power consumption, reduced datacenter footprint, ease of deployment, and overall flexibility. You can do more with less, do it more cheaply, and do it faster with more flexibility.

Does this sound too good to be true? Are you skeptical? I hope so.

It's easy to be swept up in the hype and cut corners in planning and research, resulting in a less-than-optimal experience. Too often, we've run into people who have heard about the benefits of virtualization but who don't understand how it changes other IT aspects such as system and application monitoring, high availability, patch management, backups, and security. Like any disruptive technology, virtualization can provide solutions to many problems but also introduce new challenges. This book is a great way to avoid any pitfalls.

At Microsoft, we listen closely to our customers. One consistent message from is that they want high-performance, easy-to-use, hypervisor-based virtualization. Not a technology that only the high-end enterprises with deep pocketbooks can afford. We agree. With all the benefits that virtualization provides, we want to make this technology available to everyone, whether you're a small business, in a branch office, or a global Fortune 500 company. Toward that end, we're pleased to offer Hyper-V both as a role included with Windows Server 2008 and as a free standalone product, Microsoft Hyper-V Server 2008.

Since the Hyper-V release, customer reaction has been overwhelmingly positive, resulting in over 600,000 downloads of Hyper-V technology in just over the first six months of its release. Within Microsoft, Hyper-V has been extensively deployed throughout the company; thousands of Hyper-V virtual machines run a substantial portion of our day-to-day production infrastructure. In addition, if you've been to a Microsoft Web site, you've most likely interacted with a Hyper-V virtual machine. Why? Because some of Microsoft's largest Internet sites including TechNet, MSDN (both receive a few million hits *per day*), and Microsoft.com (*more than a billion hits per month*) are hosted with Hyper-V. These examples demonstrate the performance, scalable, and reliability that Hyper-V has to offer while running some of the largest Internet properties on the planet.

If you're not employing virtualization today—if you haven't tried Hyper-V yet—I strongly urge you to do so with this book in hand. There's never been a better time to get started, and we have a long roadmap ahead.

—*Jeffrey Woolsey*
  Principal Group Program Manager, Microsoft Virtualization

Introduction

Welcome to the best book we've ever written about Microsoft's hypervisor technology: Hyper-V! Hyper-V is a foundational virtualization technology released in 2008 by Microsoft, and this book is intended to be a resource for systems administrators looking to use it in a cost effective and efficient manner. Other books may be written about Hyper-V, but no others so far have appeared on the landscape written by those who helped shape or support the product.

The book is meant to cover the essentials of using Hyper-V, giving you the information necessary to get up and running quickly. The book includes technical depth (some not found anywhere else), but it isn't intended as a comprehensive guide to all aspects of Hyper-V.

What Is Virtualization?

At its simplest, *virtualization* is the abstraction of computing from computers. Separating software from hardware isn't a new concept. Administrators have done it for many years on all sorts of platforms. Nearly any system or system component can be somehow pulled away or separated from the hardware or software on which it depends. In Windows-centric environments, complete operating system instances can be virtualized using Hyper-V, Virtual Server, and Virtual PC. Windows systems can also be virtualized with products from other companies, including VMware. This full-system virtualization is only one type of computing abstraction.

Virtualization can happen at nearly any computing boundary within a system. The broad definition and interpretation of virtualization has led to a virtualization frenzy in all forms. It seems as if every software and hardware company has a virtualization offering of some kind. For good or for bad, the word *virtualization* has been tagged onto products and solutions across the computing industry. It sounds like virtualization is the *next great thing* in computing. It's already here, so it actually *was* the next great thing! In all its present forms, virtualization is providing value to enterprises and individuals and has been doing so for some time.

Microsoft's Approach to Virtualization

Some software companies address virtualization from a single direction. VMware, for example, focuses on virtualizing and managing operating-system instances. Microsoft has been more thoughtful and less myopic in its approach. Microsoft's articulated virtualization direction is in five key areas:

- *Server*—Hyper-V and Virtual Server 2005 for server services

- *Desktop*—Virtual PC for client-centric, local operating-system instances

♦ *Presentation*—Terminal Services providing remote desktop and application access

♦ *Application*—SoftGrid/AppV for application encapsulation

♦ *Profile*—Roaming profiles for personal-experience encapsulation

All these approaches are tied together by Windows as a platform and managed by the System Center family of products to enable administration of virtual and physical resources.

You can benefit from this multipronged approach to virtualization, which is unified by a common platform and management suite.

It's All Windows

The great thing about virtualization technology from Microsoft is that it's integrated with Windows. Windows is a platform well known to administrators and users alike. You don't need special training to use Microsoft's virtualization offerings because they're already familiar. You don't need to be a virtualization specialist to use Hyper-V, Terminal Services, or AppV (as you might with VMware). You can have virtualization as a competency, just as you might with other focus areas of Windows administration.

System Center Manages All Worlds Well

You manage and monitor each of these virtualization offerings with the same System Center tools that you may already have in your environment for physical system management. Some virtualization-management tools only provide insight into the virtualization layer and can't dive further into running operating systems or applications (they're essentially half blind). Using a unified, familiar tool set that can correlate data between physical, virtual, and application software can magnify the benefits of virtualization.

Mixing and Matching with Virtualization

You can use these separate directions of virtualization together with the others to provide more value. You can combine the different focuses of virtualization—server, desktop, presentation, application, and profile—to meet the needs and requirements of changing enterprises. Why not rapidly provision Hyper-V–based virtual machines for thin-client access to meet dynamic demands? How about combining AppV with Terminal Services to alleviate application coexistence issues and reduce server count?

Where Hyper-V Fits

Hyper-V is Microsoft's efficient hypervisor that enables operating-system virtualization in a server environment. Hyper-V is a core technology pillar of Microsoft's virtualization strategy and the focus of this book. It's an installable feature of Window Server 2008 and is available as a no-cost download as Hyper-V Server. Even with other virtualization solutions already installed, Hyper-V can be part of any contemporary Windows Server infrastructure, based on availability and price.

Why We Wrote This Book

Just before the release of Hyper-V, we realized there were few books on the horizon addressing this important and industry-altering technology. We agreed that a book should be written to bring together the combined available information and knowledge we had in developing, using, and managing Hyper-V. We had all read books written by professional authors about technology and felt that the insight of those closer to the product (not professional authors) could serve the needs of administrators well.

Who Should Read This Book

Everyone and anyone interested in understanding Hyper-V and how to use it should read this book. We developed the content specifically for Windows administrators. IT professionals with some experience using Windows Server 2003 or Windows Server 2008 will get the most out of the book. Some chapters are more technical than others, but notes, tips, and pointers to necessary resources are included to make every (aspiring server administrator) reader productive.

Readers are expected to be familiar with Windows and have some experience with and understanding of Windows Server 2008. You don't need extensive server-administration experience to benefit from the book, only a desire to learn more about Hyper-V and how to use it.

How the Book Is Organized

The book is organized and written with a crawl, walk, run philosophy. We'll introduce you to server virtualization and Hyper-V administration and then lead you along to expose you to enterprise management concepts and tools for virtualization. We've purposely organized the book into three distinct sections to address separate levels of interest and to provide you with three different perspectives on Hyper-V. Each section of the book is written by a different author who has specialized knowledge and expertise in that area.

The first section (Chapters 1 through 5), or the *crawling* section, is geared toward making you productive with Hyper-V as quickly as possible. These chapters are focused on introducing Hyper-V, setting it up, and running virtual hosts in an efficient and secure manner using little more than the Hyper-V console:

Chapter 1: Introduction to Hyper-V

Chapter 2: Installing Hyper-V and Server Core

Chapter 3: Configuring Hyper-V

Chapter 4: Virtualization Best Practices

Chapter 5: Hyper-V Security

The second, *walking* section (Chapters 6 through 10) builds on knowledge from the earlier chapters. The middle of the book dives into more advanced manual administration tasks and concepts. Here we wade into complicated and necessary topics including virtual machine migration, backup and recovery, failover clustering, and automation through scripting. We show you how to handle advanced administration tasks manually or through custom automation:

Chapter 6: Virtual Machine Migration

Chapter 7: Backup and Recovery

Chapter 8: High Availability

Chapter 9: Understanding WMI, Scripting, and Hyper-V

Chapter 10: Automating Tasks

The final section of the book (Chapters 11 through 13) is the *running* or *soaring with eagles* part of the book. These chapters introduce you to the most effective way to manage an enterprise virtualization environment with several members of the Microsoft System Center family of products. One chapter is devoted to each of three products that are commonly used for server virtualization management (Operations Manager, Virtual Machine Manager, and Data Protection Manager):

Chapter 11: System Center Virtual Machine Manager 2008

Chapter 12: Protecting Virtualized Environments with System Center Data Protection Manager

Chapter 13: System Center Operations Manager 2007

Final Thoughts

The best way to learn about Hyper-V is to be hands-on with it. If you can, take some time to load Windows Server 2008 with Hyper-V on a capable system. This book provides lots of great tips and tricks for using Hyper-V, and trying them firsthand is a great way to develop your understanding and expertise.

Inexpensive systems available today include hardware-assisted virtualization support (as well as x64 support) and make serviceable Hyper-V test systems. You don't even need new systems for Hyper-V—just a host with Intel VT or AMD-V support. Many of the examples in the book were developed and tested on laptops and desktop systems more than two years old. An older desktop or laptop may not be in any way suitable for production use with Hyper-V, but it can be perfect for you to build a better understanding of this important and useful virtualization technology.

Chapter 1

Introduction to Hyper-V

With the release of Windows Server 2008, Microsoft has included a built-in virtualization solution, Hyper-V. Hyper-V is a role of Windows Server 2008 that lets administrators create multiple virtual machines. A *virtual machine* is a separate, isolated environment that runs its own operating system and applications.

Virtual machine technology isn't new—it's been available from Microsoft in both Virtual PC and Virtual Server since late 2003 and from other vendors since the 1970s. By including it in the operating system, Microsoft has made an extremely feature-rich product available at no extra cost.

Hyper-V takes the concept of virtualization to the mainstream IT environment by including it in the operating system. Previous Microsoft virtualization solutions ran on top of the operating system—a significant difference from the way Hyper-V is designed. Inclusion in the operating system also provides a seamless management experience when paired with the System Center family of products.

In this chapter, we'll review the following elements of Hyper-V:

- Key scenarios for Hyper-V
- Hyper-V architecture
- Hyper-V features
- Hardware and software requirements

Scenarios for Hyper-V

Hyper-V was developed with a several key scenarios in mind. When Microsoft started developing Hyper-V, the development team spent a great deal of time meeting with customers who were using virtualization—small businesses, consultants who implement virtualization on behalf of their customers, and large companies with multimillion dollar IT budgets. The following key scenarios were developed as a result of those meetings; they represent customer needs, demands, and wants.

Server Consolidation

Systems are becoming increasingly powerful. A couple of years ago, it was rare to find a quad-processor server at a price most customers could afford. Now, with major processor manufacturers providing multicore functionality, servers have more and more processing power. Multicore technology combines multiple processor cores onto a single die—enabling a single physical processor to run multiple threads of execution on separate cores. Virtualization and multicore technology work great together: If you're combining multiple workloads onto a single server, you need to have as much processing power as possible. Multicore processors help provide the optimal platform for virtualization.

Businesses are increasingly likely to need multiple systems for a particular workload. Some workloads are incredibly complex, requiring multiple systems but not necessarily using all the power of the hardware. By taking advantage of virtualization, system administrators can provide a virtualized solution that better utilizes the host hardware—thus allowing administrators to get more out of their expenditure.

Workloads aren't the only driving item behind virtualization. The power and cooling requirements of modern servers are also key driving factors. A fully loaded rack of servers can put out a significant amount of heat. (If you've ever stood behind one, you're sure to agree—it's a great place to warm up if you've been working in a cold server room.) All that heat has to come from somewhere. The rack requires significant power.

But for companies in high-rise buildings in the middle of major cities, getting additional power is incredibly difficult, if not impossible. In many cases, the buildings weren't designed to have that much power coming in—and the companies can't add more power without extensive retrofitting. By deploying virtualization, more workloads can be run on the same number of servers.

Testing and Development

For people working in a test or development role, virtualization is a key to being more productive. The ability to have a number of different virtual machines (VMs), each with its own operating system that's ready to go at the click of a mouse, is a huge time-saver. Simply start up whichever VM has the operating system. You no longer need to install a clean operating system. Also, by using the snapshot functionality, users can quickly move between known states in the VM.

With Hyper-V's rich Windows Management Interface (WMI) interfaces, testing can be started automatically. By scripting both Hyper-V and the operating system to be tested, testers can run a script that starts the VM, installs the latest build, and performs the necessary tests against it.

A Hyper-V virtual machine is also portable. A tester can work in the VM; if an issue is found, the tester can save the state of the VM (including the memory contents and processor state) and transfer it to the developer, who can restore the state at their convenience. Because the state of the VM is saved, the developer sees exactly what the tester saw.

Business Continuity and Disaster Recovery

Business continuity is the ability to keep mission-critical infrastructure up and running. Hyper-V provides two important features that enable business continuity: live backup and quick migration.

Live backup uses Microsoft Volume Shadow Services functionality to make a backup of the entire system without incurring any downtime, as well as provide a backup of the VM at a known good point in time. The system backup includes the state of all the running VMs. When a backup request comes from the host, Hyper-V is notified, and all the VMs running on that host are placed into a state where they can be backed up without affecting current activity; they can then be restored at a later time.

Quick migration is the ability to move a VM from one host to another in a cluster using Microsoft Failover Cluster functionality. During a quick migration, you save the state of the VM, move storage connectivity from the source host to the target host, and then restore the state of the VM. Windows Server 2008 added support for the virtual-machine resource type to the Failover Clustering tool, enabling you to make a VM highly available using functionality included with the operating system. For more information about both of these features of Hyper-V, refer to Chapter 7, "Backup and Recovery."

Disaster recovery is becoming a requirement for increasing numbers of businesses. With natural disasters such as Hurricane Katrina fresh in the minds of system administrators, enterprises are seeking ways to keep their businesses running throughout such events. You must consider more than just big disasters, though—small disasters or even simple configuration issues can lead to a mission-critical service being unavailable. Hyper-V includes support for geographically dispersed clusters (a new feature of Windows Server 2008).

Dynamic IT

Microsoft's idea of a dynamic IT infrastructure involves self-managing dynamic systems—systems that adjust automatically to the workload they're running. By using Hyper-V in conjunction with the systems-management functionality present in the System Center family of products, enterprises can take advantage of the benefits of virtualization to meet the demands of a rapidly changing environment.

Now that we've covered Hyper-V's key targeted scenarios, let's review the architecture of Hyper-V to see how Microsoft has implemented support for them.

Architecture

Before we examine the architecture of Windows Server 2008 with the Hyper-V role, it's useful to understand how Windows Server 2008 works without this role.

As shown in Figure 1.1, Windows Server 2008 operates in both kernel mode and user mode. Kernel mode (also known as Ring 0) is where the Windows kernel lives, as well as all the device drivers for the hardware installed in the system. User mode (Ring 3) is where applications are run. This ring separation is a key feature of the x86 architecture—it means that a rogue application shouldn't be able to take down the operating system.

A default installation of Windows Server 2008 doesn't include any active roles or features. Windows Server 2008 was designed to be as secure as possible. As part of the development process, Microsoft worked with and received feedback from many users about how they deploy servers. A frequent customer request was an easy way to deploy a server to perform a particular task—for example, a file server or print server. That's where the concept of a role or feature came into play.

Now that you understand the meaning of roles and features in Windows Server 2008, let's talk about the Hyper-V role. We'll cover installation of the role in Chapter 2, "Installing Hyper-V and Server Core."

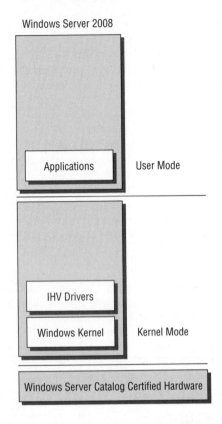

FIGURE 1.1
Simplified architecture for a clean install of Windows Server 2008

Figure 1.2 shows that once the role is installed, some pretty significant changes happen to the installed copy of Windows Server 2008.

A *role* in Windows Server 2008 is a task for the server, whereas a *feature* can (and often does) supplement a role. A great example of this role/feature distinction is a web server. IIS functionality is a role of Windows Server 2008, and features that go hand in hand with IIS include Network Load Balancing and Windows PowerShell. Each of those features can be installed on an as-needed basis.

Looks quite a bit different, doesn't it? Let's break down each of the changes.

Parent Partition

The installation of Windows is now running on top of the Windows hypervisor, which we'll describe later. One of the side effects of running on top of the hypervisor is that the installation is technically a VM. We'll refer to this as the *parent partition*.

The parent partition has two special features:

- It contains all the hardware device drivers, as well as supporting files, for the other VMs. We'll look at the functions of each of those drivers later in the chapter.

- It has direct access to all the hardware in the system. In conjunction with the virtualization service providers, the parent partition executes I/O requests on behalf of the VM—sending disk traffic out over a fibre channel controller, for example.

FIGURE 1.2
Simplified architecture for Windows Server 2008 with the Hyper-V role added

The following best practices provide a secure and stable parent partition, which is critical to the VMs running on the host:

♦ Don't run any other applications or services in the parent partition. This may seem like basic knowledge for system administrators, but it's especially crucial when you're running multiple VMs. In addition to possibly decreasing stability, running multiple roles, features, or applications in the parent partition limits the amount of resources that can otherwise be allocated to VMs.

♦ Use Windows Server 2008 in the Core role as the parent partition. We'll discuss Windows Server Core in Chapter 2.

WINDOWS HYPERVISOR

The Windows hypervisor is the basis for Hyper-V. At its heart, the hypervisor has only a few simple tasks: creating and tearing down partitions. (A partition is also known as the basis for a VM) and ensuring strong separation between the partitions. It doesn't sound like much, but the hypervisor is one of the most critical portions of Hyper-V. That's why development of the hypervisor followed the Microsoft Security Design Lifecycle process so closely—if the hypervisor is compromised, the entire system can be taken over, because the hypervisor runs in the most privileged mode offered by the x86 architecture.

One of Microsoft's design goals was to make the Microsoft hypervisor as small as possible. Doing so offered two advantages:

◆ The Trusted Computing Base (TCB) is smaller. The TCB is the sum of all the parts of the system that are critical to security. Ensuring that the hypervisor is small reduces its potential attack vectors.

◆ The hypervisor imparts less overhead on the system. Because all VMs (as well as the parent partition) are running on top of the hypervisor, performance becomes a concern. The goal is to minimize the hypervisor's overhead.

KERNEL-MODE DRIVERS

A Windows kernel-mode driver is one of two types of drivers in Windows. Kernel-mode drivers execute in Ring 0. Because this type of driver is executing in kernel mode, it's crucial that these drivers be as secure as possible: An insecure driver, or a crash in the driver, can compromise the entire system.

Hyper-V adds two kernel-mode drivers:

VMBus   VMBus is a high-speed in-memory bus that was developed for Hyper-V. VMBus acts as the bus for all I/O traffic that takes place between the VMs and the parent partition. VMBus works closely with the virtualization service provider and virtualization service client, which we'll describe later in this chapter.

Virtualization Service Provider (VSP)   The Virtualization Service Provider (VSP) enables VMs to securely share the underlying physical hardware by initiating I/O on behalf of all VMs running on the system. It works in conjunction with the hardware vendor drivers in the parent partition—which means that no special "virtualization" drivers are necessary. If a driver is certified for Windows Server 2008, it should work as expected with Hyper-V. Each class of device has a VSP present—for example, a default installation of Hyper-V has a networking VSP as well as a storage VSP. The VSPs communicate with the matching Virtualization Service Client (VSC) that runs in the VM over VMBus. We'll cover the VSC when we look at the different types of VMs.

USER-MODE APPLICATIONS

User-mode applications are, strangely enough, applications that run in user mode. They execute in Ring 3, which is where all unprivileged instructions are run. Many of the applications that run in Windows are user-mode applications—for example, the copy of Notepad that you use to look at a text file is executing in user mode.

Hyper-V has a number of different user-mode applications:

Virtual Machine Management Service (VMMS)   The VMMS acts as the single point of interaction for all incoming management requests. It interacts with a number of processes, two of which we'll refer to here.

WMI providers   Hyper-V has a rich set of WMI interfaces. They provide a way to manage the state and health of the VMs as well as get settings information and some performance information. All the WMI interfaces are fully documented on http://msdn.microsoft.com.

Worker processes   When a VM is started up, a worker process is created. The worker process represents the actions that are taking place in the virtual processor, as well as all emulated devices and the virtual motherboard. Each VM that is running on a host has a worker process.

Now that we've shown you what's happening in the parent partition, let's look at the VMs. After you create a VM and power it on, you can install a wide variety of x86/x64-based operating systems. Even though these are VMs, they can run the same operating systems without modification as a physical computer. But operating systems that are supported by Microsoft include new synthetic drivers, which work in conjunction with the matching VSP running in the parent partition.

Let's first examine how a fully emulated operating system handles I/O.

Virtual Machine

A VM can have two different types of devices: emulated and synthetic. Although synthetic devices are encouraged due to their superior performance, they aren't available for all operating systems. Emulated devices are present in Hyper-V mainly for backward compatibility with non-supported operating systems. VMs running certain distributions of Linux have synthetic device support as well. Let's examine each type of device.

EMULATED DEVICES

Emulated devices in Hyper-V exist primarily for backward compatibility with older operating systems. In an ideal world, all applications would run on the latest version of the operating system they were designed for, but that's far from reality. Many companies have systems in production that run on older copies of operating systems because one of their applications doesn't run on anything newer. An older operating system may not be supported under Hyper-V, which means it can't take advantage of the high-performance I/O. That's not a total loss, however: If you consolidate those older systems onto a newer Hyper-V host, the advantages of moving to a more up-to-date hardware platform can provide a performance boost.

Emulated devices have another key role. During the installation of the VM, operating systems don't have support for the synthetic devices that may be installed in the VM. For that reason, you must use emulated devices—otherwise, the operating-system installation can't function. For Hyper-V, it's easy to move from emulated to synthetic devices.

The emulated devices presented to a VM are chosen for their high degree of compatibility across a wide range of operating systems and in-box driver support. As you can see in Figure 1.3, the video card is based on an S3 video card, and the network card is an Intel 21140-based Ethernet adapter.

Emulated devices under Hyper-V don't perform as well as the new synthetic devices. Thanks to part of the work that was done to harden the entire virtualization stack, emulated devices execute in the worker process—specifically, in user mode in the parent partition.

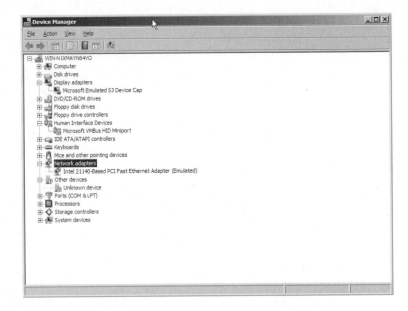

How does I/O happen with emulated devices?

Figure 1.4 goes into considerable detail about how emulated storage requests are handled. Emulated networking is handled in a similar fashion. I want to point out a few specific items:

◆ Context switches are used. A *context switch* is a switch from executing a particular processor instruction in kernel mode to user mode. When paired with virtualization, a context switch is an "expensive" operation. There's no money involved, but the CPU cost for such an operation is very high. That time could be spent doing other tasks.

◆ The path that the data packet traverses is long, especially compared to the synthetic case (which we'll review next).

◆ The path illustrated in the figure is repeated hundreds of times for a 10 kilobyte write to disk. Imagine if you're doing a large SQL transaction that involved writing hundreds of megabytes to disk, or running a popular website being served up from IIS running in the VM. You can see that it won't scale well.

SYNTHETIC DEVICE DRIVERS

Synthetic devices provide much higher performance than their emulated counterparts. By taking advantage of VMBus, synthetic devices can execute I/O transactions at a much faster rate.

Synthetic devices, such as the Microsoft Virtual Machine Bus Network Adapter shown in Figure 1.5, don't have real-world counterparts. They are purely virtual devices that function only with Hyper-V—loading the drivers on a physical system does nothing. These new synthetic devices rely on VMBus.

FIGURE 1.4
I/O for emulated
storage devices

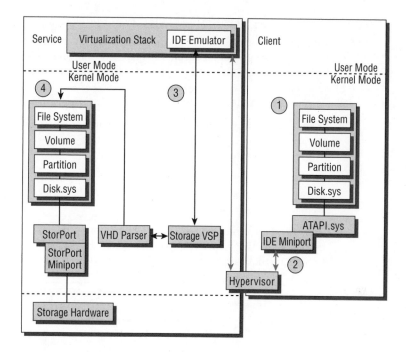

FIGURE 1.5
Device Manager
for a Windows
Server 2008 virtual
machine, showing
synthetic devices

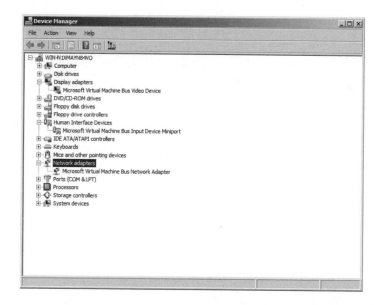

Synthetic device drivers are available only for operating systems that are supported by Microsoft. (For reference, a list of supported operating systems for Hyper-V is available at www.microsoft.com/virtualization.) If you're running an operating system in the VM that isn't supported by Microsoft, you'll need to use the emulated devices in the VM.

Much like the emulated storage request chart shown earlier in Figure 1.4, Figure 1.6 presents a lot of data. Here are a few key differences:

◆ In the beginning, the data path is similar to the emulated data path. However, the synthetic storage device in Hyper-V is a SCSI-based device—so the last driver it hits before getting put on VMBus is the StorPort driver.

◆ When a packet makes it to the miniport driver, it's put on VMBus for transport to the Storage VSP in the parent partition. Because VMBus is a kernel-mode driver, no context switches are necessary.

◆ After the data packet crosses over to the parent partition, the correct destination is determined by the VSP, which routes the packet to the correct device. In Figure 1.6, the destination is a virtual hard disk (VHD) file.

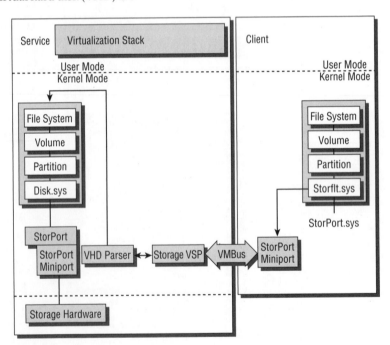

FIGURE 1.6
I/O for synthetic storage devices using VMBus

Installing Synthetic Device Drivers

It's easy to install synthetic device drivers in the VM. After you've installed the operating system, select Action ➤ Insert Integration Services Setup Disk. An installer launches and automatically installs the drivers for you. When you reboot, the VM can take advantage of the new architecture.

NOTE   A special synthetic driver deals with the boot process: Optimized Boot Performance. Because the synthetic drivers rely on VMBus, you can't boot off hard drives that are connected to the SCSI controller. All isn't lost—during the boot process, after the VMBus driver is loaded, all the IDE boot traffic is automatically routed through the same infrastructure that is used for SCSI traffic. This means the boot process and all disk traffic (reads and writes) perform at the same accelerated speed.

LINUX DEVICE DRIVERS

No, that's not a typo—certain distributions of Linux are supported under Hyper-V. Not only is the operating system supported, but a full set of device drivers also enable synthetic device support under Linux (see Figure 1.7). The drivers include the Hypercall adapter—a thin piece of software that runs in the Linux VM and increases performance by translating certain instructions to a format that Hyper-V can understand.

FIGURE 1.7
Synthetic device support under Linux

Features

Now that we've gone over both the scenarios and architecture of Hyper-V, let's dive into some of the features of Microsoft's virtualization platform:

32-bit (x86) and 64-bit (x64) VMs   Hyper-V provides support for both 32-bit as well as 64-bit VMs. This lets users provision both architectures on the same platform, easing the transition to 64-bit and providing legacy 32-bit operating systems.

Large memory support (64 GB) within VMs   With support for up to 64 GB of RAM, Hyper-V scales out to run the vast majority of enterprise-class workloads. Hyper-V can also use up to a total of 1 terabyte (TB) of RAM on the host.

SMP virtual machines   Symmetric Multi Processor (SMP) support allows VMs to recognize and utilize four virtual processors. As a result, server applications running in a Hyper-V VM take full advantage of the host system's processing power.

Integrated cluster support for quick migration and high availability (HA)   Windows Server 2008 Hyper-V and HA go hand in hand. As we'll discuss later in the book (see Chapter 8, "High Availability"), it's easy to create a failover cluster of VM hosts that your VMs can live on. After you set up the failover cluster, you can quickly and easily move a VM from one host to the other from the Failover Cluster Manager or from other management tools (such as System Center Virtual Machine Manager).

Volume Shadow Service integration for data protection   Hyper-V includes a Volume Shadow Services (VSS) provider. As we discussed earlier, in the list of scenarios, VSS lets backup applications prepare the system for a backup without requiring the applications (or VMs) to be shut down.

Pass-through high-performance disk access for VMs   When a physical volume is connected directly to the VM, disk I/O–intensive workloads can perform at their peak. If the Windows Server 2008 system can see the volume in the Disk Management control panel, the volume can be passed through to the VM.

Although you'll see faster performance with pass-through disk access, certain features (such as snapshots, differencing disks, and host-side backup) that you get from using a VHD file aren't available with pass-through disks.

VM snapshots   Snapshots let administrators capture a point in time for the VM (including state, data, and configuration). You can then roll back to that snapshot at a later point in time or split from that snapshot to go down a different path. The snapshot is a key feature for the test and development scenario, because it lets users easily maintain separate points in time. For example, a user may install an operating system inside a VM and take a snapshot. The user can perform a number of tasks and then take a second snapshot. Then, the user can return to either of those snapshots later, saving configuration time and effort.

New hardware-sharing architecture (VSP/VSC/VMBus)   By using the new VMBus communication protocol for all virtual devices, Hyper-V can provide higher levels of performance than were previously seen with Microsoft virtualization products.

Robust networking: VLANs and NLB   Virtual Local Area Network (VLAN) tagging—also referred to as the IEEE standard 802.1q—provides a secure method for multiple networks to use the same physical media. Hyper-V supports VLAN tagging (802.1q) on the virtual network interfaces and specifies a VLAN tag for the network interface.

Network Load Balancing (NLB) support in Hyper-V allows VMs to participate in an NLB cluster. An NLB cluster is different from a failover cluster, such as those used for VM quick migration. NLB clusters are configured with front-end nodes that handle all incoming traffic and route it to multiple servers on the back-end.

DMTF standard for WMI management interface   The Distributed Management Task Force (DMTF) is a standards body that provides a uniform set of standards for the management of IT environments. Microsoft has worked closely with the DMTF to ensure that all the management interfaces for Hyper-V adhere to the standards, allowing management tools from multiple vendors to manage the system.

Support for full or Server Core installations   Hyper-V can run on a full installation of Windows Server 2008 as well as the Server Core option. We'll discuss Server Core in more depth later.

Now that we've gone through the list of Hyper-V features, let's look at the system requirements.

ADVANTAGES OVER VIRTUAL SERVER

Windows Server 2008 Hyper-V has a number of advantages over Virtual Server 2005 R2 SP1:

◆ Support for SMP and 64-bit VMs. Virtual Server was limited to 32-bit uni-processor virtual machines.

◆ Support for more than 3.6 GB of RAM per VM.

◆ Support for mapping a logical unit number (LUN) directly to a VM.

◆ Increased performance from VSP/VSC architecture.

◆ Hyper-V management via a MMC-based interface instead of the web-based console.

However, it's impossible for users who have only 32-bit hardware in their environment to move to Hyper-V (because it's a feature of the 64-bit version of Windows Server 2008).

Requirements

Because Hyper-V is included as a role of Windows Server 2008 x64 Edition, it inherits the same hardware requirements. However, a few areas require special attention for Hyper-V.

Hardware Requirements

Some of the requirements for Hyper-V are hard requirements, such as the type of processor, whereas others are best practices to ensure that Hyper-V performs optimally.

PROCESSOR

Hyper-V requires a 64-bit capable processor with two separate extensions: hardware-assisted virtualization and data-execution prevention.

Hardware-assisted virtualization is given a different name by each vendor—Intel calls it Virtualization Technology (VT), and AMD calls it AMD Virtualization (AMD-V). Almost all processors now ship with those features present, but check with your processor manufacturer to make sure.

Although the functionality is required in the processor, it's also required to be enabled in the BIOS. Each system manufacturer has a different way of exposing the functionality, as well as a different name for it. However, most, if not all, manufacturers provide a way to enable or disable it in the BIOS. You can enable it in the BIOS, but some systems don't enable the feature unless there's a hard-power cycle—shutting off the system completely, for example. *We recommend that the system be completely powered off.*

Data-execution prevention (DEP) goes by different names depending on the processor manufacturer—on the Intel platform, it's called eXecute Disable (XD); and AMD refers to it as No eXecute (NX). DEP helps protect your system against malware and improperly written programs by monitoring memory reads and writes to ensure that memory pages marked as *Data* aren't executed. Because you'll be running multiple VMs on a single system, ensuring stability of the hosting system is crucial.

STORAGE

As we talked about earlier, Hyper-V's architecture lets you use standard Windows device drivers in conjunction with the VSP/VSC architecture. As such, any of the storage devices listed in the Windows Server Catalog will work with Hyper-V. These include SCSI, SAS, fibre channel, and iSCSI—if there's a driver for it, Hyper-V can use it. Of course, you'll want to take some considerations into account when planning the ideal Hyper-V host. We'll talk about those more in Chapter 10, "Automating Common Tasks."

Here are some of the areas where extra attention is necessary:

Multiple spindles and I/O paths   Most disk-intensive workloads, such as database servers, need multiple spindles to achieve high performance. Hyper-V's storage architecture enables those workloads to be virtualized without the traditional performance penalty. When multiple disk-intensive workloads share the same disk infrastructure, they can quickly slow to a crawl.

Having multiple disks (as well as multiple I/O paths) is highly recommended for disk-intensive workloads. Even two workloads sharing a host bus adapter with a single fibre channel can saturate the controller, leading to decreased performance. Having multiple controllers also can provide redundancy for critical workloads.

Disk configurations for optimal performance   Hyper-V has a number of different ways to store the VM's data, each with its own pros and cons:

◆ Pass-through disks:

 ◆ Pros: Pass-through disks generally provide the highest performance. The VM writes directly to the disk volume without any intermediate layer, so you can see near-native levels of performance.

 ◆ Cons: Maintaining the storage volumes for each VM can be extremely challenging, especially for large enterprise deployments.

- Fixed virtual hard disks:

  - Pros: These are the best choice for production environments using VHD files. Because you allocate all the disk space when you create the VHD file, you don't see the expansion penalty that occurs with the dynamically expanding VHD.

  - Cons: Because all the space for the VHD is allocated at creation, the VHD file can be large.

- Dynamic virtual hard disks:

  - Pros: A dynamically expanding VHD expands on demand, saving space on the system until it's needed. Disks can remain small.

  - Cons: There is a small performance penalty when a disk is expanded. If large amounts of data are being written, the disk will need to be expanded multiple times.

Snapshots   Snapshots are extremely useful in the test and development environment. However, what can be helpful in one environment can be harmful in another. You shouldn't use snapshots in a production environment because rolling back to a previous state without taking the proper precautions can mean data loss!

Networking

Much like storage, networking with Hyper-V inherits the rich driver support of Windows Server 2008. Many of the caveats for storage apply to networking as well—ensure that multiple NICs are present so a single interface doesn't become the bottleneck.

The following list identifies areas where you should pay special attention with networking:

- Hyper-V supports Ethernet network adapters, including 10, 100, 1000, and even 10Gb-E network adapters. Hyper-V can't use ATM or Token Ring adapters, nor can it use wireless (802.11) adapters to provide network access to the VMs.

- During the Hyper-V role installation (which we'll cover in Chapter 2), you can create a virtual network for each network adapter in your system.

- We recommend that you set aside a single NIC to manage the host. That NIC shouldn't be used for any VMs (no virtual switch should be associated with it). Alternatively, you can use out-of-band management tools to manage the host. Such tools typically use an onboard management port to provide an interface to the system.

Software Requirements

Hyper-V is a feature of Windows Server 2008 x64 Edition only. There's no support for Hyper-V in the x86 (aka 32-bit) Edition or the Itanium versions of Windows Server 2008. The x64 Edition is required for a couple of reasons:

Kernel address space   The 64-bit version of Windows Server 2008 provides a much larger kernel address space as compared to the 32-bit edition. This directly translates into the support of larger processes, which is crucial for virtualization.

Large amount of host memory   Hyper-V supports up to 1 TB of RAM on the host. x86 versions of Windows Server 2008 support only up to 64 GB of RAM on the host, which would severely limit the number of VMs you could run.

We're frequently asked to explain the differences with Hyper-V between versions of Windows Server 2008. There's no difference—the features of Hyper-V are the same, regardless of whether you're running the Standard, Enterprise, or Datacenter product. However, differences in the versions of Windows Server 2008 affect key virtualization scenarios:

Processor sockets   Windows Server 2008 Standard Edition is limited to four sockets, whereas Enterprise Edition supports eight sockets.

Memory   Windows Server 2008 Standard Edition supports up to 32 GB of RAM, and Windows Server 2008 Enterprise Edition supports up to 2 TB of RAM.

Failover clustering   Windows Server 2008 Standard Edition doesn't inclu de the failover-clustering functionality required for quick migration.

Virtual image use rights   As summarized in Table 1.1, Windows Server 2008 includes the rights to run virtual images of the installed operating system. The number of those virtual images is tied to the edition.

TABLE 1.1   Virtual Image Usage Rights

EDITION	VIRTUAL IMAGE USAGE RIGHTS
Standard Edition	1
Enterprise Edition	4
Datacenter Edition	Unlimited

Summary

Are you intimidated yet? In this chapter, we've provided a great deal of information about Hyper-V. From its scenarios to its architecture to its features, we've laid the groundwork. In the upcoming chapters, we'll go into depth about many of the items we touched on here. Keep reading to find out why you should deploy Hyper-V in your environment.

Chapter 2

Installing Hyper-V and Server Core

In Chapter 1, "Introduction to Hyper-V," we spent a great deal of time talking about the "why" for Hyper-V. Now, let's look at how to actually start using Hyper-V. Because Hyper-V is a built-in role of the operating system, installation is quite simple. However, you need to take certain steps to ensure that you're using the latest version of Hyper-V.

In this chapter, we'll look at three different usage scenarios. First, we'll look at a clean installation—installing Windows Server 2008 and Hyper-V on a clean system. Then, we'll look at upgrading from the beta version of Hyper-V included with Windows Server 2008 to the final RTM version of Hyper-V.

Finally, we'll end with a discussion of the use of Windows Server Core as a host operating system and address some of the common pitfalls that system administrators run into when getting used to this new installation option of Windows Server 2008. We'll also examine some of the significant benefits that using Windows Server Core brings to administrators.

We'll cover the following topics in this chapter:

◆ Clean installation of Hyper-V

◆ Updating from beta

◆ Windows Server Core

◆ Installing Windows Server 2008 as a Core installation

Clean Installation of Hyper-V

You have two different choices for installing Hyper-V. Both installation methods result in the same binaries being installed—it all depends on how you as an administrator perform system updates. Although some of the intermediate steps are different, both installation paths begin and end the same way.

Before we get started, let's address perhaps the most burning question—why do we have to apply this update? When Windows Server 2008 shipped, it included the beta version of Hyper-V. In a perfect world, the Windows Server 2008 media would have included the final version of Hyper-V. However, software development is rarely a perfect world, so it was decided that the Hyper-V RTM update would be released after Windows Server 2008 shipped. These instructions will cover how to install the RTM update for Microsoft Hyper-V.

Installation Requirements

Before you start the installation of Windows Server 2008, confirm that the system meets the requirements of the version that's being installed. Each version of Windows Server 2008 has a different set of hardware requirements as well as supported features.

For example, the Standard edition of Windows Server 2008 doesn't include the failover-clustering functionality (required for Quick Migration, covered in Chapter 8, "High Availability"). The other versions, Enterprise and Datacenter, include that functionality (which enables Quick Migration) as well as additional virtualization usage rights. We'll cover what virtualization usage rights bring your enterprise later. Table 2.1 covers the processor sockets, memory, virtual image rights, and other features across all three versions of Windows.

TABLE 2.1   Comparison of Windows Server 2008 Versions

	WINDOWS SERVER 2008 STANDARD	WINDOWS SERVER 2008 ENTERPRISE	WINDOWS SERVER 2008 DATACENTER
Processor sockets supported	4	8	64
Memory	32GB	2TB	2TB
Virtual image rights	1	4	Unlimited
Failover clustering	Not included	Included	Included

NOTE   Microsoft has a tool that helps system administrators evaluate their current IT infrastructure and provides an easy-to-read report specifying what Microsoft technologies are best for the given environment. You can download the Microsoft Assessment and Planning Toolkit Solution Accelerator from http://go.microsoft.com/fwlink/?LinkId=111000.

To install Windows Server 2008, follow these simple steps:

1. Start the Windows setup process by starting up your system with the Windows Server 2008 DVD in the drive or by booting the system to a Pre-boot eXecution Environment (PXE) deployment server over the network.

2. If you're prompted to enter a product key, enter the key that came with the copy of Windows Server 2008.

3. After you type in the product key, you're presented with a list of available installation choices. Select the version for which the system is licensed.

4. The installer automatically proceeds and reboots a few times. After the installation is complete, the login screen appears.

Now that you have installed the base OS, you have two separate ways to update the installed version of Hyper-V to the final RTM release.

Updating via Windows Update

Windows Update is one of the ways that Microsoft distributes updates. You can configure it a number of different ways—for example, to apply updates automatically or only after approval of an administrator. Updates that are posted to Windows Update are assigned a priority, ranging from *Optional* to *Recommended*.

To update from the installed beta version of Hyper-V to RTM (Release to Manufacturing) via Windows Update, follow these steps:

1. Open Windows Update. Browse to Start ➤ All Programs ➤ Windows Update.

2. By default, Automatic Updating is turned off. You can enable it by clicking the Turn On Now button. Clicking the button will caused updates to be installed automatically every day at 3 A.M.

Click the View Advanced Options link, and you're presented with a number of options for how Windows Update will update the system. These options provide more control over what updates are applied, at the cost of manual approval of updates. The last option, Never Check For Updates, does exactly what it says: your system won't be updated.

NOTE Group Policy settings can set the default action and block users from making changes.

Regardless of the choice, you need to make one before you can proceed.

3. To do a manual check for updates, click the Check For Updates button. Doing so contacts the server for a listing of the updates that apply to the system.

4. In the list of applicable updates, Update For Windows Server 2008 x64 Edition (KB950050) should be listed. Ensure that the check box is selected. This option updates the offline package store on the system so that when the Hyper-V role is added, the RTM version will be used.

5. Select any other updates to be applied, and click the Install button.

Updating via Download Center

If your system doesn't have access to the Internet (and therefore can't use the Windows Update functionality), you can download the Hyper-V RTM update from the following website:

http://support.microsoft.com/kb/950050

Copy the downloaded file to the new Hyper-V host, and run it. Doing so updates the offline package store on the system so when the role is added, the final version will be used.

NOTE   Don't download the update from any website other than Microsoft's.

Adding the Hyper-V Role

Now that you've updated the binaries to the RTM version of Hyper-V, you need to add the Hyper-V role. To do so, you use Server Manager (see Figure 2.1), which is a central console for most administration tasks against a host computer. Follow these steps:

1. From the Start menu, open Server Manager, and expand the Roles option on the left side of the window.

2. Server Manager uses a wizard to walk you through adding a role to a system. Click the Add Roles link on the right to start the wizard.

3. After an introductory page, the Add Roles Wizard lists all the roles that are available to add to the server. Select the Hyper-V role, and then click Next.

FIGURE 2.1
Server Manager
on a clean
install
of Windows
Server 2008

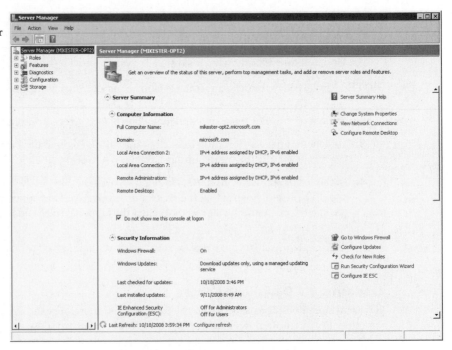

After the introductory page for Hyper-V appears, which describes what Hyper-V does, you see the screen shown in Figure 2.2.

As we'll discuss in Chapter 3, "Configuring Hyper-V," a virtual machine has three different types of virtual networks that can be used for network traffic. The setup process for Hyper-V provides an easy-to-use method for creating external virtual networks; this process allows virtual machines to send traffic over physical network adapters that are installed on the host.

NOTE   What if Hyper-V isn't listed? There are a few possible causes for this:

- ◆ Are you using the x64 version of Windows Server 2008? Hyper-V isn't included in the x86 versions of Windows Server 2008.

- ◆ Did you use an installation disc that has Windows Server 2008 without Hyper-V?

- ◆ When you add the role, does the Hyper-V Manager say beta? If so, the update didn't apply successfully.

FIGURE 2.2
Create Virtual Networks in Server Manager

4. To create a virtual network, select the check box next to the name of the Ethernet card installed on the host.

NOTE   It's highly recommended that you set aside one network interface card (NIC) for remote administration of the host and that you not create a virtual network on it. We'll cover this topic in more detail in Chapter 4, "Virtualization Best Practices."

5. Select the virtual networks to be created, and click Next.

After confirming the installation choices, the system performs the installation and then reboots. The Hyper-V role has now been installed.

6. Browse to Administrative Tools in the Start menu, and launch the Hyper-V Manager to start using Hyper-V.

TIP If you're installing on a number of systems, it's possible to slipstream the Hyper-V RTM update into the installation media. For more information, refer to this blog post: http:// tinyurl.com/76ykex, where the author reviews how to integrate the final version of Hyper-V into the installation media.

Updating from Beta

As we discussed earlier, the released version of Windows Server 2008 included the beta version of Hyper-V. Before you update to the RTM version, you must perform several steps to protect against data loss.

Pre-update Configuration

Unfortunately, there is no central site for configuration data. Therefore, you must follow the following four steps for basic configuration before you apply the update:

◆ *Record the static IP configuration.* If the virtual machine is set up to use a static IP address, write it down. As part of the upgrade process, the virtual machine will need to be re-created using the old virtual hard disk (VHD). Because the new virtual machine will have a new Media Access Control (MAC) address for the Ethernet controller, the old static IP address won't be recognized.

◆ *Shut down all virtual machines.* Saved states from earlier versions of Hyper-V can't be used when moving forward to a newer version.

◆ *Commit all snapshots.* Snapshots aren't compatible between the beta version and the RTM of Hyper-V. Additionally, because virtual machines will need to be re-created, actively using a snapshot when the RTM update is applied can possibly lead to data loss.

◆ *Record virtual network names.* Any virtual networks that were created under the beta of Hyper-V will need to be re-created. If you wish to maintain the same names after the update is applied, record the name of each virtual network so it can be re-created after updating.

Now, follow the steps outlined earlier in this chapter to apply the Hyper-V RTM update to your host via Windows Update or the Microsoft Download Center.

Post-update Configuration

After you've applied the Hyper-V RTM update, follow these steps to configure your system:

◆ *Re-create virtual networks.* Create any custom virtual networks that were present in the earlier version of Hyper-V. We'll cover how to do this in Chapter 3.

◆ *Re-create virtual machines.* If virtual machines were running on the host before you updated to the RTM version of Hyper-V, they will need to be re-created. Follow the steps in Chapter 3, Creating a new virtual machine, to create a virtual machine from an existing VHD file.

◆ *Update integration components.* The Hyper-V RTM update includes new integration components that need to be updated in the virtual machine. Information about how to apply the updated integration components can be found in Chapter 4.

Windows Server Core

Until now, we've been talking about the full installation of Windows Server 2008 as the parent partition. Another installation option for Windows Server 2008, called Windows Server Core, has some significant differences that may make you think twice about using a full installation of Windows Server 2008.

What Is Windows Server Core?

Windows Server Core is an installation option of Windows Server 2008. A full installation of Windows Server 2008 includes the full user interface. This is the only installation option that has been present for Windows Server until now. Having the full user interface means that local applications can be run on the system, including management or configuration tools.

Windows Server Core, on the other hand, is a new minimal installation option for Windows Server 2008 that removes the Windows Explorer shell from the operating system and instead presents only a command line (see Figure 2.3). Windows Server Core is included in all of the Windows Server 2008 versions—Standard, Enterprise, Datacenter, and Web.

FIGURE 2.3
Windows
Server 2008,
Enterprise Edition,
in the Core
installation

Windows Server Core contains a subset of the roles and features of a full installation of Windows Server 2008. This means a Core installation can't do everything that a full installation can do, but the lower overhead (both on disk and in memory) and reduced attack surface make it an ideal parent partition for virtualization.

Windows Server Core Architecture

The architecture of Windows Server Core is extremely similar to a full installation of Windows Server 2008. Windows Server Core uses the same device drivers, has the same kernel installed on disk, and behaves the same as a full installation of Windows Server. The main difference is that the graphical subsystem of Windows, as well as the .NET Framework and other products and services, are absent from a Core installation. This means that any application that relies on any of those pieces of functionality won't run, such as websites that rely on the ASP.NET framework. Some applications, such as SQL Server 2008, also won't work on a Windows Server 2008 Core installation. Additionally, items such as Internet Explorer and Windows Mail have been removed.

BENEFITS

Windows Server Core offers a number of benefits, regardless of its intended use:

Reduced maintenance By default, a Windows Server Core system has very few binaries installed. When a role is added, only the components that are necessary for the role are installed. The binaries are still present on the system, which allows for those components to be updated during normal patch cycles. No longer will your Windows Servers need updates for little-used components. Systems running Windows Server Core can see up to 40 percent fewer patches compared to systems running Windows Server 2003.

Reduced attack surface Because fewer applications and services are running on the server, there are fewer avenues to exploit. Exploits aimed at components that don't exist on the server don't get a chance to work.

Reduced management Because fewer components are installed on the system, there's less administrative overhead.

Less disk space required Fewer binaries being installed on disk mean that less disk space is required. Windows Server Core requires only 10GB of disk space, as opposed to 20GB for a full installation of Windows Server 2008.

DISADVANTAGES

Although the Server Core installation option sounds great in theory, administrators need to be aware of the following concerns:

Remote management Because Windows Server Core provides no local GUI-based administration tools, you perform the bulk of administration for the system from another system with a full installation of Windows Server 2008 or enterprise-management tools. Many of the Windows administration tools that are accessed through the Microsoft Management Console (MMC) can be configured to administer other computers in either a workgroup or a domain setting.

Command line The only interface presented at a console or remote logon at a Windows Server Core system is the command line. For some administrators, that's preferred—and those administrators probably use batch files (.BAT) and command scripts (.CMD) to perform mundane administration tasks. Not all administrators prefer that approach, however.

No PowerShell Because Windows Server Core doesn't include the .NET Framework, the PowerShell feature isn't available. You can still use PowerShell from another system to perform administrative tasks against the Windows Server Core system via Windows Management Interface (WMI).

Inability to transition from Core to full   A Windows Server Core installation can't be "upgraded" to a full installation of Windows Server. To move to a full installation of Windows Server 2008, you must reinstall the system.

Managing Windows Server Core

Windows Server Core can be managed a number of different ways:

Local command prompt   Many of the command-line utilities present in a full installation of Windows Server 2008 also exist in a Core installation. This allows administrators to perform the same tasks using a common toolset.

Terminal Server   Windows Server Core supports Terminal Services Remote Administration mode. Administrators can connect to the Server Core system from another Windows system for administrative purposes. The user experience is identical—the user logging in from the remote system will only get a command prompt in their Remote Desktop session.

NOTE   Terminal Services Remote Administration is disabled by default, just as it is on a full installation of Windows Server 2008. We provide instructions on how to enable Terminal Services Remote Administration later in this chapter.

WS-Management   Web Services for Management (WS-Management) is a relatively newly defined standard in the IT world. It provides a common method for systems to access and exchange management information across the entire IT infrastructure. Many management tools, including System Center Virtual Machine Manager, use WS-Management to communicate between the client and the server.

Windows Remote Shell   By adding this feature, administrators can execute commands on a Server Core system from another system via the command line. Windows Remote Shell uses WS-Management to pass the commands from one system to another.

From the Windows Server Core system, run the following command:

```
WinRM quickconfig
```

Now, from a separate Windows Server 2008 or Windows Vista system, you can execute commands against the Windows Server Core system like this:

```
Winrs -r:<server_core_system> dir
```

This generates a directory listing of the remote Windows Server Core system.

Windows Script Host   Windows Server Core includes the cscript.exe application, allowing you to run scripts for administrative purposes. You can write scripts in a variety of different languages—Jscript, VBScript, and so on (providing the scripting engine for that language is installed).

Installing Windows Server 2008 as a Core Installation

We've spent a great deal of time talking about the advantages and disadvantages of Windows Server Core. Let's look at how to deploy Hyper-V on a Windows Server 2008 Core installation.

Installation Considerations and Requirements

As we detailed earlier in this chapter, there are advantages and disadvantages to running Windows Server Core. Before you implement Windows Server Core, system planners should ensure that their tools and scripts work as expected in the Windows Server Core environment and that administrators are comfortable in the command-line environment. Additionally, you should confirm system-management and anti-virus tool functionality. Management agents (such as the Microsoft System Center Operations Manager Agent) can't have any dependencies on the Windows shell or GUI, nor can they use managed code.

The installation requirements for Windows Server Core are nearly the same as for a full installation of Windows Server 2008, which we talked about earlier in this chapter (see Table 2.2). The main difference is in the amount of disk space required. Because Windows Server Core has fewer binaries on disk, it requires less disk space.

TABLE 2.2   Installation Requirements for Full Installation vs. Core Installation

	WINDOWS SERVER: FULL	**WINDOWS SERVER: CORE**
Processor	1.4GHz or faster processor minimum, 2GHz or faster recommended	1.4GHz or faster processor minimum, 2GHz or faster recommended
Memory	512MB minimum, 2GB recommended	512MB minimum, 2GB recommended
Disk	20GB space minimum, 40GB or more recommended	10GB space minimum, 40GB or more recommended
Other	DVD-ROM drive, keyboard, mouse	DVD-ROM drive, keyboard, mouse

Performing a Core Installation

Installing Windows Server Core is exactly the same as performing a full installation:

1. Start the Windows setup process by starting up the system with the Windows Server 2008 DVD in the drive or by booting the system to a PXE deployment server over the network.

2. If you're prompted to enter a product key, enter the key that came with the copy of Windows Server 2008.

3. After you type in the product key, you're presented with a list of available installation choices (see Figure 2.4). Select the version for which the system is licensed in the Server Core Installation—this will install Windows Server 2008 in the Server Core configuration.

4. Select the volume for installation, and the installer automatically proceeds and reboots a few times. After the installation is complete, the login screen appears. In the full server install only, you must set the password for the administrator as the initial step.

Initial Configuration

Because Windows Server Core has no graphical elements, you need to use the command line to configure the system. We'll cover some of the most common configuration steps in this section. We can't discuss all of the configuration steps in this chapter, but you can find additional information about configuration at the Windows Server TechCenter: www.microsoft.com/windowsserver2008.

Activate a Windows Server Core system To activate a Windows Server Core system, run the following command:

```
cscript.exe %windir%\system32\slmgr.vbs -ato
```

This command attempts to activate the installed copy of Windows over the Internet. It's also possible to activate the newly installed copy of Windows against a corporate Key Management Services (KMS) server, but steps for that are beyond the scope of this book.

Configure a static IP address for a management NIC We'll talk about a management NIC in more detail in Chapter 4. With Windows Server Core, you have no graphical tools for the configuration of the NIC's properties—you must configure it from the command line. Specifically, the `netsh` command-line tool provides the functionality to set the IP addresses on the NIC, among other things. To set the management NIC to use a static IP address, run the following commands:

```
Netsh interface ipv4
show interfaces
set address name="ID" source=static address=StaticIP mask=SubnetMask
gateway=DefaultGateway
add dnsserver name="ID" address=DNSIP index=1
netsh interface set interface name name="OLD_NAME" newname="Management NIC"
```

Set the machine name   To set the name of the Windows Server Core system, run the following command:

```
Netdom.exe renamecomputer %computername% /newname:<new_computer_name>
```

Join a domain (if desired)   Use netdom.exe to join the system to a domain. Run the following command:

```
Netdom.exe join %computername% /domain:<domain_name> /userd:<user_name> /
password:<password>
```

Add users to the administrator's group   Logging in as the local administrator, especially in a domain environment, is usually a very bad idea. By adding individual administrators to the administrator's group, you can audit actions in case of issues.

To add a user account to the administrator's group, run the following command:

```
net localgroup administrators /add <user_account>
```

OTHER HELPFUL SCRIPTS FOR THE COMMAND LINE

Here are a few extra tips that aren't related to virtualization but are still good techniques to know.

To enable Remote Administration, run the following command:

```
Cscript.exe \windows\system32\scregedit.wsf /ar 0
```

To enable Remote Administration to accept connections from systems before Windows Vista or Windows Server 2008, run the following command:

```
Cscript.exe \windows\system32\scregedit.wsf /cs 0
```

To enable Automatic Updates, run the following commands:

```
Cscript.exe \windows\system32\scregedit.wsf /au 4
net stop wuauserv
net start wuauserv
```

To disable the Windows Firewall, run the following command:

```
netsh firewall set opmode disable
```

You can find additional functionality in the \windows\system32\scregedit.wsf script.

Installing Hyper-V under Windows Server 2008 Server Core

Installing Hyper-V under Windows Server Core requires the same series of steps as installing Hyper-V on a full installation of Windows Server 2008. We covered those steps earlier in this chapter in "Adding the Hyper-V Role." However, due to the command-line interface, there are a few differences. Follow these steps:

1. Apply the Hyper-V RTM update. The released media for Windows Server 2008 includes the beta version of Hyper-V and must be updated. You can update the role by copying the MSU package to the Windows Server Core system and then running it from the command prompt (see Figure 2.5).

FIGURE 2.5
Applying the Hyper-V RTM update on Windows Server 2008 Core

2. Browse to where the file is located, and run it. For the Hyper-V RTM update, the filename is `Windows6.0-KB950050-x64.MSU`.

3. After the update succeeds, you must restart the system.

NOTE If you ran Automatic Updates via Windows Update, then the Hyper-V RTM update may have been applied, depending on your Windows Update settings.

Now that you've updated the offline package store, you need to install the role:

1. After the system restarts, log in. When the command prompt appears, run the following command:

```
Start /w ocsetup Microsoft-Hyper-V
```

NOTE The capitalization of this command is critical—the command will fail if it isn't capitalized exactly as shown in step 1.

The system installs all the necessary files for Hyper-V. After it completes, a prompt appears, as shown in Figure 2.6.

FIGURE 2.6
Reboot prompt after successful application of the Hyper-V RTM update

2. Click Yes to reboot the system.

NOTE As part of the installation of the Hyper-V role, all firewall ports required by Hyper-V are opened.

3. The system is ready to run virtual machines. From another system, use the Hyper-V Manager to connect as the local administrator account on the Server Core host.

NOTE Ensure that the system where the Hyper-V MMC is being used has also been updated to the RTM version of Hyper-V. Administration of an RTM Hyper-V host from an earlier version of the Hyper-V Manager MMC isn't supported.

4. Before you create a virtual machine, you must create virtual networks. From the Hyper-V Manager MMC, select the Hyper-V host on the left, and then select Virtual Network Manager in the Actions section at right. From there, create the necessary external, internal, and private virtual networks for the virtualized workloads on the host (see Figure 2.7).

NOTE Ensure that an external virtual network isn't created on the NIC being used as the management NIC.

For more information about the different types of virtual networks, refer to Chapter 3, Configuring Hyper-V.

FIGURE 2.7
Virtual Network
Manager showing
no virtual net-
works created

Congratulations! You can now use the system to run virtualization workloads on top of a Windows Server Core system.

Summary

In this chapter, we've detailed how administrators can lay the groundwork for implementing virtualization in your environment. By having Hyper-V as a role of Windows Server 2008, Microsoft has provided an easy deployment scenario, allowing users to add the virtualization layer to Windows.

For production servers where the host is running only the Hyper-V role, Windows Server Core is easily the best choice. By removing from the system a number of the applications that are rarely used and pairing the system with the targeted role and feature functionality of Windows Server 2008, you've got the base platform for a great virtualization host. It may take a little while to adjust to the command-line equivalents of graphical tools you're used to, but the benefits of Windows Server Core make it the optimal platform for your production virtualization needs.

Chapter 3

Configuring Hyper-V

In the first two chapters, we've provided an introduction to why system administrators and developers would want to use virtualization, and specifically Hyper-V.

In this chapter, we'll look at the Hyper-V Manager, the main administration console for Hyper-V. The Hyper-V Manager is a powerful management interface that provides easy-to-use wizards for tasks such as new virtual-machine creation, shows an all-up view of all virtual machines on a host, and has multiple-host-management built in.

After we review the Hyper-V Manager, we'll dig in to how to create a new virtual machine using the New Virtual Machine Wizard. We'll edit the settings of the newly created virtual machine and then finish by looking at some more advanced topics.

Ready? Let's get started! In this chapter, we'll cover the following topics:

◆ The Hyper-V MMC

◆ Creating a new virtual machine

◆ Virtual-machine settings

◆ New Virtual Hard Disk Wizard

◆ Virtual Network Manager

Getting Started: The Hyper-V MMC

To start working with Hyper-V, click the Start menu, select Administrative Tools, and then select Hyper-V Manager (see Figure 3.1). If the Hyper-V Manager isn't present, or for information about adding the Hyper-V Manager to a system, keep reading.

Although the initial window for the Hyper-V Manager is sparse, it'll fill up quickly when you begin creating virtual machines (VMs). Let's look at each area of the Microsoft Management Console (MMC).

On the left is list of all the Hyper-V hosts managed by this instance of the Hyper-V Manager. By default, only one host is listed: the local host on which the MMC is running. To add hosts to the MMC, right-click the Hyper-V Manager text, and select Connect To Server. After typing in the host name in the Another Computer text box, you can perform all Hyper-V administrative tasks against that system.

FIGURE 3.1
Window for
Hyper-V
Manager

The center of the Hyper-V Manager window is broken up into three sections as follows.

The top section is a list of all the VMs that are registered on the selected host. Because you haven't created any VMs, this list is empty. This section also lists the status of all the VMs—including the state (running, off, saved, and so on), central processing unit (CPU) utilization, the amount of time the VM has been running, and operations that are currently taking place against the VM.

The middle section lists all the snapshots for the selected VM. The snapshot functionality is one of the new features in Hyper-V. A *snapshot* is a point-in-time representation of a VM. As an administrator, you can move back and forth between snapshots and easily perform tasks like, for example, resetting a test environment.

NOTE Snapshots should not be used as a backup tool in a production environment. For more information about snapshots, see Chapter 7, "Backup and Recovery."

The bottom section provides a small thumbnail of the virtual-machine console session, as well as the VM's created date and notes. We'll cover where to enter notes later in this chapter.

On the right is a list of actions that you can take against the selected host. These include creating a VM (which we'll cover next) as well as changing the host settings and starting/stopping the Hyper-V service. If you create a VM and select it here, more options appear below; these are actions you can take against the selected VM and are dependent on the state of the VM.

NOTE   It's possible to add the Hyper-V Manager to a Windows Server 2008 or Windows Vista SP1 system that isn't running the Hyper-V role. This enables you to remotely configure and control a Hyper-V host.

To add the Hyper-V Manager on a Windows Server 2008 system, launch Server Manager from the Start menu. Select Features, and then select Add Features. Under Remote Server Administration Tools, browse to Role Administration Tools, select Hyper-V Tools, and then click Install. After installation, you can launch the Hyper-V Manager from Administrative Tools ➢ Hyper-V Manager.

To add the Hyper-V Manager on a Windows Vista SP1 system, download the Update for Windows Vista (KB952627) from the Microsoft Download Center. After installation, you can launch the Hyper-V Manager from Administrative Tools ➢ Hyper-V Manager. (Make sure you select the correct package to download—packages for both x86 and x64 architectures are available.)

Creating a New Virtual Machine

To create a new VM, use the New Virtual Machine Wizard. To launch this wizard, select New ➢ Virtual Machine. It will walk you through the initial configuration of the VM:

1. The Before You Begin page of the wizard is a simple introduction that provides an overview of the wizard (see Figure 3.2). It also provides a check box that you can select to prevent the page from appearing again, which can be a time-saver if you're creating multiple VMs.

FIGURE 3.2
First page of
the New Virtual
Machine Wizard

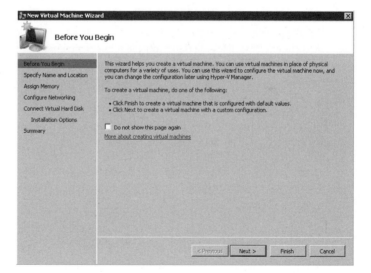

2. On the Specify Name And Location page, you can set the VM's name as well as the location of its supporting files (see Figure 3.3).

FIGURE 3.3
Specify Name And
Location page in
the wizard

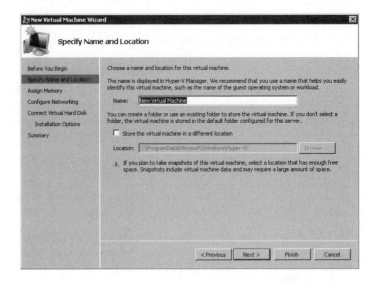

WARNING The name of the VM as set here is separate from the name that will be assigned to the virtual operating system that is installed. One common gotcha is assigning the same name to two different VMs. Because the displayed name is a friendly form for a long, globally unique identifier behind the scenes, Hyper-V Manager doesn't check to see whether the name already exists.

The VM's location is where the configuration file and all the associated files will be created. These files include the `.BIN` and `.VSV` files. When a VM is powered on, both `.BIN` and `.VSV` files are created. The `.BIN` file is used when the VM is powered on, and it's the same size as the memory assigned to the VM. This file ensures that, in case of a system shutdown, the VM can be saved. When the state of the VM is saved, the `.VSV` file holds the VM's memory so it can be restored at a later time.

One common reason to change the default location of the VM is so you can create a *highly available* VM. If you're going to do so, then you need to create the VM on a shared volume. We'll cover that more in Chapter 8: "High Availability."

3. On the Assign Memory page, the memory assigned to the VM is set. By default, it's set at 512MB of RAM (see Figure 3.4). The maximum amount of RAM that can be assigned is one of two values: the amount of memory installed in the host, or 64GB (whichever is smaller).

FIGURE 3.4
Assign
Memory page

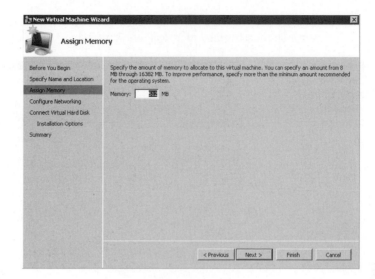

We'll cover memory best practices in Chapter 4, "Virtualization Best Practices."

4. By default, the wizard will add a single virtual network adapter to the VM, as you can see on the Configure Networking page shown in Figure 3.5. The network adapter can be connected to any virtual network that has already been created. If you're going to install the operating system (OS) via Pre-boot eXecution Environment (PXE), then make sure you select a valid virtual network on this page. If you leave the Connection option set to Not Connected, PXE can't be used for OS installation (as you'll see in step 6).

FIGURE 3.5
Configure
Networking page

5. The Connect Virtual Hard Disk page controls where the OS for the VM will go. There are three options, two of which deal with virtual hard disk (VHD) files (see Figure 3.6).

FIGURE 3.6
Options available on the Connect Virtual Hard Disk page

◆ Create A Virtual Hard Disk. This option creates a new VHD file for OS installation. The newly created VHD is completely blank. You can set the location as well as the size here.

When you create a new VM via the wizard, the VHD type is a dynamically expanding disk. For other types, such as a fixed size disk or a physical disk, you must configure the VM's settings after the wizard completes. We'll cover that later in this chapter.

◆ Use An Existing Virtual Hard Disk. This option allows you to use a VHD that you've already created. We'll cover how to create a library of VHD files in Chapter 4.

◆ Attach A Virtual Hard Disk Later. Select this option if you plan to use a physical disk or a fixed-size VHD file. If you select this option, you can modify the VHD in the settings for the VM.

6. The Installation Options page provides a number of different ways that you can install the OS within the VM (see Figure 3.7):

◆ Install An Operating System Later. If you choose this option, an OS isn't installed in the VM.

◆ Install An Operating System From A Boot CD/DVD-ROM. You can install operating systems either by using the physical CD/DVD-ROM drive on the host computer or by using an ISO file. An ISO file is an exact file copy of the contents of a physical piece of

CD/DVD-ROM media. Many software companies now ship electronic copies of OSs in the ISO file format. Installs that take place from an ISO file are generally faster than from the physical CD/DVD-ROM drive, because the installation is reading from a fast disk as opposed to a slower optical drive. Additionally, you can set up a central network share for multiple systems to access a library of ISO files.

NOTE   The Installation Options page appears only if you created a new VHD in step 5. If you select a VHD file that already exists, the wizard assumes that the existing VHD has an OS installed.

FIGURE 3.7
Installation
Options page

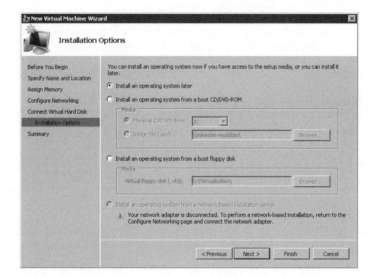

NOTE   Only one VM at a time can install an OS from the physical CD/DVD-ROM drive.

NOTE   If you have a network share with operating system ISO files, they can be shared with all the Hyper-V hosts in your environment. Simply add the machine account to the share permissions—for example, HYPERV1$.

◆ Install An Operating System From A Boot Floppy Disk. Some operating systems require the use of a boot floppy disk to start the installation. By selecting this option, you must use a virtual floppy disk (VFD) file. A VFD file is similar to an ISO file—it's a file-based representation of the physical medium.

NOTE   Hyper-V can't directly access the physical floppy disk drive on the host computer.

◆ Install An Operating System From A Network-Based Installation Server. Hyper-V includes the capability to boot the VM over the network using the PXE protocol. You can install a variety of operating systems over the network by using the PXE protocol, including Windows Server 2008. In order to perform a network-based installation, you must use a legacy network adapter.

If you selected a virtual network earlier in the setup process, and you then select the Install An Operating System From A Network-Based Installation Server option, the network adapter added to the VM will be a legacy network adapter, and the boot order will be modified to boot over the network first.

7. Completing The New Virtual Machine Wizard appears next. Finally, the VM creation is complete. The last screen provides a summary of the newly created VM (see Figure 3.8).

FIGURE 3.8
Completing the
New Virtual
Machine
Wizard page

Virtual Machine Settings

Now that you've created a new VM using the wizard, let's look at the VM's setting. To do so, select the newly created VM in the Hyper-V Manager, and click Settings.

The Settings dialog is broken into two sections: Hardware and Management. The hardware options control the hardware that's available to the VM, and the management options control the VM's administrative tasks. We'll look at all the options available.

Hardware

Just like a physical system, a VM consists of a variety of (virtual) hardware devices. In the settings for a VM, you can modify that hardware—including adding processors, network adapters, and hard disks.

ADD HARDWARE

You can modify the configuration of the VM by adding hardware, such as a small computer system interface (SCSI) controller or additional network interface, to the VM (see Figure 3.9). The VM must be powered off to add hardware to the VM. After you add the virtual hardware to the VM and power on the VM, the OS will recognize the new hardware.

FIGURE 3.9
Adding hardware
for a new VM

BIOS

Hyper-V doesn't allow direct access to the Basic Input/Output System (BIOS), so the only BIOS settings you can modify are exposed here (see Figure 3.10):

◆ Num Lock. Selecting this check box triggers Num Lock in the VM to be active on boot.

◆ Startup Order. This option controls the order in which devices will be queried for boot. The top-most option will be tried first, and if it fails, then the next option will be tried. By default, the boot order is CD, IDE, legacy network adapter, and then floppy.

FIGURE 3.10
Looking at the BIOS for a new VM

MEMORY

You can adjust the amount of memory allocated to the VM (see Figure 3.11). This can range from 8MB to the maximum amount of RAM in the system. There are some caveats:

◆ Once the VM is powered on, the memory is allocated to the VM and can't be reclaimed until the VM is saved or turned off.

◆ Memory allocated to a VM can't be shared. If multiple VMs are running the same OS, Hyper-V doesn't provide the capability to share common pages of memory between the VMs.

◆ Hyper-V doesn't provide support for allocating more memory than is available on the host. This limits the amount of memory available to allocate to VMs to about 1GB less than the maximum amount of RAM in the host.

We'll discuss some of the best practices for memory in Chapter 4.

FIGURE 3.11

Setting memory

PROCESSOR

The Processor Settings dialog has a number of options, as you can see in Figure 3.12.

As we discussed in Chapter 1, "Introduction to Hyper-V," Hyper-V supports up to four virtual processors in the VM. Those virtual processors are scheduled as threads on the physical processors. A VM can't have more virtual processors allocated than are present in the host. That means that in order to create a four-core VM, the host system must have at least four cores.

NOTE It's important to know the differences between a *logical processor* and a *virtual processor*. Logical processors are the foundation of today's multicore processors. A system with a single core and without Hyper-Threading has a single logical processor. Adding additional cores increases the logical processor count. For example, a system with two physical processors, each processor having two cores, has a total logical-processor count of four. A virtual processor is seen on the host as a single thread of execution, which can then be scheduled on any of the logical processors in the system.

FIGURE 3.12
Modifying the
number of proces-
sors for a new VM

The upper limit of total virtual processors you can allocate on a host is eight times the number of logical processors. A single dual-socket, dual-core server (exposing 4 processors to the host) can support a total of 32 virtual processors. You should keep a very close eye on performance to ensure that the system can handle all the running VMs as well as the host.

Additionally, the Processor Settings dialog is where you set the resource-control options for the VM. This dialog includes the following options:

◆ **Virtual Machine Reserve.** This reserves a set amount of processor power for the VM. You can think of this reserve as a guaranteed amount of processor resources.

◆ **Virtual Machine Limit.** This is a hard cap on the amount of processor power that the VM can take from the host.

◆ **Relative Weight.** The relative weight is another method of assigning a value of importance between multiple VMs. You can set this option to any value from 1 to 10,000. If two VMs have the same VM reserves and limits, the VM with a higher relative weight will receive more processing power.

◆ **Processor Functionality.** The last check box in the processor settings controls the processor functionality. By selecting this option, you'll let older OSs, such as Windows NT or earlier, work with Hyper-V.

IDE Controller

Hyper-V includes a dual-channel IDE controller much like many standard hardware PCs. By default, a single VHD is connected to the primary IDE controller in the primary connection, with a CD/DVD drive connected to the primary connection of the secondary controller (see Figure 3.13).

FIGURE 3.13
IDE controller options

The VM can boot only from a VHD connected to the IDE controller. Although this does seem strange and counterintuitive for performance reasons, this arrangement is necessary because of the architecture of Hyper-V. The synthetic devices in Hyper-V aren't seen in the OS without the integration components being installed.

NOTE   After you install the integration services in the VM, you'll notice near-identical performance from disks connected to the IDE controller and disks connected to the SCSI controller.

By clicking the IDE controller, you can add a new hard disk or DVD drive to the specific IDE controller. (DVD drives can be connected only to the IDE controllers.) If you select a hard disk, you have a number of options to choose from.

At the top, you can select the specific location where the VHD file will be connected the top (see Figure 3.14). If no SCSI controllers have been added to the VM, then you can add the new

VHD to one of the pre-existing IDE controllers only. However, if you added a SCSI controller to the VM's configuration, then the SCSI controller and all available locations will be listed as well.

FIGURE 3.14
Specifying the path for a VHD with the IDE controller

After you've assigned the new VHD to a specific location, you can set up the specifics of the disk. A number of Hard Drive settings are available, including creating a new VHD, using an existing disk, or editing or inspecting an existing disk.

The New, Edit, and Inspect buttons all map back to the New Virtual Hard Disk Wizard. This wizard provides a one-stop interface for all tasks having to do with VHD files. We'll cover the New Virtual Hard Disk Wizard later in this chapter.

The bottom option, Physical Hard Disk, lets you directly connect a physical logical unit number (LUN) to a VM. This allows the VM to use directly storage volumes that are connected to controllers on the host—including fibre channel, Internet SCSI (iSCSI), or direct-attached SCSI storage. The use of physical hard disks lets you treat your VMs the same way as physical machines, and you get an increase in performance compared to the default dynamically expanding VHD.

In order to connect a physical hard disk to a VM, you must mark the physical disk Offline on the host. You can do this by opening the Disk Management MMC snap-in, selecting the disk, and then right-clicking it and selecting Offline. Take care that you don't bring the same volume online while the VM has it mounted, or you may lose data.

NETWORK ADAPTER

You have several items to choose in the Network Adapter Settings window, and you can change the same settings regardless of the type of network adapter—normal or legacy (see Figure 3.15).

FIGURE 3.15
Network Adapter
window

- ◆ Network. Each network adapter defined in the Settings dialog can be connected to a single virtual network.

- ◆ MAC Address. The Media Access Control (MAC) address of a network adapter is what makes each network adapter unique. The role of the MAC address in the network stack is beyond the scope of this book.

Hyper-V gives you the ability to assign a static MAC address to each network adapter in the VM or to use a dynamically generated MAC address. Some applications use the MAC address of a system for a number of purposes. To set a static MAC address, click the Static radio button and enter the value.

Dynamic MAC addresses under Hyper-V always start with 00:15:5D, with the last three octets randomly chosen based on the MAC address of the host's physical adapter.

- ◆ Enable Virtual LAN Identification. If the VM needs to communicate over a specific virtual local area network (VLAN) using the 802.1q protocol, enter the VLAN ID here. Multiple virtual network adapters can be connected to different VLANs.

COM PORT

The COM ports in the VM can either be left unconnected (the default selection) or be connected to a named pipe (see Figure 3.16). *Named pipes* are a special way of communicating between two different systems.

To connect a virtual COM port to a named pipe on the local system, enter the name of the pipe in the Pipe Name text box. There's no need to format it in the traditional \\.\pipe\pipe syntax; the dialog box takes care of that. To connect to a remote pipe on another system, select the Remote Computer check box and enter the name of the computer.

FLOPPY

A VM has a single virtual floppy disk drive (see Figure 3.17). The virtual floppy drive has no access to the physical floppy disk drive—rather, it uses virtual floppy disks (VFD files). You can create VFD files by using the Virtual Disk Wizard (New ➢ Floppy Disk).

Virtual Machine Management

Now that we've covered all of the VM's hardware settings, let's look at the management options available in the VM's configuration.

NOTE To use the same VFD file in multiple VMs, make sure the file is locked in Windows Explorer. To lock a file, right-click the file, select Properties, and select the Read-Only check box.

FIGURE 3.17
Setting the virtual
floppy disk

NAME

The name, as you would expect, controls the display name of the VM. Additionally, the text box lets you enter notes about the VM; these can include the OS installed, the patch level, and applications installed. These notes are displayed in the Hyper-V MMC (see Figure 3.18).

FIGURE 3.18
Setting the display
name for a VM

INTEGRATION SERVICES

When integration services are installed in a VM, they provide a number of additional features to the OS (if the OS supports them). You can select which of those features are enabled on a per-VM basis, as shown in Figure 3.19. These features include the following items:

FIGURE 3.19
Choosing integration services

◆ Operating System Shutdown. When you select Shut Down in the Hyper-V Manager, the integration services attempt to shut down the OS cleanly. If you don't select this option, then the only way to shut down a VM is to log in and manually issue a shut-down command (or to turn off the power to the VM).

◆ Time Synchronization. By default, Hyper-V syncs the clock of the VM and the host when the VM is first powered on. If the integration services are installed, the time-synchronization functionality will keep the two clocks in sync.

◆ Data Exchange. The data-exchange component allows the host and the VM to exchange data via a set of Registry key pairs. This data includes the host on which the VM is running on well as the name of the VM as defined in the Hyper-V Manager. You can obtain additional data via the data-exchange component, including the version of the OS in the VM and the values for the GetVersionEx function defined in MSDN.

◆ Heartbeat. The heartbeat service allows the Hyper-V host to identify whether a VM is running. If the heartbeat integration component is running in the VM and the check box is selected, then the VM sends a heartbeat back to the host every two seconds. The state of the heartbeat is displayed in the bottom panel of the Hyper-V Manager, and you can query it through Windows Management Interface (WMI) to determine whether the VM is still active and responding.

◆ Backup (Volume Snapshot). Hyper-V includes a Volume Shadow Services (VSS) writer that, when signaled by a VSS-aware backup application, prepares the VM for backup and signals the VSS request into the VM. This ensures that when the VM is restored from the backup medium, it's in an application-consistent state from which it can recover.

SNAPSHOT FILE LOCATION

By default, the location where snapshot files are created is the same location where the VM is created. You can modify the location of snapshot files on a per-VM basis by changing the path (see Figure 3.20). If you're going to take a large number of snapshots, it's recommended that the location where you take them have sufficient disk space.

FIGURE 3.20
Snapshot File
Location

AUTOMATIC START ACTION

You can set VMs to perform different actions when the Hyper-V host system starts (see Figure 3.21). These actions include Nothing, Automatically Start If It Was Running When The Service Stopped (default), and Always Start This Virtual Machine Automatically. If you select the automatic-start option, you can also choose a delay time; doing so helps prevent disk contention if multiple VMs are set to start at the same time.

FIGURE 3.21

Settings for Automatic Start Action

FIGURE 3.21

Settings for Automatic Start Action

AUTOMATIC STOP ACTION

Similar to the automatic-start actions, you can specify different actions to taken when the Hyper-V host system is shut down (see Figure 3.22). These include saving the state of the VM (default), turning off the VM, or shutting down the OS. In order to shut down the OS automatically, the integration components must be installed in the guest OS.

FIGURE 3.22

Settings for Automatic Stop Action

NOTE   If the host experiences a loss of power, then all the VMs will be turned off as well.

New Virtual Hard Disk Wizard

We need to cover two more important items in the Hyper-V Manager: the Virtual Network Manager and the New Virtual Hard Disk Wizard. Both of these items are important for different reasons: The New Virtual Hard Disk Wizard covers advanced disk configurations, including fixed disks and differencing disks. You'll learn more about the Virtual Network Manager in the next section.

You start the New Virtual Hard Disk Wizard by selecting New ➤ Hard Disk from the main page of the Hyper-V Manager.

NOTE   When starting the New Virtual Hard Disk Wizard, ensure that the correct Hyper-V host is selected from the list in the left pane of the Hyper-V Manager.

When the New Virtual Hard Disk Wizard starts, an introductory page appears. Clicking Next provides three separate choices of VHDs to create (see Figure 3.23). You follow the same steps to set up a dynamic or a fixed VHD. However, one step is different when you set up a differencing VHD. Let's start by reviewing each type of VHD.

FIGURE 3.23
Choosing the type of VHD

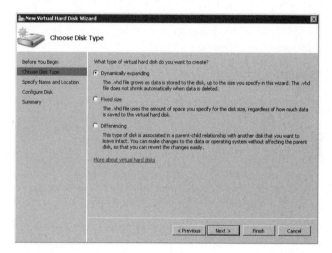

Types of Virtual Hard Disks

A *dynamic* VHD starts off small (approximately 1MB) but will expand to the maximum size specified as data is written to the disk. These types of disks are great for scenarios, like test and development, where disk space is at a premium (see Figure 3.24). However, we don't recommend using dynamic disks in production, because the expansion could slow performance.

FIGURE 3.24
Dynamic VHD

A *fixed-size* VHD has all the space allocated on the host's disk when the disk is created (see Figure 3.25). This obviously requires that the space exist on the host system. A fixed-size VHD is ideal for production deployments. Check out Chapter 6, "Virtual Machine Migration," for more information on import and export.

FIGURE 3.25
Fixed VHD

A *differencing* VHD is a special type. This is a disk that stores all the changes to a parent disk to a separate disk. Differencing disks are another great tool for test and development environments, where multiple VMs can be started from a single parent disk that contains a preinstalled OS. Differencing disks do present a number of unique concerns, which we'll discuss in Chapter 4.

Now that we've reviewed the three types of disks that can be created via this wizard, let's walk through the wizard.

Using the Wizard to Create Virtual Hard Disks

The first step to creating a new VHD file is to assign it a name and a location on the host OS. The name should give some sort of indication as to the contents of the VHD file. If you're creating a dynamic disk, ensure that there's enough space on the volume where the disk is being placed to hold the fully expanded disk.

NOTE   If a dynamic VHD can't expand because of lack of space on the volume where it resides, then the VM will pause, and an event will be logged in the event viewer notifying the administrator of the issue.

The next step depends on the type of disk you're creating:

Dynamic disk or fixed-size disk   For these two types of disk, you have two options: You can set the maximum size of the disk (the maximum size of a VHD file is a little less than 2TB), or you can select an existing physical disk. If you select an existing physical disk, then a new VHD file is created that is the same size as the existing physical disk. After the disk is created, the contents of the physical disk are copied to the new VHD file.

Differencing disk   For differencing disks, the next step after entering the name and location of the new disk is to define the parent. The *parent* VHD is the disk that the new VHD reads from while redirecting all writes to the newly created differencing disk.

The final page is a summary that details the actions selected during previous steps of the New Virtual Hard Disk Wizard. The summary page lest you confirm that the selected actions are correct before they're executed.

Virtual Network Manager

The Virtual Network Manager is the central administration point for ensuring that VMs have access to the correct network resources. Virtual networks differ from the virtual network adapters that are defined in the configuration—the virtual network adapters connect to the virtual networks. Multiple VMs, and multiple virtual network adapters, can connect to the same virtual network.

You access the Virtual Network Manager from the Actions pane of the Hyper-V Manager.

Types of Virtual Networks

There are three types of virtual networks, and each has a specific function:

External An external network is bound to the selected physical network adapter. This type of virtual network provides access to the network that the physical network is connected to. If a VM is serving data to other physical computers, for example, an external virtual network is the type to use.

Internal An internal virtual network isn't bound to a physical network adapter. A VM that's connected to an internal virtual network can communicate with all the VMs that are connected to the virtual network, as well as the host computer. An internal virtual network provides the functionality to connect from the host to the VM(s).

Private A private virtual network, like an internal virtual network, isn't bound to a physical network adapter. Private virtual networks only allow communication between all the VMs connected to the virtual network. This is incredibly useful for virtualized environments where the need to keep data from going out "over the wire" is critical.

Creating a virtual network is simple:

1. From the Hyper-V Manager, select Virtual Network Manager on the right under Actions. A list of all the virtual networks appears on the left, with an option at right to create a new virtual network.

2. Click the Add button to open the settings for the new virtual network (see Figure 3.26):

   ◆ Name. This is the display name for the virtual network. It's recommended that it reference the virtual network's intended use as well as the physical network connection (if it's an external network).

   ◆ Notes. This field is for notes regarding the virtual network. Again, providing a description of the virtual network is highly recommended in case you need to troubleshoot.

   ◆ Connection Type. Set this to the type of virtual network you're creating.

   ◆ Enable VLAN Identification For Parent Partition. This is a different setting from the setting in the virtual network adapter. If you're using the same network adapter both for VM traffic (as an external virtual network) and to provide network access to the host on a specific VLAN, then enter the correct VLAN ID here.

NOTE If an external virtual network is created on a host remotely using the Hyper-V Manager, there is a possibility of a loss of connection. The Virtual Network Manager will alert you to that fact before it's created.

3. After you enter all the correct data, click OK to create the virtual network and close the Virtual Network Manager.

FIGURE 3.26
Virtual network
properties

Summary

By now, you should have a good grasp of the Hyper-V Manager—what it does, how to create VMs, and how to modify the settings of the VMs you create. Additionally, we reviewed the New Virtual Hard Disk Managers and Virtual Network Manager, which provide even more control and functionality for complex configurations. We'll cover more advanced configurations, including best practices, later in this book.

Chapter 4

Virtualization Best Practices

After you put Hyper-V into use in an environment, the next logical step is to look at performance and how you can use Hyper-V more efficiently. Tuning a Hyper-V host isn't much different from tuning any other high-performance server. In addition to checking the host's performance, though, it's critical to tune the virtual machines being used.

We'll look at best practices from two points of view: that of the host, including processor, memory, networking, and storage; and that of the virtual machine, including integration services, using the Sysprep tool, and patching virtual machines.

In this chapter, we'll cover the following topics:

◆ Host best practices

◆ Virtual machine best practices

Host Best Practices

Once you decide to deploy Hyper-V in a production role, a number of areas need advanced planning and thought. Because the Hyper-V host will be running multiple production workloads, it's critical that such planning take place before the system is put into use. By identifying the workloads that will be run in virtual machines (VMs) on the host, planning can help you identify potential bottlenecks in the host system. These best practices help in two key areas:

◆ Host sizing

◆ Ongoing host performance

This chapter will help with both areas.

Choosing a Processor

As of this writing, Hyper-V provides support for up to 24 cores in the parent partition. A *core* is a unit of processing power. Both Intel and AMD have released processors that consist of multiple processor cores on a single processor. These processors plug into sockets on the computer's motherboard. Having multiple processor cores on a single die allows even a single-socket system to execute multiple threads of execution at the same time. Although 24 cores sounds like a lot of processing power (and in most cases, it certainly is!), virtualization can easily use all of it.

You must consider three key factors about processors as you work through the planning stages:

◆ Number of processors in the system

◆ Number of cores on the processors in the system

◆ Speed of the processors in the system

Because one of the key features of virtualization is the ability to achieve higher density (running multiple VMs on a single physical host), administrators naturally gravitate toward the processor as a key bottleneck. After all, if a host runs out of processing power, those virtualized workloads may not be able to keep up with the demand being placed on them.

You need to answer a couple of key questions for the host:

◆ How many processors are necessary for this virtualization host?

◆ Do the processors need to provide t wo, four, or even six cores per processor?

The answer to these two questions is usually, "It depends." Two schools of thought apply here, which bring up two more questions: Do you want to use more dual-socket systems, which usually have a lower price point? Or do you want to achieve maximum consolidation by going with quad-socket systems?

The price advantage of dual-socket systems is significant. At the time of writing, you can deploy three physical dual-socket systems for the price of one quad-socket system. You can then cluster those three dual-socket systems together in a high-availability configuration to ensure continuous uptime for the workloads running in the VMs. With the three-system configuration, however, you need to consider some other costs. Having three systems means further expenses for operating system licenses, management software licenses, and the administration of three servers. You also need to factor in the power costs of the three servers.

The other option, which uses only one quad-socket virtualization host, doesn't provide any sort of backup or high availability—meaning that if the single host goes down, all the virtualized workloads will go down with it. But quad-socket servers generally provide a bit more in terms of expansion and I/O scalability, which could result in additional VMs being deployed on a single host.

Some enterprises are also considering the use of blade servers. Although the up-front cost of the enclosure is higher, the ability to use 14 systems in 7 units of rack space (for example) could be a better fit for some companies.

As you can see, there's no simple answer when you're deciding on the best configuration for your host.

FASTER PROCESSORS AND PERFORMANCE

In some cases, the speed of the processors leads to better performance. However, this isn't always the case. For example, let's consider a VM created by using a physical-to-virtual conversion. This workload was previously running on an older Pentium 3 Xeon processor at 700MHz and is running a custom line-of-business (LOB) application.

Now that it's in a VM, will the workload run more quickly? Depending on the type of application, it may not. That doesn't mean the extra processing power from faster processors goes to waste, because it provides extra headroom for workloads to grow and a resource for other VMs. But you do need to take this fact into account.

CPU-BOUND OR I/O-BOUND WORKLOADS

Not all workloads are capped by the processing power available to the VM. Some workloads, such as a SQL Server, are generally bound to a greater extent by the limits of memory and the disk subsystem than by the processor. In this case, buying a faster processor won't necessarily provide faster performance to the VMs—use the money you save to invest in memory or a faster storage subsystem.

Once the host has been deployed, administrators often use management tools to determine how the host is performing. But because of the virtual nature of the processors, monitoring a virtual system isn't as simple as looking at the Task Manager.

PERFMON

Traditionally, administrators used Windows Task Manager to get a quick glance at what was happening on the system (see Figure 4.1). However, because of the architecture of Hyper-V, Task Manager doesn't show the CPU usage of VMs. Task Manager running in the parent partition has no way of displaying that information; instead, you need to use Perfmon.

FIGURE 4.1
Windows Task
Manager
shows system
performance

WHAT'S PERFMON?

Perfmon, short for Performance Monitor, is Microsoft's tool to examine performance data. This data can be as simple as CPU utilization or as complex as context switches between Ring 0 and Ring 3.

By looking at the Hyper-V performance counters through Perfmon, you can determine if the system has room for more VMs or, conversely, if the system is oversubscribed (too many VMs running on the host).

Using Perfmon to monitor the host is easy. From the Start menu, select Administrative Tools, and then select Reliability And Performance Monitor. Click Performance Monitor in the list on the left (see Figure 4.2).

FIGURE 4.2
Performance
Monitor for VMs

By default, only one item is tracked in Perfmon: % Processor Time. Unless you're interested in the processor utilization of the parent partition only, you'll need to add some counters.

The processor-performance counters refer to the number of logical processors (LPs) in the system. A *logical processor* is a unit of processing power—for example, if you have a system with a single CPU socket and a single-core, non-hyperthreaded processor, you have one LP. Change that processor to a dual-core processor, and you have two LPs. Adding Hyper-Threading? Make it four logical processors.

NOTE Before you add a virtualization-related counter, make sure a VM is running. If no VMs are running, the counters won't appear.

To add a performance counter, you click the green + sign or press Ctrl-I. A large number of Hyper-V–related performance counters are available, but we're interested in a couple in particular (see Figure 4.3):

Hyper-V Hypervisor Virtual Processor, % Total Run Time   Under Instances Of Selected Object, you'll see a few options. _Total provides a sum of all the VPs allocated to all running VMs. You can also add individual VPs allocated to a VM.

Hyper-V Hypervisor Root Virtual Processor, % Total Run Time   This is the percentage of the time that the logical processors selected are executing instructions in non-Hypervisor–based code in the root/parent partition.

Adding these two values gives you the total CPU utilization of the host executing virtualization-related code. The closer the value gets to 100%, the more heavily loaded the system is.

FIGURE 4.3

Processor counters
for a Hyper-V host

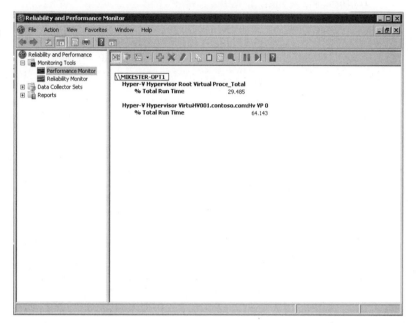

How Much Memory Is Enough?

Memory is another key area to consider when you set up virtualization. After all, you can have all the processing power in the world, but unless you have enough memory to run those VMs at the same time, you'll be stuck with extra processing power.

Hyper-V doesn't support the concept of allocating more memory than is available in the host system. This prevents you from affecting the performance of the host. (If you started a VM using 4GB on a system with 2GB of RAM, the system would need to use virtual memory to provide the extra memory beyond what was available on the host.)

How much memory is necessary for the host? The usual answer applies here: It depends on a number of factors.

Number of VMs running, and their allocated memory   How many VMs will be running on the host, and how much memory will be allocated to each one? The amount of memory each VMs needs is entirely dependent on the workload running within the VM. A SQL Server running in a VM will require much more memory than a departmental file server.

Other workloads running on the host   Although it's recommended that Hyper-V be the only role running on the host, it's possible that this won't be the case. If so, it's critical that enough memory be available to service all the other workloads running on the system. Refer to the memory requirements of the other workload(s) that will be running on the host, and add that amount to the total amount of memory required for the VM.

Host reserves It's recommended that you set aside 512MB of RAM for the host. That memory is used by Hyper-V's virtualization stack that runs in the parent partition, as well as by any services running in the parent partition. Hyper-V won't allow a VM to launch unless at least 32MB of RAM is available.

Other VMs (for quick-migration scenarios only) If the host is part of a Windows Server 2008 cluster for quick migration, ensure that there are sufficient resources across all nodes of the cluster in case one node goes down. If a node hosting VMs goes offline for any reason, those VMs will attempt to restart across all other nodes in the cluster. However, if there's not enough memory on the cluster's remaining active nodes, the VMs may not be able to start. For more information, refer to Chapter 6, "Virtual Machine Migration," which covers quick migration in depth.

NOTE In some rare cases, a VM may not be able to start even when plenty of memory is available. This is most commonly seen when large file copies are performed in the parent partition. Microsoft has released a hotfix for this as KB953585.

Luckily, monitoring the amount of available memory on a Hyper-V host is significantly easier than monitoring processor utilization, because memory utilization appears in Task Manager. You can also monitor the host's memory utilization using the Memory ➤ Available Mbytes counter.

Storage: How Many Drives Do I Need?

Storage can be one of the most complicated areas to plan for virtualization deployments. It's rare that you'll know exactly how large your VMs will grow, which may lead to either too much or not enough storage being allocated to a particular virtualization host. You can avoid both situations with some planning and monitoring.

When you're planning a virtualization deployment, knowing the basics of the workload and expected growth is critical to ensuring that enough storage is provisioned to the host. However, the way that storage is provisioned is as critical as the amount. Allocating 2TB of storage to a host for VM usage may sound great; but if it's two 1TB drives connected to a Serial Advanced Technology Attachment (SATA) controller on the motherboard, it's highly unlikely that it will perform under load.

Storage planning involves two main areas of concern: storage controllers and the number of drives connected to those controllers. The type of storage on the back end also matters:

Storage controllers The number of storage controllers installed in the system is a common bottleneck. A VM will do as much I/O as a physical system. If a VM is doing significant amounts of I/O, it can and will saturate the storage controller. Performance will suffer for any other VMs that are using virtual hard disks (VHDs) available from that storage controller.

That's why it's absolutely critical to have multiple paths available to the storage pool, for both performance reasons and failover in case of a loss of connection. Having multiple controllers available eliminates the single point of failure that can cripple a large-scale virtualization deployment.

Number of drives As we mentioned earlier, provisioning storage for virtualization doesn't always mean getting the largest drive available. In many cases, just as with many high-performance workloads, it's preferable to have multiple smaller disks as opposed to fewer larger disks. Having multiple disks available lets you spread the work across multiple physical disks that are part of a Redundant Array of Independent Disks (RAID).

Storage type   The type of storage connected to the host is of slightly less importance. As long as the storage is on the Windows Server 2008 hardware compatibility list, it will work with Hyper-V. This includes small computer system interface (SCSI), serial-attached SCSI (SAS), Internet SCSI (iSCSI), fibre channel, and even Intelligent Drive Electronics (IDE) and SATA.

You'll see the difference in the rotational speed of the disk, as well as the amount of cache available on the disk. The performance gains from moving from a 7,200 RPM disk to a 10,000 RPM or even 15,000 RPM disk are significant and can increase even more past that level. Similarly, moving from 4 or 8MB of cache to 16 or 32MB will increase performance.

Volume management   When you pair storage with highly available VMs, the best practices get a bit more complicated. VMs that are made highly available as part of failover clustering have a limitation of one VM per logical unit number (LUN) if individual failover per VM is desired. This means you must carefully plan the provisioning of LUNs.

NOTE   Microsoft doesn't yet have a filesystem that supports multiple VMs on a LUN, but that doesn't mean it's not possible. Check out Chapter 8, "High Availability," for more information.

After your Hyper-V host is up and running, you should watch a few performance counters related to storage:

- Physical Disk, % Disk Read Time

- Physical Disk, % Disk Write Time

- Physical Disk, % Idle Time

These three counters provide a good high-level view of disk activity. If the read and write times are high (consistently greater than 75%), then disk performance is likely to be affected. Additional counters to monitor include these:

- Physical Disk, Avg. Disk Read Queue Length

- Physical Disk, Avg. Disk Write Queue Length

High levels for these counters (greater than 2) may indicate a disk bottleneck.

Networking

Networking requires a significant amount of planning for virtualization. You need to account for a number of different scenarios, and all of them depend on the workloads running in the VM on any given host.

Some questions you'll need to answer include the following:

- Does the server have an out-of-band server-management controller?

- How many VMs will be running on the host, and what is their network utilization?

- Is iSCSI-based storage in use?

- How much network bandwidth is available on the back end?

For the purposes of this section, let's assume you have a host system that is hosting three VMs. The host has four network adapters and doesn't have an out-of-band management controller. Let's examine how you can best put these interfaces to use in a number of different scenarios, while answering the previous questions.

HOST MANAGEMENT

The first area to consider is host management. Because the system doesn't have an out-of-band management controller, which would let you access the host and act like you were sitting in front of it, you need to dedicate one interface for host management. You can do so in one of two ways:

◆ During installation, leave one of the interfaces on the host unselected (see Figure 4.4).

◆ If the installation has already taken place, delete the virtual network that's bound to the network adapter you want to use for management of the host.

FIGURE 4.4
Leaving a physical network adapter unselected for host management while adding the Hyper-V role

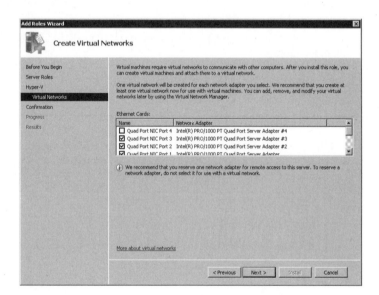

WORKLOADS

Now, let's look at the workloads running in the VMs on this host. Three VMs are running, and analyzing the data indicates that two of the VMs don't generate much network traffic and the third generates a significant network load. You decide to create two virtual networks—one for the VMs that don't generate significant network traffic, and one for the VM that does.

You can do this three ways:

◆ During installation, select two ports on the Create Virtual Networks tab (see Figure 4.5).

◆ If the installation has already taken place, use the Virtual Network Manager to modify the existing virtual networks.

FIGURE 4.5

Leaving two physical network adapters unselected for iSCSI usage while adding the Hyper-V role

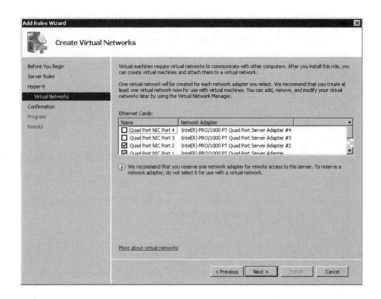

♦ Use a series of scripts to create a new virtual network without creating a virtual network adapter in the parent partition. This can be accomplished by running four VBScripts, as follows:

1. Create a new virtual switch. The following script takes one parameter, which is the name of the virtual switch to be created. (You can find the original script at `http://msdn.microsoft.com/en-us/library/cc136783(VS.85).aspx`.)

```
option explicit

dim objWMIService
dim switchService
dim fileSystem

const wmiStarted = 4096
const wmiSuccessful = 0

Main()

'--------------------------------------------------------------------
' Main
'--------------------------------------------------------------------
Sub Main()

    dim name, friendlyName, learnableAddress
    dim computer, objArgs, createdSwitch

    set objArgs = WScript.Arguments
    if WScript.Arguments.Count = 3 then
      name = objArgs.Unnamed.Item(0)
```

```
        friendlyName = objArgs.Unnamed.Item(1)
        learnableAddress = objArgs.Unnamed.Item(2)
    else
        WScript.Echo "usage: cscript CreateSwitch.vbs name friendlyName
learnableAddress"
        WScript.Echo "Example: CreateSwitch FirstSwitch ""My First Switch"" 1024"
        WScript.Quit(1)
    end if

    set fileSystem = Wscript.CreateObject("Scripting.FileSystemObject")
    computer = "."

    set objWMIService = GetObject("winmgmts:\\" & computer &
"\root\virtualization")
    set switchService = objWMIService.ExecQuery("select * from
Msvm_VirtualSwitchManagementService").ItemIndex(0)

    set createdSwitch = CreateSwitch(name, friendlyName, learnableAddress)

    if createdSwitch Is Nothing then
        WriteLog "CreateSwitch failed."
        WScript.Quit(1)
    else
        WriteLog "Done"
        WScript.Quit(0)
    end if

End Sub

'------------------------------------------------------------------
' Create a virtual switch by calling CreateSwitch WMI method
'------------------------------------------------------------------
Function CreateSwitch(name, friendlyName, learnableAddress)

    dim objInParam, objOutParams

    set CreateSwitch = Nothing
    set objInParam = switchService.Methods_("CreateSwitch").InParameters.
SpawnInstance_()
    objInParam.FriendlyName = friendlyName
    objInParam.Name = name
    objInParam.NumLearnableAddresses = learnableAddress
    objInParam.ScopeofResidence = null
```

```
    set objOutParams = switchService.ExecMethod_("CreateSwitch", objInParam)

    if objOutParams.ReturnValue = wmiSuccessful then
        set CreateSwitch = objWMIService.Get(objOutParams.CreatedVirtualSwitch)
    else
        WriteLog Format1("CreateSwitch failed with error code {0}",
objOutParams.ReturnValue)
    end if

End Function


'-------------------------------------------------------------------
' Create the console log files.
'-------------------------------------------------------------------
Sub WriteLog(line)
    dim fileStream
    set fileStream = fileSystem.OpenTextFile(".\CreateSwitch.log", 8, true)
    WScript.Echo line
    fileStream.WriteLine line
    fileStream.Close

End Sub


'---------------------------------------------------------------------------
' The string formatting functions to avoid string concatenation.
'---------------------------------------------------------------------------
Function Format1(myString, arg0)
    Format1 = Replace(myString, "{0}", arg0)
End Function
```

2. Connect to the virtual switch a network adapter that currently isn't in use. The follow-ing script also takes one parameter: the name of the network adapter. Use the "friendly" name, which you can find in Network Connections. An example friendly name would be similar to Intel(R) Pro/1000 PT Quad Port Server Adapter. (Original script source: http://msdn.microsoft.com/en-us/library/cc136768(VS.85).aspx.)

```
option explicit

dim objWMIService
dim switchService
dim fileSystem

const wmiSuccessful = 0
```

```
Main()

'-----------------------------------------------------------------
' Main
'-----------------------------------------------------------------
Sub Main()
    dim computer, objArgs, externalEthernetPort, firendlyName

    set objArgs = WScript.Arguments
    if WScript.Arguments.Count = 1 then
        firendlyName = objArgs.Unnamed.Item(0)
    else
        WScript.Echo "usage: cscript BindExternalEthernetPort
ExternalEthternetPortFriendlyName"
        WScript.Echo "Example: BindExternalEthernetPort ""Intel(R) PRO/1000 PM
Network Connection"""
        WScript.Quit(1)
    end if

    set fileSystem = Wscript.CreateObject("Scripting.FileSystemObject")
    computer = "."

    set objWMIService = GetObject("winmgmts:\\" & computer &
"\root\virtualization")
    set switchService = objWMIService.ExecQuery("select * from
Msvm_VirtualSwitchManagementService").ItemIndex(0)


    set externalEthernetPort = GetExternalEthernetPort(firendlyName)

    if (externalEthernetPort Is Nothing) then
        WriteLog Format1("Unable to find external Ethernet Port {0}", firendlyName)
        WScript.Quit(1)
    end if

    if BindExternalEthernetPort(externalEthernetPort) then
        WriteLog "Done"
        WScript.Quit(0)
    else
        WriteLog("BindExternalEthernetPort failed")
        WScript.Quit(1)
    end if
End Sub
```

```
'-------------------------------------------------------------------
' Retrieve the external Ethernet port
'-------------------------------------------------------------------
Function GetExternalEthernetPort(externalEthernetPortFriendlyName)
    dim objNTInfo, computerName, query, computer
    dim externalEthernetPort, externalEthernetPorts

    set GetExternalEthernetPort = Nothing
    set objNTInfo = CreateObject("WinNTSystemInfo")
    computerName = lcase(objNTInfo.ComputerName)

    query = Format1("select * from Msvm_ComputerSystem where Name = '{0}'",
computerName)
    set computer = objWMIService.ExecQuery(query).ItemIndex(0)

    query = Format1("ASSOCIATORS OF {{0}} WHERE resultClass =
Msvm_ExternalEthernetPort", computer.Path_.Path)
    set externalEthernetPorts = objWMIService.ExecQuery(query)
    for each externalEthernetPort in externalEthernetPorts
        if lcase(externalEthernetPort.ElementName) =
lcase(externalEthernetPortFriendlyName) then
            set GetExternalEthernetPort = externalEthernetPort
            Exit Function
        end if
    next

End Function


'-------------------------------------------------------------------
' Bind the External Ethernet Port by calling BindExternalEthernetPort
'-------------------------------------------------------------------
Function BindExternalEthernetPort(externalEthernetPort)
    dim objInParam, objOutParams

    BindExternalEthernetPort = false
    set objInParam =
switchService.Methods_("BindExternalEthernetPort").InParameters.SpawnInstance_
()
    objInParam.ExternalEthernetPort = externalEthernetPort.Path_.Path

    set objOutParams = switchService.ExecMethod_("BindExternalEthernetPort",
objInParam)

    if objOutParams.ReturnValue = wmiSuccessful then
        BindExternalEthernetPort = true
```

```vbscript
        else
            WriteLog Format1("BindExternalEthernetPort failed with error code {0}",
    objOutParams.ReturnValue)
        end if

End Function


'---------------------------------------------------------------------
' Create the console log files.
'---------------------------------------------------------------------
Sub WriteLog(line)
    dim fileStream
    set fileStream = fileSystem.OpenTextFile(".\BindExternalEthernetPort.log", 8,
true)
    WScript.Echo line
    fileStream.WriteLine line
    fileStream.Close

End Sub


'---------------------------------------------------------------------------
' The string formating functions to avoid string concatenation.
'---------------------------------------------------------------------------
Function Format1(myString, arg0)
    Format1 = Replace(myString, "{0}", arg0)
End Function
```

3. Create a port on the virtual switch. This script takes two parameters: the name of the virtual switch you created in step 1 and a generic port name—for example, HyperVExternalPort1. (Original script source: http://msdn.microsoft.com/en-us/library/cc136782(VS.85).aspx.)

```vbscript
option explicit

dim objWMIService
dim switchService
dim fileSystem

const wmiSuccessful = 0

Main()


'---------------------------------------------------------------
' Main
'---------------------------------------------------------------
Sub Main()
```

```
    dim computer, objArgs
    dim switch, switchName,  name, friendlyName, createdSwitchPort

    set fileSystem = Wscript.CreateObject("Scripting.FileSystemObject")
    computer = "."

    set objWMIService = GetObject("winmgmts:\\" & computer &
"\root\virtualization")
    set switchService = objWMIService.ExecQuery("select * from
Msvm_VirtualSwitchManagementService").ItemIndex(0)

    set objArgs = WScript.Arguments
    if WScript.Arguments.Count = 3 then
      switchName = objArgs.Unnamed.Item(0)
      name = objArgs.Unnamed.Item(1)
      friendlyName = objArgs.Unnamed.Item(2)
    else
      WScript.Echo "usage: cscript CreateSwitchPort SwitchName Name FriendlyName"
      WScript.Echo "Example: CreateSwitchPort MyFirstSwitch FirstVirualSwitchPort
""First VirualSwitch Port"""
      WScript.Quit(1)
    end if

    set switch = GetVirtualSwitch(switchName)
    if Not (switch Is Nothing) then
       set createdSwitchPort = CreateSwitchPort(switch, name, friendlyName)
       if Not(createdSwitchPort Is Nothing) then
          WriteLog "Done"
          WScript.Quit(0)
       End if
    else
       WriteLog "CreateSwitchPort failed"
       WScript.Quit(1)
    end if
End Sub


'-----------------------------------------------------------------
' Retrieve VirtualSwitch
'-----------------------------------------------------------------
Function GetVirtualSwitch(firendlyName)
    dim query
    set GetVirtualSwitch = Nothing
    query = Format1("select * from Msvm_VirtualSwitch where ElementName = '{0}'",
firendlyName)
    set GetVirtualSwitch= objWMIService.ExecQuery(query).ItemIndex(0)
End Function
```

```
'-------------------------------------------------------------------
' Create a virtual switch by calling CreateSwitch WMI method
'-------------------------------------------------------------------
Function CreateSwitchPort(virtualSwitch, name, friendlyName)
    dim objInParam, objOutParams

    set CreateSwitchPort = Nothing
    set objInParam =
switchService.Methods_("CreateSwitchPort").InParameters.SpawnInstance_()
    objInParam.FriendlyName = friendlyName
    objInParam.Name = name
    objInParam.VirtualSwitch = virtualSwitch.Path_.Path
    objInParam.ScopeofResidence = null

    set objOutParams = switchService.ExecMethod_("CreateSwitchPort", objInParam)

    if objOutParams.ReturnValue = wmiSuccessful then
        set CreateSwitchPort = objWMIService.Get(objOutParams.CreatedSwitchPort)
    else
        WriteLog Format1("CreateSwitchPort failed with error code {0}",
objOutParams.ReturnValue)
    end if
End Function


'-------------------------------------------------------------------
' Create the console log files.
'-------------------------------------------------------------------
Sub WriteLog(line)
    dim fileStream
    set fileStream = fileSystem.OpenTextFile(".\CreateSwitchPort.log", 8, true)
    WScript.Echo line
    fileStream.WriteLine line
    fileStream.Close

End Sub


'-------------------------------------------------------------------
' The string formatting functions to avoid string concatenation.
'-------------------------------------------------------------------
Function Format1(myString, arg0)
    Format1 = Replace(myString, "{0}", arg0)
End Function
```

4. Connect the newly created port on the virtual switch to the network adapter in step 2. Robert Vierthaler, an escalation engineer with Microsoft Germany, has created a script that will do this task. This script takes three parameters: the switch name from step 1, the port name from step 3, and the friendly name of the network interface card (NIC) from step 2. The script to perform this task can be found at the following URL:

```
http://blogs.msdn.com/robertvi/archive/2008/08/27/howto-create-a
-virtual-swich-for-external-without-creating-a-virtual-nic-on-the
-root.aspx
```

iSCSI

The next step for proper network planning and utilization involves iSCSI. Will the VMs be using iSCSI, or will the host be using iSCSI? Regardless of whether it's a host or a guest, you should set aside a separate interface for each instance of iSCSI traffic. If the host is using iSCSI (for failover clustering, for example), then it should have a separate adapter port that is different from any adapter port being used for guest VMs using iSCSI.

NOTE   iSCSI can be used in a VM—in fact, it's the only way to set up a cluster of VMs. It's recommended that if a VM is using iSCSI, you should create a separate virtual network to ensure sufficient bandwidth.

VLAN Tagging

Will any of the VMs be using virtual local area networks (VLANs)? *VLAN tagging*, also known as 802.1q, assigns a specific *tag* to packets if it's in use. This tag allows separate traffic streams to go out over the same wire while maintaining isolation, because the packets can't be snooped or sniffed. This is especially useful in larger deployments of Hyper-V in enterprises with the infrastructure already in place.

As we discussed in Chapter 3, "Configuring Hyper-V," you can use VLAN tagging on each individual virtual adapter that's assigned to a VM. To do so, select the network adapter from the settings for the VM, and enter the correct VLAN ID.

Switch Uplink Bandwidth

Until now, we've been looking at the adapters that are available on the host, as well as the virtual adapters available to the VM. There's one area that we've yet to touch on: the hub or switch that the physical interfaces are plugged in to. A wide variety of switches are available, and each of them is slightly different. It's important that the switch have enough bandwidth to support multiple-gigabit interfaces and to send the data upstream. If a switch has eight 1GB network ports and each port is sending 1GB of traffic, a single-gigabit uplink port won't be able to handle all the traffic coming out of the switch, leading to less than optimal performance.

Monitoring virtual networks in Hyper-V is relatively painless. In Perfmon, the Hyper-V Virtual Network Adapter provides counters for each virtual network you've created. Careful monitoring of those counters can alert you to the saturation of a particular virtual network.

NOTE   "What if my system has only a single network adapter?" This question comes up frequently for users in a test/development scenario. In this case, many of the items we've discussed don't apply.

If only a single Ethernet port is available, all the traffic from all VMs will share the same port. We recommend that at least two network interfaces be available on the system, which lets you reserve one network adapter for host administration.

Host Operating System Best Practices

Now that we've covered hardware best practices, let's look at what you can do on the software side. As we discussed in Chapter 2, "Installing Hyper-V and Server Core," you can run Hyper-V on either a full installation of Windows Server 2008 or a Core installation. Each installation has its benefits and drawbacks; but the core Hyper-V binaries are exactly the same, regardless of your installation choice.

For a more secure and possibly more stable virtualization platform, using Windows Server 2008 Core is your best choice. Windows Server 2008 Core has a smaller attack surface and slightly less overhead for the parent partition. Those benefits help provide a more robust virtualization platform for large deployments.

RUNNING OTHER APPLICATIONS OR SERVICES IN THE PARENT PARTITION

Two additional factors can help to reduce bottlenecks in the parent partition and lead to faster performance:

- ◆ Don't run any applications in the parent partition.

- ◆ Don't run other server roles in the parent partition.

Running other applications or server roles in the parent partition can degrade performance. It's critical to keep the parent partition as unencumbered as possible. Keeping the parent partition lean and mean means more resources are available to the VMs.

NOTE Running a lean parent partition is generally acceptable for a datacenter-based deployment of Hyper-V, but branch offices typically deploy only a few servers per branch. With limited processing power available, it might seem to make more sense to run lightweight workloads on the parent partition alongside the Hyper-V role. Doing so can impact the stability of the Hyper-V role, so it's generally best to run those workloads inside VMs.

VIRUS SCANNERS: DON'T LET THEM IMPACT PERFORMANCE

You should set your virus scanners to ignore virtualization-related files. If a virus scanner is running in the parent partition, constant scanning of virtualization-related files may slow disk performance. Many antivirus programs don't have a way to look at the contents of those files, so it's best to set up scanning exemptions in your antivirus software of choice.

The process varies depending on the antivirus software you use. You can typically block scanning either by file type or by folder. The following file types should be excluded from scanning (see Figure 4.6):

- ◆ Virtual hard disk (.vhd)

- ◆ Memory placeholder file (.bin)

- ◆ Saved-state files (.vsv)

- ◆ File-based representations of physical CD/DVD media (.iso)

FIGURE 4.6
Possible file extensions to exclude when using an antivirus scanner

Alternatively, you can exclude a directory from real-time scanning and then set the engine to ignore the configuration and VHD directories as defined in the host settings (see Figure 4.7).

FIGURE 4.7
Excluding directories

Virtual-Machine Best Practices

Although you can do a significant amount of work on the host to ensure that your VMs are performing as well as possible, you can also do quite a bit of work within the VM. In addition to sizing the VM correctly, running integration services in the VM increases performance significantly.

You can also set up a library of VHD files that have been prepared for quick deployments. If the operating systems running in the VM are Microsoft Windows, then those VHD files should be Sysprepped for hands-off deployment.

Finally, after you've Sysprepped a library of images, how do you keep them up to date? Microsoft has a tool to help, called the Offline Virtual Machine Servicing Tool. We'll cover how this tool updates VHDs.

Integration Services: Guest Drivers

Integration services are a set of drivers and services that run in the VM. They're installed after you install the operating system in the VM. (We discussed integration services briefly in Chapter 1, "Introduction to Hyper-V.")

Integration services are available for the following operating systems:

◆ Windows Server 2008, x86 and x64 editions

◆ Windows Server 2003 SP2, x86 and x64 editions

◆ Windows 2000 Server/Advanced Server

◆ Windows Vista SP1, x86 and x64 editions

◆ Windows XP SP2 or 3, x86 and x64 editions

◆ SUSE Linux Enterprise Server 10 SP2, x86 and x64 editions

These services contain the following drivers:

IDE   This driver provides optimized paths for IDE traffic, redirecting such traffic from the emulated device path to the synthetic (Virtual Machine Bus [VMBus]) device path.

SCSI   This driver provides support for the synthetic SCSI device in the VM. SCSI controllers in Hyper-V can have up to 64 devices per controller, with a maximum of 4 controllers per VM.

Networking   This driver provides support for the Microsoft VMBus network adapter, which provides much greater performance than the older emulated device.

Video/mouse   The video and mouse drivers work together to provide a seamless experience when you use VMConnect to access a VM.

In addition to the optimized virtualization drivers, additional services are made available to the VM once you install the integration components:

Operating System Shutdown   Operating System Shutdown lets you shut down the operating system within the VM without having to log in. It's very similar to pushing the power button on a hardware system to power it down.

Time Synchronization   Time Synchronization keeps the VM's clock and the host clock in sync. When the VM is powered on, the clock in the VM is synced to the clock on the host. This driver keeps the two in sync afterward.

Data Exchange   By using the Key Value Pair (KVP) mechanism, VMs and their hosts can communicate by key pairs. This allows both systems to get information from each other—for example, the VM can query the host and get the name of the host. The VM can only modify the HKEY_LOCAL_MACHINE\Software\Microsoft\Virtual Machine\Guest keys. This functionality is available only on Windows-based VMs.

Heartbeat   If integration services are installed in the VM, a heartbeat service will run in the VM. That heartbeat service sends a notification to the host if it's still responding. You can observe the heartbeat status in the Hyper-V Manager as well as through the Windows Management Interface (WMI) interfaces.

Online Backup The Online Backup component is a Volume Shadow Services (VSS) writer. VSS provides a method for taking a backup of the state of a disk at any given point in time; the backup is application consistent. When you start a VSS backup, all running VMs with integration services installed are notified, and data is flushed to disk.

To install integration services in the VM, select Action ➤ Insert Integration Services Setup Disk in the Virtual Machine Connect application. Doing so mounts the installation image in the VM. When that's complete, the autorun functionality in Windows starts the installer. If autorun is disabled, browse to the support\x86 directory and double-click setup.exe.

NOTE Installing integration services in a Linux VM requires a download, because the components aren't included in-box with Hyper-V. For more information about integration services for Linux, go to http://www.microsoft.com/virtualization.

Sysprep: Creating a Master Base Image

For environments where you must rapidly deploy VMs, a library of prebuilt drive images can be a real time-saver. If those VMs are running Windows, though, it's not as simple as installing Windows once and then copying the VHD file. You need to remove the name and unique identifier of the operating system that's installed. Microsoft has made a tool available that will perform those tasks; it's called Sysprep.

When you Sysprep a VM, certain information is deleted and marked for re-creation on the first boot. This information includes the username, the product key, and your acceptance of the End User License Agreement (EULA). This process makes it extremely easy to create a library of prebuilt VMs—and then deploy them without having to install a new copy of the operating system.

Sysprepping a VM is a very quick process. With Windows Vista and Windows Server 2008, the tool is included in the operating system. (For older operating systems, refer to the documentation to learn where Sysprep is located.) Open a command window, browse to %WINDIR%\system32\sysprep, and launch sysprep.exe.

The Sysprep tool, when run with its defaults, clears the VM's Security Identifier (the SID) and removes the registered owner. It also sets the operating system to enter what Microsoft calls *Mini-Setup*, which lets you set some parameters for the VM such as the machine name and the new administrative password.

NOTE To create a master copy of a Windows operating system in a VHD file and prepare it for future deployments, it's best to perform a clean install of the operating system, apply any available updates and/or patches, and install the integration services. Then, run the Sysprep tool (see Figure 4.8) and select Shutdown Options ➤ Shutdown. When the VM shuts down, you've got a clean master copy of the operating system that can be saved for future deployment.

FIGURE 4.8
Sysprep tool

Offline Patching

After you follow the steps we've discussed and create a library of VMs, you need to keep them up to date with patches. Microsoft has released a solutions accelerator called the Offline Virtual Machine Servicing Tool 2.01. This tool works in conjunction with System Center Virtual Machine Manager (SCVMM) and either Windows Server Update Services (WSUS) 3.0 or System Center Configuration Manager 2007 (SCCM) to provide a safe and secure method for applying updates to VM images.

The workflow for the tool is simple:

1. The VM is deployed on a maintenance host—a special host type defined by SCVMM.

2. A job is triggered within the VM that starts the software-update cycle.

3. The VM is shut down and returned to the library, fully patched.

To find out more about the Offline Virtual Machine Servicing Tool, or to download your free copy, browse to `http://www.microsoft.com/solutionaccelerators`.

Summary

In this chapter, we've looked at a number of ways that you can configure your systems for optimal performance. By ensuring that the physical system is tuned and can stand up to the VMs running on the host, you can ensure that the choice to deploy virtualization results in a positive experience for users and administrators alike.

Chapter 5

Hyper-V Security

In the first four chapters of this book, we covered a wide variety of topics, including installation of Hyper-V, creation of virtual machines, and best practices. Now that we've covered the basics and set up a level playing field, let's dig into the security features of Hyper-V.

Security is a hot-button topic these days, especially when it comes to virtualization. With workload consolidation happening on a major scale after virtualization is deployed, you want to ensure that virtualized workloads are well isolated and that you grant the right access privileges to the right people.

In this chapter, we'll cover:

◆ Hypervisor security model

◆ Virtualization machine-access security model

◆ Working with the Authorization Manager (AzMan)

The Hyper-V Security Model

Because the Hypervisor sits below all other components (see Chapter 1, "Introduction to Hyper-V," for the architectural overview), it's naturally the first attack target of those looking to compromise a Hyper-V host.

One of the most talked-about items related to security of hypervisors (not specific to Hyper-V) is Blue Pill. The term Blue Pill harkens back to the film *The Matrix*—if you ingested the blue pill, you had no idea that you actually lived inside the Matrix. The Blue Pill concept was written by Joanna Rutkowska and presented at the Black Hat Security Conference in 2006; it referred to the possibility of malware being injected into a hypervisor-aware platform without the user's knowledge. Needless to say, it caused quite a stir when people learned that a hypervisor could be subverted so easily.

Hyper-V was developed with a number of security assumptions in mind:

◆ The parent partition is trusted by the hypervisor, and the virtual machines (child partitions) trust the parent partition.

◆ None of the virtual machines (VMs) running on a host are trusted. They can be used for nefarious deeds.

◆ The code running in VMs must be run unmodified, must use all features of the x86 instruction set, and can execute in any ring necessary.

◆ The hypercall interface, which child partitions can use to access functions of the hypervisor, is publically available and fully documented. A (potentially) untrusted VM can attempt to execute any of the hypercalls.

◆ A VM can detect that it's running on a hypervisor.

In this section, we'll review the security of the hypervisor as well as the security of the virtualization stack.

Hypervisor Security

Microsoft has done a number of things to ensure a secure hypervisor:

Security Development Lifecycle   The Microsoft Security Development Lifecycle (SDL) is one of the main ways that Microsoft assures quality software. In place since 2004, the SDL has improved product quality by implementing strict quality gates, process improvements, and other guidance throughout the entire software-development process. By being put in place at the earliest possible time, before a line of code has been written, the SDL helps eliminate security issues before the product ships and can affect users.

For more information, you can read the following white paper, which provides guidance on how Microsoft implemented the SDL: http://www.microsoft.com/downloads/details.aspx?FamilyID=2412c443-27f6-4aac-9883-f55ba5b01814&displaylang=en.

Keep in mind that this is only a guide and that not all the steps Microsoft followed are publically available.

Separate address spaces   Both the hypervisor and the host operating system maintain separate address spaces. An *address space* refers to a specific location in memory. By ensuring that there are separate address spaces for both components, the host operating system can't read or access the hypervisor address space and vice versa.

No third-party code   The hypervisor included as part of Hyper-V doesn't include any third-party code. Other hypervisors include device drivers or other drivers that were submitted by third parties.

By having all code in the hypervisor go through the SDL, Microsoft can ensure the stability of the hypervisor as a whole.

Guest-to-guest communication   No communication that takes place between guests over synthetic devices goes through the hypervisor. This reduces the chance of a man-in-the-middle attack in the hypervisor, where someone injects a driver at the hypervisor level that sniffs data going between two VMs.

No shared memory between guests   Each guest has its own memory space. This means the memory allocated to those VMs is exclusive and can't be accessed from other VMs.

Inability of guests to affect hardware I/O   All I/O for synthetic devices in VMs is handled in the Virtualization Service Provider / Virtualization Service Client (VSP/VSC) model, which sits above the hypervisor layer. Also, the I/O model of the VSP/VSC architecture sends out requests on behalf of the VM—the VM itself doesn't send I/O requests.

Hypervisor access   The host and guests are unable to write to the hypervisor; rather, they communicate with the hypervisor via the well-defined Hypercall API. This ensures that the hypervisor can't be modified.

Virtualization Stack Security

The security work that Microsoft did with Hyper-V didn't stop at the hypervisor level:

◆ All of the binaries that are included as part of the Hyper-V role have gone through the SDL process. One part of this process adds address-space-layout randomization, which, when enabled, loads critical DLLs in random pages of memory at each boot. This helps alleviate exploits that target DLLs that load in the same memory location every time.

◆ The worker processes that represent the virtual processor to the VM have a number of safe-guards—they run in user mode, with reduced privileges, and each worker process is separate from the others.

◆ Each VM has its own instance of a virtual device. No two VMs can use the same virtual network adapter—when a VM is created, a new virtual network adapter is created for that VM.

◆ By requiring the Execute Disable/No Execute bit in the host's processor, the chance of malicious buffer overflow attacks is reduced.

Other components, such as the VSP/VSC architecture, have additional security measures in place:

◆ Each VM that is powered on has a separate instance of Virtual Machine Bus (VMBus).

◆ VMBus is a point-to-point connection between the VSP in the parent and the VSC in the guest.

◆ Because the VSC doesn't have access to the physical device, DMA (Direct Memory Access) attacks can't take place.

Virtual Machine Access Security Model

Of course, when it comes to security, ensuring your binaries and software are secure is only half the battle. One of the core tenets of security is to ensure a user has no more access than is absolutely necessary for a particular task. As we've been saying all along, this is even more important after you bring virtualization into play. In a shared host environment, for example, an administrator for the accounting department shouldn't be able to shut off the VM for the HR department. You can achieve this separation by working with the Authorization Manager (AzMan), which is part of Windows Server 2008.

Previously with Virtual Server 2005, this security was granted via access rights on the configuration file and on the virtual hard disk (VHD) file. However, with the changes made for Hyper-V, security and access rights moved into the AzMan. Rest assured, everything you could do previously with Virtual Server, you can still do with Hyper-V.

Working with the Authorization Manager

The AzMan functionality was first included with Windows Server 2003. It's undergone some enhancements with Windows Server 2008. At its heart, it's a simple role-based security architecture that allows compatible applications, such as Hyper-V, to grant users access to functionality without granting them administrative rights to the host system.

Terminology

You need to become familiar with some terms before you get started working with AzMan:

- *Role*: A set of permissions that's necessary to perform a job.

- *Operation*: The lowest level of actions you can take against a Hyper-V host. Examples of operations include creating a VM, modifying a virtual network, and viewing a list of the VMs on the host. You can't modify operations, but you can group them into tasks.

- *Task*: A group of operations. You can create tasks that group necessary operations for a particular task. An example task would include the ability to create and power on a VM.

- *Policy*: Definition of the interdependencies between roles, tasks, and operations.

Using the Authorization Manager for Hyper-V Security

In this example, the Contoso corporation has deployed a new Hyper-V host. This host will be hosting VMs for multiple departments. Each group has an administrator. The company's IT administrator wants to provide each group's administrator with the ability to turn the group's VM on or off, or reset it. The first group to get a VM provisioned on this host is the HR group.

To give the group administrator this ability, as the IT administrator you need to follow these steps:

1. Open the default store.

2. Create a new role definition in the master scope.

3. Create a new child scope for the HR organization.

4. Create a role definition for the HR team in the child scope.

5. Assign access for the HR Admin account to the role definition.

6. Assign a VM to the newly created scope.

To start with, you need to open the default authorization store. This contains all the default roles, operations, and tasks. In this store, you'll make the changes necessary for the first set of tasks.

Opening the Default Store

To open the default store, follow these steps:

1. Click the Start menu, and type in **azman.msc** in the text box. Alternatively, open a new MMC console, select Add/Remove Snap-in, and add the Authorization Manager snap-in. Next, select Action ➢ Open Authorization Store to open the window shown in Figure 5.1.

FIGURE 5.1
Opening the authorization store

NOTE   If you're modifying the access rights to a Windows Server Core system, you need to do so from a full installation of Windows Server 2008. Browse to the Windows Server Core host, and select the authorization store there.

2. Browse to the authorization store. The default authorization store is kept in the following location: C:\programdata\microsoft\windows\hyper-v\initialstore.xml.

Now that you have the store open, you can start with the changes necessary to support your scenario. Before you start, let's get familiar with the AzMan UI (see Figure 5.2).

FIGURE 5.2

The Authorization Manager UI

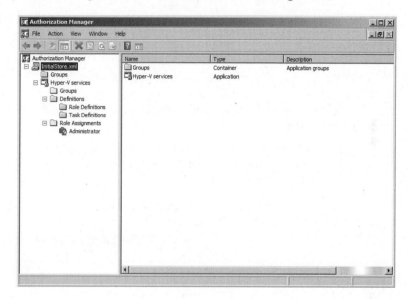

By default, a single scope is defined, named Hyper-V Services. Each child scope to the primary scope is independent of the other, but each child scope can inherit from the primary scope. Later in this exercise, you'll create a new scope.

In the Definitions folder are two items: Role Definitions and Task Definitions. By right-clicking those folders, you can create new definitions.

ASSIGNING ROLES

To get started, you need to create a new role definition. This role definition will give a user access to the VM Management Service (VMMS) and the Virtual Switch Management Service:

1. Right-click Role Definitions, and select New Role Definition.

2. For the name, type in **VM Manager Access**. Click the Add button, select the Operations tab, and select the Read Service Configuration and View Virtual Switch Management Service check boxes (see Figure 5.3). Click OK to close the New Role Definition window.

FIGURE 5.3

Creating a new role
definition

Now that you've created the role definition, you need to create a role assignment based on
that role definition.

3. Back in the Authorization Manager window, right-click Role Assignments, and select
New Role Assignment from the pop-up menu. Select the VM Manager Access check box,
and click OK (see Figure 5.4).

FIGURE 5.4

Creating a new role
assignment

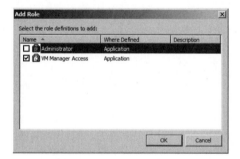

The last step adds a user account to the new role assignment you just created.

4. Right-click the VM Manager Access role assignment, and select Assign Users and
Groups ➢ From Windows and Active Directory. Type in the name of the account you
want to add (see Figure 5.5)—in this case, the HR team has an account called HRAdmin
that they'll be using for this purpose.

FIGURE 5.5

Adding a user account to the role assignment

NOTE If you're interested in just adding users to Hyper-V without requiring administrative rights to the host, add the user account to the Administrator role assignment. This grants the user administrative rights on the Hyper-V host, allowing them to perform actions against all VMs that are registered on the host.

CREATING A CHILD SCOPE

The next steps involve creating a child scope that will handle all the access permissions for the HR organization. In that scope, you'll create a new role definition that's specific to that scope. This scope will let you delegate control of the HR team's VM to the HR administrator:

1. In AzMan, right-click Hyper-V Services, and select New Scope. Name the new scope **HR** (see Figure 5.6). This creates a child scope to the master Hyper-V services scope.

2. In the HR scope, click Role Definitions, and then select New Role Definition. You'll name the new role definition HRAdmin.

3. Click the Add button, and then select the Operations tab. In this window, you can add all the options you want the HR Admin to be able to perform against all VMs that will be assigned to the scope. Select the check boxes next to the following items:

   ◆ Allow Input To Virtual Machine

   ◆ Allow Output From Virtual Machine

   ◆ Pause And Restart Virtual Machine

   ◆ Start Virtual Machine

   ◆ Stop Virtual Machine

The end result should look like Figure 5.7.

4. Like last time, you need to create a new role assignment for the role you just created. Right-click Role Assignments in the HR scope, and select New Role Assignment. Select the HRAdmin check box (see Figure 5.8), and click OK.

5. Right-click the new role assignment, and select Assign Users And Groups ➤ From Windows And Active Directory. Add the HRAdmin account in the dialog box, and click OK (see Figure 5.9).

FIGURE 5.6
Creating a new
child scope

FIGURE 5.7
Creating a new role
definition in the
child scope

FIGURE 5.8
Creating a role
assignment in the
child scope

FIGURE 5.9
Adding the user
account to the role
assignment in the
child scope

SETTING THE SCOPE OF A VIRTUAL MACHINE WITH SCRIPTS

At this point, the HR Admin user has access to the Hyper-V host. The account doesn't have the access necessary to create a VM, though. You need to create a new VM and set the scope of the VM to the HR Admin account. Hyper-V doesn't have any graphical way to set the scope of a particular VM, so you'll use a script.

You'll need four scripts for these next steps. These scripts, shown in Listings 5.1 through 5.4, were written by Tony Soper and posted on the Microsoft TechNet forums; refer to http://tinyurl.com/9d54gp for more information.

LISTING 5.1   CreateVMInScope.vbs

```
Option Explicit

Dim WMIService
Dim VMManagementService
Dim VMName
Dim VMScope
Dim VMSystemGlobalSettingData
Dim Result
Dim inParameters

VMName = InputBox("Specify the name for the new virtual machine:")
VMScope = InputBox("Specify the scope to be used for the new virtual
machine:")

'Get an instance of the WMI Service in the virtualization namespace.
Set WMIService = GetObject("winmgmts:\\.\root\virtualization")

'Get a VMManagementService object
Set VMManagementService = WMIService.ExecQuery("SELECT * FROM
Msvm_VirtualSystemManagementService").ItemIndex(0)

' Initialize the global settings for the VM
Set VMSystemGlobalSettingData =
WMIService.Get("Msvm_VirtualSystemGlobalSettingData").SpawnInstance_()

'Set the name and scope
VMSystemGlobalSettingData.ElementName = VMName
VMSystemGlobalSettingData.ScopeOfResidence = VMScope

' Create the VM
VMManagementService.DefineVirtualSystem(VMSystemGlobalSettingData.GetText_(1
)
```

LISTING 5.2   DisplayVMScopes

```
Option Explicit

Dim WMIService
Dim VMList
Dim VM
Dim VMSystemGlobalSettingData
Dim Message

'Setup start of message string
Message = "Virtual Machines and their scope of residence" & chr(10) _
        & "======================================="

'Get instance of 'virtualization' WMI service on the local computer
```

```
Set WMIService = GetObject("winmgmts:\\.\root\virtualization")

'Get all the MSVM_ComputerSystem object
Set VMList = WMIService.ExecQuery("SELECT * FROM Msvm_ComputerSystem")

For Each VM In VMList
   if VM.Caption = "Virtual Machine" then
       Set VMSystemGlobalSettingData =
(VM.Associators_("MSVM_ElementSettingData",
"Msvm_VirtualSystemGlobalSettingData")).ItemIndex(0)
       Message = Message & chr(10) & "VM:        " & VM.ElementName
       Message = Message & chr(10) & "Scope:  " &
VMSystemGlobalSettingData.ScopeOfResidence
       Message = Message & chr(10)
    end if
Next


wscript.echo Message
```

LISTING 5.3   ClearVMScope

```
Option Explicit

Dim WMIService
Dim VMList
Dim VM
Dim VMSystemGlobalSettingData
Dim VMManagementService
Dim Result

'Get instance of 'virtualization' WMI service on the local computer
Set WMIService = GetObject("winmgmts:\\.\root\virtualization")

'Get a VMManagementService object
Set VMManagementService = WMIService.ExecQuery("SELECT * FROM
Msvm_VirtualSystemManagementService").ItemIndex(0)

'Get all the MSVM_ComputerSystem object
Set VMList = WMIService.ExecQuery("SELECT * FROM Msvm_ComputerSystem")

For Each VM In VMList
   if VM.Caption = "Virtual Machine" then
       Set VMSystemGlobalSettingData =
(VM.Associators_("MSVM_ElementSettingData",
"Msvm_VirtualSystemGlobalSettingData")).ItemIndex(0)
       VMSystemGlobalSettingData.ScopeOfResidence = ""
       Result = VMManagementService.ModifyVirtualSystem(VM.Path_.Path,
VMSystemGlobalSettingData.GetText_(1))
    end if
Next
```

LISTING 5.4   ChangeVMScope

```
Dim WMIService
Dim VM
Dim VMManagementService
Dim VMSystemGlobalSettingData
Dim VMName
Dim VMScope
Dim Result

'Setup variables for the VM we are looking for, and the scope to assign it to
VMName = InputBox("Specify the virtual machine to change scope on:")
VMScope = InputBox("Specify the new scope to be used:")

'Get an instance of the WMI Service in the virtualization namespace.
Set WMIService = GetObject("winmgmts:\\.\root\virtualization")

'Get a VMManagementService object
Set VMManagementService = WMIService.ExecQuery("SELECT * FROM
Msvm_VirtualSystemManagementService").ItemIndex(0)

'Get the VM object that we want to modify
Set VM = (WMIService.ExecQuery("SELECT * FROM Msvm_ComputerSystem WHERE
ElementName='" & VMName & "'")).ItemIndex(0)

'Get the VirtualSystemGlobalSettingsData of the VM we want to modify
Set VMSystemGlobalSettingData = (VM.Associators_("MSVM_ElementSettingData",
"Msvm_VirtualSystemGlobalSettingData")).ItemIndex(0)

'Change the ScopeOfResidence property
VMSystemGlobalSettingData.ScopeOfResidence = VMScope

'Update the VM with ModifyVirtualSystem
Result = VMManagementService.ModifyVirtualSystem(VM.Path_.Path,
VMSystemGlobalSettingData.GetText_(1))
```

After you create the scripts, you can execute them from the command line. Each script has a specific function:

◆ CreateVMInScope creates a new VM with the specified name in the specified scope. For example, you can use this script to create a new VM named HR VM in the HR scope.

◆ DisplayVMScopes enumerates all the VMs on the host and displays their names as well as their scopes. If the scope field is empty, then it's accessible by all users who have access to the Hyper-V system.

◆ ClearVMScope removes the scope assignment from a particular VM.

◆ ChangeVMScope changes the scope assignment for a particular VM.

For the purposes of this section, let's assume that you already have a VM provisioned for the HR team named HRVM001. As an administrator on the Hyper-V host, from the command prompt, run ChangeVMScope.vbs. A dialog box appears, asking for the name of the VM on which the scope will be changed. Type in the name of the VM (**HRVM001**), and then click OK. Next, enter the scope you set up earlier (HR), and click OK.

To confirm that the scope was set correctly, run DisplayVMScopes.vbs. The scope of the VM should be set to HR (see Figure 5.10).

FIGURE 5.10
Confirming the scope for a virtual machine

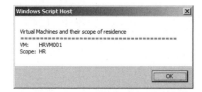

From a Hyper-V Manager console, when logged in as HRAdmin, connect to the Hyper-V host. Only one VM should be listed: HRVM001. You should be able to power on the VM as well as perform all the operations that were specified when you set up the permissions for the HR scope. You also shouldn't be able to create a new VM; if you try, an error is returned that says "Cannot create a VM in the default authorization scope."

Alternative Tools

The process that we've just covered is manual and involved. If you're looking for a short-cut, a tool is available that greatly simplifies these steps. The Hyper-V Remote Management Configuration Utility (available for download from http://code.msdn.microsoft.com/HVRemote) was written by one of the program managers on the Hyper-V team and provides a command-line interface to all the commands you used earlier.

Using the tool is extremely easy. To grant a user access to a Hyper-V host, run the following command:

```
Hvremote /add:domain\user
```

Note, however, that this grants access only to the host. If you want to restrict access by user account to a VM, then you still need to set up scopes and assign VMs to those scopes. Additional options are available that you can access by executing cscript hvremote.wsf /?.

NOTE   If you're in a domain environment, it's highly recommended that you use hvremote for granting access to a host. You need to change additional settings for Distributed COM (DCOM) to work correctly.

SCVMM and Hyper-V Security

If you're using System Center Virtual Machine Manager (SCVMM), these steps don't apply. SCVMM replaces the default store with its own authorization scheme and structure. You'll need to manage access rights, as well as all other rights, via SCVMM. For more information about SCVMM, refer to Chapter 11, "System Center Virtual Machine Manager."

Summary

In this chapter, we've looked at the work Microsoft has done to ensure a secure virtualization stack. All the components that are included as part of Hyper-V have undergone a strict security overview and in-depth analysis. We also reviewed and provided examples for granting access to a Hyper-V host without allowing administrative access to the rest of the system.

Chapter 6

Virtual Machine Migration

Existing physical systems inevitably become targets for virtualization, thanks to the savings and value it provides. Loading and configuring applications on top of a freshly installed, contemporary operating system yields the best performance and stability but may not always be feasible.

The goal of this chapter is to introduce the steps and processes required to migrate an existing system into a Hyper-V virtual machine. The chapter includes a walkthrough of the manual process to move a physical system into a virtual machine.

The best approach for converting any existing supported Windows system into a virtual machine is to use System Center Virtual Machine Manager (SCVMM). SCVMM is covered in Chapter 11, "System Center Virtual Machine Manager."

After you virtualize systems on top of Hyper-V, you may need to migrate virtual machines between physical hosts. In this chapter, we'll also discuss migrating virtual machines from one Hyper-V host to another using the provided export and import functionality.

We'll cover the following topics in this chapter:

◆ Migration challenges and drivers

◆ Migration considerations

◆ Preparing a system for migration

◆ Capturing, transposing, and deploying system configurations

◆ Capturing and deploying disk images

◆ Transposing images

◆ Walking through a physical-to virtual migration

◆ Exporting and importing in Hyper-V

Migration Challenges and Drivers

The challenges presented by a virtual migration are similar to those you would encounter moving a system from one physical host to another. Relocating (via backup/restore or disk imaging) a Windows Server 2003–based Exchange Server from an HP DL365 to a Dell 1955 might be a risky proposition. The two systems can have significant variations in hardware including CPU manufacturer, CPU architecture, CPU core count, network interface cards, disk controllers, video controllers, management services/tools, and other components. Some of the variations are insignificant. Other changes can (we hope) be detected by the operating system and addressed. Some differences in network and storage configuration often require expert attention from either specialized migration software or a knowledgeable administrator.

You may face similar configuration challenges when you move a server from a physical or virtual environment to create a new virtual instance. No physical system in the world has an exact match for the network adapter, Small Computer System Interface (SCSI) controller, Intelligent Drive Electronics (IDE) controller, and video controller presented to a Hyper-V virtual machine (VM). You need to add optimized drivers to a migrated system just as they might be required in a physical migration. Network-configuration information (static IP address, name-resolution servers, gateways, and so on) may need to be set, just as if you were installing a new network interface card (NIC) in a physical system.

NOTE   Some hardware components simply can't be virtualized. Specialized boards to perform data collection, provide voice integration, or function as interfaces to industrial equipment don't have equivalents in the virtual world. Hyper-V lacks USB support for VMs, so USB-based devices don't function (which is important for some license-key dongle devices). Although older networking adapters including Token Ring and Attached Resource Computer Network (ARCNET) cards can't be virtualized, the Ethernet adapters found in Hyper-V may be able to provide suitable replacement network service.

With all these challenges, why migrate an existing system to a VM rather than build a clean, fresh install? A new operating system could be installed, patched, and configured to provide an up-to-date platform for applications and services. It sounds like a great approach, but often building a new system isn't feasible. Reasons for pursuing a server migration rather than a replacement vary. Sometimes the expertise for configuring a system or application is no longer available. Installation source for a program may not be accessible (floppies have been lost, or the vendor is out of business). A system's configuration may be deemed too fragile to risk a reinstallation. A catastrophic hardware failure may have left only an old backup image of a system.

Whatever the reasons might be, the pain and suffering you incur to build a system can be greater than the risk and effort to forklift the system into a VM. Drivers to migrate such systems (legacy hardware maintenance costs, backup costs, recovery risk, power cost, performance limitations, and so forth) can easily justify the effort to migrate. After the system is virtualized, risks and challenges posed by a future migration are largely eliminated, because virtualized systems are portable (via export and import) and more easily recovered.

The high-level steps necessary to successfully migrate from one system to another are largely the same, regardless of the tools you use:

1. Assess the existing configuration.

2. Capture the configuration.

3. Capture the disk image(s).

4. Transpose the disk image(s).

5. Disable the legacy system.

6. Transpose the configuration.

Types of Migrations

Conversion from an existing physical host to a VM is frequently the goal of a migration, but it isn't the only type of virtualization-related system migration. In some situations, you may want to move from one virtualization platform to another or migrate a VM to physical hardware.

PHYSICAL TO VIRTUAL (P2V) MIGRATION

You use a physical to virtual (P2V) conversion to decouple a system from its hardware and create a new virtual system instance. Targets for a P2V migration often include older systems. Hardware maintenance costs and spare-part availability can conspire with vintage operating systems and application software to increase operations risk. Deep in the heart of a computer room, you may find ancient servers with unclear but critical business functions. Failure may not be an option for these systems, but fail they will—some day.

Converting the system in order to decouple it from its stone-age hardware can breathe new life into it and bring necessary longevity. Virtualizing such a system not only can extend its life by enabling it to run on contemporary hardware but can also enable entirely new backup and recovery scenarios. Often, legacy applications lacked integrated backup and recovery awareness. Successfully completing a P2V migration of such a system allows for the backup of the encapsulated VM, as detailed in Chapter 7, "Backup and Recovery."

NOTE   Migrating an older, unsupported system to a VM and hosting it on Windows Server 2008 in Hyper-V doesn't extend support from Microsoft or other vendors. If the platform or application is out of support, virtualization probably won't change its support status. But a P2V migration can *drastically reduce the risk of failure* to your organization. Regardless of vendor support status, eliminating high-risk hardware can be a good thing, and you should consider it.

Not all candidates for P2V migration are long in the tooth, high-risk servers. Contemporary mainstream systems may also be candidates for conversion to a VM. P2V processing can move you closer to the reality of a virtualized environment in conjunction with building and configuring new VMs. An automated P2V tool like that included in System Center Virtual Machine Manager (SCVMM) can save you substantial time and effort.

VIRTUAL TO VIRTUAL (V2V) MIGRATION

You may have an existing VM environment that doesn't leverage Hyper-V. Perhaps you use Virtual Server 2005, a VMware product, or another virtualization layer. Performance, software costs, or corporate standards can drive the need to move to Hyper-V, necessitating a virtual to virtual (V2V) migration.

V2V conversions are often less complicated than P2V migrations. Virtual machines don't leverage the vast array of hardware available in the physical world. The potential hardware presented to a VM is limited, so the assessment of the source VM isn't as extensive.

Common file formats used between virtualization platforms can also simplify V2V migrations. Virtual Server 2005 and Hyper-V share a common file format for virtual disks (.vhd). Moving a virtual hard disk (VHD) file from Virtual Server to Hyper-V eliminates the need to capture and convert an existing disk-image file. In this case, additional configuration is required both outside the VM (to configure similar virtual hardware resources) and within it (removing additions, installing integration components, and re-creating network configuration). It's important to note that you can't migrate a *saved* VM from one virtualization platform to another. The details of how running systems work vary by virtualization platform (how memory is mapped and managed, for example) and can't be easily converted from an in-flight operating system instance. You must shut down a VM for a successful V2V migration.

TIP Matthijs ten Seldam created a Virtual Server to Hyper-V configuration migration tool, which is available via his blog at http://blogs.technet.com/matthts/archive/2008/09/12/vmc-to-hyper-v-import-tool-available.aspx. It does a nice job of converting the configuration information, but it doesn't remove additions or install Integration Components (ICs). SCVMM does a more complete job of V2V migrations in this case.

You can easily automate V2V migrations to Hyper-V from other virtualization platforms such as Virtual Server and VMware. SCVMM includes support for Virtual Server or VMware to Hyper-V conversion.

You can move existing Hyper-V–based VMs from one host to another in a number of ways, and it really isn't considered a V2V migration. You can migrate VMs from one Hyper-V host to another using failover clustering, using export/import, or leveraging SCVMM. We'll discuss and demonstrate failover clustering in Chapter 8, "High Availability," and we cover SCVMM in Chapter 11. Export and import are discussed at the end of this chapter.

VIRTUAL TO PHYSICAL (V2P)

Occasionally, you may want to migrate a VM to dedicated physical hardware. Most often, you need to address performance requirements that can't be met from a virtual system. Although a virtual to physical (V2P) conversion is possible, it's more challenging to accomplish or automate than a P2V or V2V migration.

P2V and V2V conversions have the benefit of a known target system. The end state and target hardware come from the same pool of hardware for every migration, simplifying driver integration. The possible variations for V2P target hardware configurations are enormous and difficult to anticipate.

You must take a great deal of care to complete a successful V2P migration. Microsoft doesn't provide any supported means of performing a V2P conversion, but third parties including Acronis and Vizioncore provide tools for V2P as well as P2V and V2V. You can also use common backup and recovery tools as well as the manual processes shown later in the chapter.

Migration Considerations

As is the case when you're creating a new VM, it's important to know the performance characteristics required for a migrated system before you undertake a conversion. Assessing the system to be migrated is an important step in the overall process. Consider the following questions before you begin migration:

- How much RAM is required for the VM?

- What are the disk requirements and anticipated growth?

- How many network connections are required? Do the Media Access Control (MAC) addresses need to be preserved?

- Does the system require significant CPU capacity?

- How many processors can the system use or does it require?

- Is any software installed that may be looking for hardware that won't be in the VM?

You have to understand the constraints of the virtualization platform as well as the migration method and tools. It may be obvious to you that a physical system requiring (for example) a video-capture card to function properly won't virtualize well. It may be less clear that a network-based image-capture and -deployment tool could fail to run within Hyper-V because it lacks a suitable Hyper-V–compatible network driver. Understanding all the components of the migration process up front will save you time and effort later.

Capturing the Configuration

Creating an inventory of the physical source hardware is a common practice before undertaking a migration. Automated tools (like Microsoft's SCVMM and the older Virtual Server Migration Toolkit [VSMT]) do a thorough analysis of the source system before proceeding.

Creating a Manual Inventory

You can manually create an inventory of your physical virtualization candidates. This doesn't mean you have to shut down the system, open it up, and inspect the physical parts (although that's a good idea). Most valuable system information can be collected while the system is running, using available commands and tools. Common information to collect about the source system includes the following:

♦ Processor configuration including CPU type; quantity, speed, and number of cores; bus speed; and cache size

♦ NIC information, including MAC address, protocols, and IP address settings

♦ Amount of RAM

♦ Disk controller type(s)—SCSI, IDE, Serial ATA, and Serial-Attached SCSI (SAS) including Redundant Array of Independent Disks (RAID) support—and driver information

♦ Physical and logical disk sizes and file-system information

♦ Operating-system version and patch levels

♦ Installed applications

♦ Installed management tools

Not all of this information may be necessary for a successful P2V migration, but you'll often collect it anyway, in case you need it later. Beyond ensuring that sufficient capacity exists on the Hyper-V host (including processor, RAM, disk, and networking), modern versions of Windows can handle many of the system-reconfiguration tasks. Some system settings, like static TCP/IP configuration settings, are tied to a physical network card and will be lost if not recorded for reconfiguration purposes.

You can gather information locally or remotely from a system using Windows Management Instrumentation (WMI) and by perusing the source system's Registry. WMIC, the WMI command-line tool included in Windows XP, Windows Server 2003, and newer versions of Windows, is a convenient way to capture much of the information. The following example commands capture some configuration information for a remote system named dquad to local text files:

```
wmic /node:dquad os > c:\dquad_os.txt
wmic /node:dquad qfe > c:\dquad_patches.txt
wmic /node:dquad baseboard > c:\dquad_baseboard.txt
wmic /node:dquad cpu > c:\dquad_cpu.txt
wmic /node:dquad nic > c:\dquad_nic.txt
```

Using the MAP Toolkit

An automated tool that is free to download may provide a more expedient way to collect, save, and evaluate system information. The Microsoft Assessment and Planning (MAP) toolkit is a free download that you can use to inventory, assess, and report on your environment. You can use MAP to search your network in a secure, agentless manner and create a detailed inventory of computing resources. Running from a single network-attached system, MAP leverages Active Directory, WMI, the Remote Registry Service, and/or Simple Network Management Protocol (SNMP) to collect data. MAP can collect data from systems running the following supported versions of Windows:

- Windows 2000 Professional

- Windows 2000 Server

- Windows XP Professional

- Windows Server 2003

- Windows Server 2003 R2

- Windows Vista

- Windows Server 2008

You can find MAP on the Microsoft website, listed in the Solutions Accelerators section on the Virtualization download web page (http://www.microsoft.com/virtualization/downloads .mspx). The data and analysis provided by this toolkit can significantly simplify your planning process for migrating physical hosts and applications.

MAP includes features for gathering performance metrics from computers you're considering for migration. You can generate reports on your existing virtual environment as well as analysis of recommended placement for new VMs. The assessment performed includes an analysis of device-driver availability and recommendations for hardware upgrades that may be required.

NOTE The Microsoft Assessment and Planning toolkit does much more than collect configuration information and evaluate physical servers for migration to Hyper-V. It's a comprehensive analysis tool that you can use to document and evaluate your environment to prepare for migration to Vista and Office 2007. You can also use it to assess system-security settings and readiness for virtualization tools like SoftGrid (now called AppV). We won't be concerned with all that right now, but you should investigate MAP's other capabilities for your organization.

INSTALLING MAP

You can install the toolkit on Windows XP SP2 or later (as well as Windows Vista, Windows Server 2003, and Windows Server 2008). It leverages Microsoft Office for report creation, so it does have a number of software prerequisites, including the following:

◆ .NET Framework v3.5SP1 (3.5.30729.01)

◆ Windows Installer v4.5

◆ Microsoft Word 2007 or Microsoft Word 2003 SP2

◆ Microsoft Excel 2007 or Microsoft Excel 2003 SP2

◆ Microsoft Office Primary Interop Assemblies

◆ Any available updates for the operating system and Microsoft Office

◆ SQL Server 2008 Express

Don't be too concerned if you don't have all of the prerequisites installed before you install MAP. It will check for missing dependencies and provide clickable links to the required components (see Figure 6.1).

FIGURE 6.1
MAP installation
dependencies

NOTE   MAP will download and install SQL Server 2008 Express Edition during setup. You can use Microsoft SQL Server 2005 or Microsoft SQL Server 2008 if you create an instance named MAPS.

USING MAP

The welcome screen shown in Figure 6.2 includes links and options to perform a variety of actions.

As mentioned, the MAP toolkit application performs inventory, assessment, and reporting tasks. It also serves as a portal for migration and virtualization topics. Clicking Virtualization on the left side of the screen switches to a listing of useful virtualization resources and information accessible from MAP (see Figure 6.3).

FIGURE 6.2
MAP welcome
screen

FIGURE 6.3
Virtualization
resources

As nice as these resources are, they don't in and of themselves accomplish the inventory and assessment tasks required for a migration (your goal when using MAP). Navigating back to the Assessment area lets you prepare for data collection. But before you can begin, you must select a database from the Actions pane on the left side of the screen while in assessment mode that will function as a repository for collected information (see Figure 6.4). You can specify your own name or use an existing database.

FIGURE 6.4
MAP database definition

After you create the repository, you can collect performance and inventory data. You can gather performance data over time to help develop an accurate picture of server load, including historical measurements for the utilization of processor, network, and disk. On the other hand, you can collect inventory data all at once, including information about a system's hardware and software configuration. A detailed inventory of all assessed systems is generated in Microsoft Excel format, and it can include hardware device details like those shown in Figure 6.5 as well as summaries of installed software.

FIGURE 6.5
MAP hardware device details

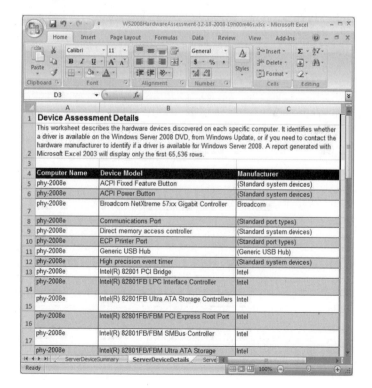

The Excel worksheets are a convenient format for reviewing system-configuration information and provide a wealth of useful information for other purposes in your environment.

Preparing a System for Migration

Some system settings are best altered before you capture the system image. Removing hardware-specific management components (hardware monitoring, audio-management tools, and legacy virtual enlightenments for V2V migrations) will save you time and frustration later. Some application installers won't run if supported hardware isn't detected on a system. Removing such tools after a migration can be difficult.

Pre-staging information and tools on the physical disk can also be a time-saver. Saving collected configuration information to the local physical disk makes it easy to find inside the VM after the migration (for example, you can save static IP settings by directing the output of IPConfig/all to a text file).

Capturing and Deploying Disk Images

After you've collected system-configuration information and evaluated a migration candidate's suitability for conversion to a VM, it's time to capture the actual files used by the system. You can collect images of the attached disks using traditional disk-imaging tools; backup and recovery products; or dedicated, automated P2V tools.

Manual Migration with Image-Capture Tools

You can manually capture and deploy disk images a number of ways—each of which involves booting the source system into a separate operating system and capturing an image of the attached disks. For many years, administrators have used Ghost disk imaging (along with other, less-well-known products). Microsoft introduced the Windows Imaging Format (WIM) and related tools to improve operating system deployments.

WIM is an integral part of Windows Vista and Windows Server 2008 installation and deployment. Like Ghost image files, WIM files can contain deployable disk images. The WIM format supports single-instance storage of disk images, meaning that you can efficiently store multiple disk images from different systems together in one file. You can mount Windows Imaging files on a system as a drive letter to manipulate their contents.

ImageX is the no-cost command-line tool for accessing and manipulating WIM files. You can use ImageX to capture and apply disk images to and from WIM files, as well as to perform other WIM management-related tasks. ImageX is available as part of the Windows Automated Installation Kit (WAIK), which you can download from Microsoft. You can use WAIK to generate a bootable Windows Pre-installation Environment (WinPE) CD that includes ImageX.

WinPE is a lightweight version of Windows intended for installing, troubleshooting, and deploying systems. Starting a system from WinPE lets you access a system's physical resources through a command-line interface. You can boot WinPE from a CD, an .ISO image (if supported), or even a USB thumb drive. A well-built WinPE image has the advantage over older tools (like those based on DOS) of providing access to attached USB devices as well as networking support. This chapter includes a walkthrough of how to create a simple WinPE CD, as well as a manual P2V migration using WinPE and ImageX.

Other imaging and pre-installation tools exist that you can use for image capture. Disk-imaging tools are available from Acronis, Symatec, and others; and pre-installation environments and tools include BartPE, WinBuilder, and VistaPE.

Using Traditional Backup and Recovery Tools

The backup and recovery tools you (we hope) use every day can often be leveraged to perform a P2V migration. Capturing a full system backup and restoring it into a VM can be just as effective as a manual P2V migration with disk-imaging tools. You'll encounter the same issues around the hardware abstraction layer (HAL), system activation, drivers, and network configuration already mentioned. Using traditional backup and recovery tools isn't a supported P2V migration method, but then neither is the use of manual tools we reviewed earlier. Using SCVMM is the best approach for physical-to-virtual migration; SCVMM was designed with Windows P2V migration scenarios in mind, and it's Microsoft's supported method for P2V migration to Hyper-V.

Microsoft Data Protection Manager does a fantastic job of backing up physical and virtual systems and could be a cost-effective way to recover a system into a VM. System Center Data Protection Manager (DPM) is covered in Chapter 12. Rather than go over ground we will walk on again, let's use another (wicked simple) backup and recovery tool to demonstrate this concept.

Cheating with Home Server

In 2007, Microsoft introduced a file server for home use called Windows Home Server. You can use this file server to provide centralized backup and recovery for systems. Windows Home Server includes a recovery ISO image (a format defined by the International Organization for Standardization commonly used for CD and DVD authoring) that allows for the quick and easy recovery of backed-up systems.

NOTE   Using Windows Home Server to back up any version of Windows Server isn't supported; nor is it a supported P2V method. But it works pretty well for simple systems, and it can be used to illustrate the process for a manual, backup-based P2V migration.

Acquiring or building a Windows Home Server appliance can be more cost-effective and time-efficient than other manual P2V solutions.

Installing the Home Server agent on a physical host is a simple process, and you can do so in a few minutes. Windows Home Server takes advantage of single-instance storage of files and stores backups in a space-efficient manner. Recovering into a VM is a simple process of booting the Windows Home Server ISO image in a properly configured VM.

NOTE   Network drivers for the Hyper-V synthetic NIC aren't yet included in any pre-configured recovery or PE CD. The initial configuration of VMs to be imaged over a network link should include a Legacy Network Adapter.

Similar to some backup and recovery tools, Windows Home Server won't restore a disk image to a disk that's smaller than the original source disk, regardless of the volume of data. If you use Windows Home Server (or another backup/recovery tool), be certain that you create VHD files with sufficient capacity to successfully restore the system.

Booting a newly created VM from the provided recovery CD starts the network-aware recovery console for Windows Home Server. Stepping though the recovery process allows you to connect to your Windows Home Server, select a machine backup set to recover, initialize the target disk, and begin a restore over the network, as shown in Figure 6.6.

FIGURE 6.6

Windows Home Server Restore console

The result of the successful restore is shown in Figure 6.7.

FIGURE 6.7

Windows Home Server restore into a VM

After the restore process is complete, you can address common configuration opportunities within the VM (HAL re-detection, installation of integration components, addition of a synthetic NIC, removal of a legacy NIC, and so on).

Using Microsoft-Supported P2V Tools

You may be getting tired of hearing about the System Center family of products. They're central to Microsoft's strategy for systems management for both physical and virtual systems. System Center Virtual Machine Manger 2008 is the automated and supported way to perform P2V Windows migrations. SCVMM does a great job and is discussed in Chapter 11.

Microsoft also released the Virtual Server Migration Toolkit (VSMT) to automate migrations to Virtual Server 2005. The VSMT is a free download and relies on Automated Deployment Services (ADS). ADS is a tool for the rapid deployment of Windows Servers (using Windows Server 2003) that has since been superseded by better deployment tools. VSMT used lots of scripting to assess, capture, and deploy images. Although the price was right (free), a P2V migration using VSMT was somewhat clunky. VSMT did support the migration of Windows NT 4.0 Server systems to Virtual Server 2005. VSMT and ADS are still available from Microsoft (as is Virtual Server 2005).

Using Third-Party Tools

Other companies, including Acronis, PlateSpin, and Vizioncore, provide automated P2V solutions that work with Hyper-V. If you've worked with third-party P2V tools for VMware migrations, you may notice that many of these same companies offer P2V solutions for other virtualization platforms, including Hyper-V.

Transposing Images

Updating a captured disk image to accommodate hardware changes is inevitable in nearly any P2V migration. You should remove unnecessary software components before you capture an image. Uninstall hardware-specific system-management tools (such as HP System Insight Manager and Dell OpenManage tools) and other unnecessary components for a virtualized system (audio-management tools, video control panels, NIC teaming software, and so on).

You can make other changes before the initial boot of the VM, such as pre-staging drivers or virtualization-management tools for later installation. For supported Windows-based VMs moving to Hyper-V, you can usually add required drivers after startup by inserting the Integration Services Setup Disk using the Actions menu.

Modern versions of Windows do a good job of detecting new hardware components, and many changes to the operating system can be made automatically. Changes to the number of processors (cores) or processor type shouldn't present a problem for currently supported versions of Windows. If you do encounter a problem at startup, the Repair option available with the original Windows installation media can correct many startup anomalies, including those related to storage changes. Other than obtaining application software to manage missing hardware, you shouldn't encounter insurmountable migration issues with Windows XP, Windows Server 2003, Windows Vista, and Windows Server 2008.

For older operating systems, plug-and-play may not be available to help your new VM get over the shock of a system migration. Altering system software for changes in support of Advanced Configuration and Power Interface (ACPI) or uni/multiprocessor capabilities can be challenging. For Windows 2000, you may need to reinstall the operating system over the existing installation (as per KB246236) or take other actions (as described in KB249694). Automated migration tools can detect and address many troublesome migration issues more easily than you might.

The last step in making your migrated server feel at home is the installation of enlightenments.

ENLIGHTENMENTS, INTEGRATION SERVICES, AND INTEGRATION COMPONENTS (ICS) ARE PRETTY MUCH THE SAME THING

You may hear software that makes a child or guest operating system run better while virtualized or "aware" that it is not actually running on physical hardware referred to as an *enlightenment*, *integration service*, *Integration Component*, or *IC*.

For Hyper-V based VMs, this means the Integration Components that you can install via the Hyper-V Console or VMConnect.exe.

Walking through a Physical-to-Virtual Migration

As explained in earlier sections, you can manually capture and deploy disk images a number of ways. Each involves booting the source system into a separate operating system and capturing an image of the attached disk. We'll walk through a manual image capture using a WinPE boot disk and leveraging ImageX to demonstrate the process.

Collecting and Creating Your Imaging Toolkit

Assembling the right tools to accomplish a manual migration can take some time if you don't normally perform disk-imaging tasks. For server administrators in larger organizations, a fantastic time-saver can be to borrow a preconfigured WinPE CD from another team that handles desktop deployment.

Desktop teams often have prebuilt tools for capturing and deploying images to physical systems. A usable WinPE CD at minimum needs to include compatible storage drivers for the source system and ImageX to capture disk images. The WinPE image can also include compatible network drivers for the source and target (VM). If you don't have access to a suitable prebuilt WinPE disk, you can create your own using the WAIK.

CREATING A WINPE DISK WITH THE WAIK

The Windows Automated Installation Kit (WAIK) is designed to help corporate IT professionals customize and deploy Windows operation systems. It can help you perform unattended Windows installs, capture Windows images with ImageX, and create Windows PE images. You can download the WAIK from Microsoft in the form of an ISO image file.

NOTE Several different versions of the WAIK are available for download. When this chapter was written, the most current version was 6001.18000.080118-1840-kb3aik1_en.iso for Vista SP1 and Windows Server 2008. It's always advisable to use the latest version of the WAIK.

You can install the WAIK on a physical Windows system by creating a DVD from the downloaded ISO file and auto-starting the disk (mounting the ISO directly in a VM may be easier!).

The installation is straightforward: click Windows AIK Setup on the Welcome screen (see Figure 6.8).

FIGURE 6.8
WAIK Welcome screen

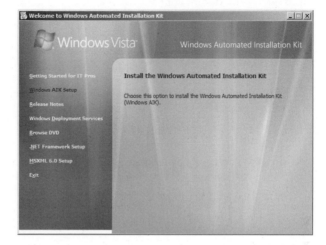

Walking through the installation installs the WAIK in the default location. The documentation included with the WAIK is useful and extensive; the included *Windows Preinstallation Environment (WinPE) User's Guide* details the processes you can follow to create and customize WinPE. (The options for customizing WinPE are extensive and not entirely applicable here for your image capturing and deployment purposes.) The following steps to create a WinPE ISO are adapted from this user guide.

CREATING A SIMPLE WINPE CD WITH THE WAIK

With the WAIK installed, you can quickly create a simple WinPE disk of your own that includes ImageX for image capture and deployment. Follow these steps:

1. Click Start, navigate to Microsoft Windows AIK, and then select Windows PE Tools Command Prompt. Doing so opens a command window with the environment prepared for you to create your own WinPE CD, as shown in Figure 6.9.

FIGURE 6.9
WinPE tools prompt

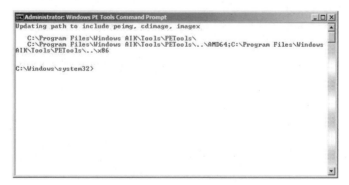

You don't need to concern yourself with lots of configuration options (unless you want to). You simply want to generate a bootable WinPE ISO image that includes ImageX. To do this, you'll run through several commands in the window.

2. Copy the necessary files for your selected processor architecture to a new directory, c:\MyWinPE:

```
copype.cmd x86 c:\MyWinPE
```

3. Copy ImageX to the appropriate spot in the newly created directory structure so that it will be part of the ISO image you create:

```
copy "c:\program files\windows aik\tools\x86\imagex.exe" c:\MyWinPE\iso
```

4. Create the following small imaging-related configuration file named wimscript.ini, which will smooth the imaging process. Place the file in the same directory as ImageX:

```
[ExclusionList]
ntfs.log
hiberfil.sys
pagefile.sys
"System Volume Information"
RECYCLER
Windows\CSC

[CompressionExclusionList]
*.mp3
*.zip
*.cab
\WINDOWS\inf\*.pnf
```

5. After the files are in place, create the ISO file using the following command line:

```
oscdimg -n -bc:\MyWinPE\etfsboot.com c:\MyWinPE\ISO c:\MyWinPE\MyWinPE.iso
```

This process creates c:\MyWinPE\MyWinPE.iso, which includes ImageX.exe. You can then burn the file to a writable CD using standard CD-burning software, including the free CDBurn.exe that is part of the Windows Server 2003 Resource Kit.

That's it! You're now armed with a simple P2V tool that will work with many physical systems. Unfortunately, not all hardware drivers are included in your new WinPE CD, including drivers for new or less common storage and network controllers. You can integrate original equipment manufacturer (OEM)–supplied driver packages, but adding drivers to WinPE can be a cumbersome process using the WAIK. You can use the Microsoft Deployment Toolkit to simplify the integration of required storage or network drivers.

ADDING DRIVERS WITH MICROSOFT DEPLOYMENT TOOLKIT

Microsoft Deployment Toolkit (MDT) connects the tools and processes required for deployment. It includes a collection of guidance for deployment, and it functions as a wrapper for other

Microsoft tools and technologies including the WAIK. Although MDT can help you automate countless deployment tasks, the benefit to you is the simplified process for generating a customized WinPE CD. You can use MDT (leveraging the WAIK) to add specialized storage and network drivers as well as other tools to a customized WinPE image.

TIP You don't need MDT to create WinPE images or to integrate drivers. It can be useful, and that's why it's mentioned here.

MDT is a tiny download compared to the WAIK. After it's downloaded and installed, you can use it to integrate driver packages from OEMs by using the Out-Of-Box-Drivers option highlighted in Figure 6.10.

FIGURE 6.10
Deployment Workbench's Out-Of-Box Drivers option

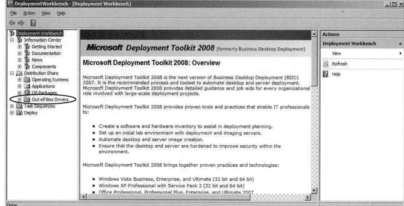

Capturing the Image

Before you capture your disk image, it's a good idea to save key information onto the disk, such as IP configuration/MAC if required for later use (IPCONFIG /ALL >c:\Net.txt and/or perhaps WMIC NIC GET >> c:\Net.txt). For the walkthrough, you'll save an image to an attached USB drive—and it's best to connect the USB drive before WinPE starts. Follow these steps:

1. Restart the system, booting from the WinPE image.

2. Assuming you have the proper storage drivers integrated, you can access the system's attached storage for imaging. To locate the drives on the system, use the diskpart command:

```
diskpart
list disk
list vol
exit
```

3. The example system has only one volume to capture. The following command works to capture an image of the C: drive and write the file sata.img on an attached USB device (E:):

```
imagex /capture c: e:\sata.img "vista"
```

4. After the image is completely captured, turn off the source host, remove the WinPE CD, and detach the USB drive.

NOTE Because WinPE provides network support, you can save images to a network drive instead of an attached USB device. This can work well for you as long as your WinPE CD has the drivers for both the physical and virtual network cards in your environment.

Defining the Virtual Machine

Creating the VM configuration is a straightforward process of mimicking the configuration of the physical system. Define a VM that corresponds to your desired configuration, taking into account RAM, processor, disk, and networking requirements. If necessary, you can use the MAC address(es) of a source system within the VM.

TIP It may make sense to include a Legacy Network Adapter to provide network access until you can add ICs. Drivers for the Legacy Network Adapter should be available in a newer WinPE disk and most supported versions for Windows. Note that an x64 driver for Windows XP and Windows Server 2003 was never released, so x64 versions of these operating systems won't work with this adapter.

Deploying the Image

With the image captured to a WIM file, you can now deploy it as a VM. After defining the VM, the image must be accessible for deployment. You'll use the pass-through disk feature of Hyper-V to expose the image file to the VM:

1. Attach the USB drive to the Hyper-V host, and off-line the disk in Disk Manager on the physical system (see Figure 6.11).

Off-lining the USB disk containing the WIM image allows the newly defined VM to mount the disk as an additional drive via pass-through, as shown in the Hyper-V settings in Figure 6.12.

2. Boot the WinPE disk inside the new Hyper-V–based VM, and identify the source and target volumes. If the VHD file is new, you'll need to prepare it before the image can be applied. You should use diskpart to identify and (possibly) prepare your VHD for the image:

```
diskpart
list disk
select disk 1
create part primary
list vol
exit
format e: /fs:ntfs /q
```

FIGURE 6.11
Offline USB
source disk

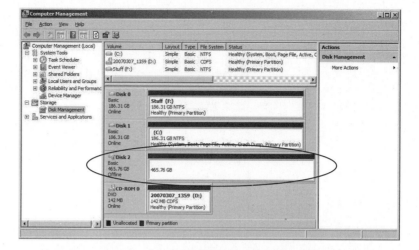

FIGURE 6.12
Settings to access
pass-through

These commands assume that you didn't pre-create a partition on disk 1 (the VHD file). After the partition was created by this process, it was assigned drive E:, which was then formatted.

3. When the drive is formatted, you can apply the image to E: using ImageX:

```
imagex /apply c:\sata.img "vista" e:\
```

After you apply the image, the VM reboots, and the newly formatted drive appears as C:.

If you pre-created the VHD file with a partition and file system, the drive probably would show up as C: from the beginning of the process in WinPE. Figure 6.13 shows this entire process with a VHD that was preconfigured before imaging.

FIGURE 6.13

Checking the disk and applying the image

Applying the image to the VHD can take some time. The overall imaging speed is fast, but it depends on the size of the image to be applied as well as the speed of storage. A successful image application is shown in Figure 6.14.

4. After you apply the image, shut down the VM, remove the pass-through disk, dismount the captured CD, and restart the VM. The VM should boot the captured operating-system instance.

NOTE In some circumstances, the volume may not have been properly initialized. This can happen if, for instance, you use a WinPE image that isn't based on the same version of Windows that you're deploying. The simplest way to correct this condition is to re-create the volume (in the VHD) using the install media for the operating system in question. If you're working with a Vista image, start the installation of Vista to the VHD, and re-create the volume. After the installation begins, shut down the VM and apply the image again.

FIGURE 6.14

Successful imaging

Performing System Updates

Similar to a character in a horror movie, the newly created VM may go into a state of shock when it starts up and finds itself living in a new body. The system may not have expected to have its hardware drastically altered. Now it must either adjust or die. Contemporary versions of Windows do a good job of detecting system changes and adjusting where possible. Minor changes can be accommodated after startup within the normal operations, like those shown in Figure 6.15.

FIGURE 6.15
Successful startup

Figure 6.15 shows that Windows Vista has found new hardware that requires drivers. It has also detected the loss of sound support. The drastic change in hardware has also triggered the Windows activation process. In some cases, you can trigger hardware change detection. You can kick off (for example) a HAL redetection on Windows Vista an Windows Server 2008 by running MSConfig, selecting the Boot tab, and selecting Detect HAL (see Figure 6.16).

FIGURE 6.16
Detect HAL

Not all hardware changes can be easily addressed within Windows. Changes to the underlying storage can cause the operating system to fail, as shown in Figure 6.17.

FIGURE 6.17
Nasty startup error

In this case, the source system depended on SATA for the system volume. You can rectify this error condition with the original installation media for the operating system. Boot the VM with the proper Windows Vista installation DVD, and select the Repair Your Computer option on the startup screen (see Figure 6.18) to correct the issue (see Figure 6.19).

Storage-related issues may be your biggest headache for manual P2V migrations. The variety and complexity of storage available for server hardware can make manual P2V migrations too complicated for some hardware and operating-system configurations. You should use automated and supported P2V tools (such as SCVMM) in these cases.

After your VM is running, you'll also want to install the Hyper-V Integration Components in order to use the higher-performance synthetic NIC, improved mouse integration, and other performance enhancements.

NOTE   Occasionally, you may encounter an error message while installing the Integration Components in Windows Vista, indicating that the ICs require "a newer version of Windows." Applying SP1 to Vista will allow the ICs to successfully install.

FIGURE 6.18
Vista Welcome
screen

FIGURE 6.19
Vista repair

Exporting and Importing in Hyper-V

V2V migrations between different virtualization platforms require steps similar to those in the P2V examples shown earlier. You can move VMs between Hyper-V hosts without all these steps by leveraging the built-in export and import functionality.

Export and import aren't truly V2V processes, but they allow you to move VMs from one Hyper-V host to another, and they fit well into a chapter focused on migration. You can also use failover cluster to migrate a VM from one host to another, but this requires you to configure clustering on similar hosts. SCVMM has a capability that you can use to move VMs from one host to another without export and import. (SCVMM is covered in Chapter 11.)

Exporting a Virtual Machine

The Hyper-V Console enables you to export and completely duplicate the configuration of a stopped or saved VM. This capability lets you move or copy an entire VM and configuration (more than simply copying a VHD file). To do so, select the VM in the console, and choose Action ➤ Export (see Figure 6.20).

FIGURE 6.20

Export option

You can also right-click a VM and select Export, or select Export from the actions listed for the selected VM on the right side of the console. Any of these techniques will open the Export dialog, allowing you to select a directory location for the data (see Figure 6.21).

FIGURE 6.21

Selecting the
export location

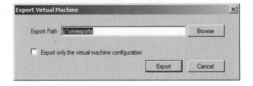

TIP The destination of the export must be accessible to the parent system. A locally attached volume is usually your best bet (including an Internet SCSI [iSCSI] attached disk). The parent partition won't typically have access to a network share unless you first configure constrained delegation.

The export process runs in the background, duplicating the VM configuration information, memory contents (if the VM is saved), and disks (VHD and AVHD snapshot files). If you choose, you can export only the VM configuration by selecting the Export Only The Virtual Machine Configuration check box in the dialog shown in Figure 6.21. This can be useful if you back up the VM disk files using another process, like those described in Chapter 7.

You can view the progress of the export in the Hyper-V Console (see Figure 6.22).

FIGURE 6.22
Export progress

After you complete the export, you can copy or move the entire export directory hierarchy and contents to a local disk on the target Hyper-V host.

NOTE The folder created during the export process *under* the specified export directory is the repository of the VM's information. The folder is named the same as the display name of the VM. This is the folder hierarchy to move or copy to a target host. The folder contains all the information necessary to import the VM on a new host.

Importing a Virtual Machine

You import the VM in the reverse order that you export it (see Figure 6.23). The import process takes very little time.

FIGURE 6.23
Starting an import

Selecting the Import action on the target host reads in the configuration data from the unique directory containing the exported VM. If the VM is unique to your environment, you can choose to reuse the VM's existing identification information (see Figure 6.24).

FIGURE 6.24
Selecting an import

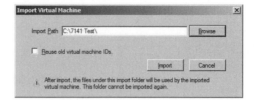

The import process reads the information and creates the VM configuration on the target host. Keep in mind that **you can do an import only once**, unless you save the export folder and file hierarchy elsewhere. You should also consider that the location of the VM you specify during this import will be the final resting place for the VM. The VM will run from this directory after import, so you should be certain your exported VM is in the right location before importing.

You must remember to make the same resources available to the imported VM that it had on the source system. Be sure you define identically named virtual networks and that mounted ISO files registered when exported are available on the new physical host. Missing resource (networks and ISO files) will result in warning messages or cause imports to fail (see Figure 6.25).

FIGURE 6.25
Import warning

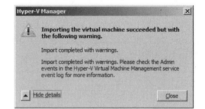

Summary

Migrating existing physical systems to VMs is a necessary part of moving to a virtual environment. You can convert systems manually, but you need the right tools, expertise, and time. Fully automated methods for migrating physical systems and existing VMs to Hyper-V VMs exist. SCVMM is the recommended and supported means for P2V and V2V migration; it's covered in Chapter 11.

Chapter 7

Backup and Recovery

Companies often move to virtualization in order to separate a server-based application from *at risk* physical hardware and thus guard against failure. When you migrate "that scary server in the corner that we don't have the install CDs for anymore" to a virtual machine, you can perpetuate a key business function well into the future.

When you encapsulate virtual machine (VM) information inside a single virtual hard disk (VHD), you can back up, migrate, and restore server-based services and applications, which you can't always easily accomplish with a physical server. A coordinated *save* or *shutdown* of a VM hosting an application without backup awareness allows an otherwise impossible recovery in the event of a failure.

With all of its promise, virtualization introduces huge disruptions to traditional operational procedures and processes. How is it possible to quickly back up a dozen running VMs, each of which uses tens of gigabytes of VHD files? Where will you store these backups to make them quickly recoverable? How will you recover the configurations for each VM, as well as critical configuration data for the physical host, in a timely manner?

The aim of this chapter is to explore important considerations for backup and recovery of VMs as well as common backup and recovery approaches. In the latter part of the chapter, we'll walk through two approaches for host-based backup that don't require additional third-party software licensing.

This chapter will cover the following areas:

◆ Virtual machine backup considerations

◆ Manually backing up and recovering a virtual machine

Virtual Machine Backup Considerations

For any administrator, the goal of a backup is to allow computer-based data or services to be easily restored. Your organization may be driven by different requirements, such as compliance, business continuity, disaster recovery, application development, and testing. Data volumes, timing, network bandwidth, security, heritage backup solutions, and budget concerns can influence how your company implements a solution.

The considerations that drive plans and solutions for backing up VMs and their host systems are the same as for traditional server backups. The benefits of virtualization (abstracting software from hardware and encapsulating storage in VHDs) give you new options for rapid backup and recovery.

You can often replicate the bulk of VM data by copying associated VHD files to a new location or host. But remember that a VM is defined by more than the data contained in VHDs. The VM's configuration also contains critical information necessary for the smooth and rapid recovery of a virtual operating-system instance. Virtual networks are defined on the Hyper-V host system—outside of VM configurations—and may also be required in many recovery scenarios. You must consider backup and recovery for multiple components of an entire virtualization environment (more than simply a VHD) when you develop backup and recovery solutions.

Classic Backup/Recovery Options and Challenges

Other than the obvious challenge of physically connecting a tape drive to a VM (which you can't do), you can use traditional backup and recovery processes with VMs. You'll find common, tested, network-based backup solutions that often install agents that back up and restore data on physical and virtual machines. As noted earlier, virtualization may disrupt the rhythm of existing backup and recovery processes if you don't take its impact into account.

USING THE VOLUME SHADOW COPY SERVICES

Before Microsoft introduced the Volume Shadow Copy Services (VSS), administrators often performed application backup operations on Windows Server systems by first shutting down a service or application. Not all backup processes required service interruption, but administrators could ensure that file input/output activity ceased and that files were duplicated reliably for later recovery.

Microsoft introduced VSS as part of Windows Server 2003. VSS lets you coordinate necessary actions to create a consistent point-in-time copy (also known as a *shadow copy* or *snapshot*) of data for backup purposes. You can copy these shadow copies to separate disk or tape-based storage without affecting data files used by an active application or service.

Four key components must be present for a service or application to take advantage of VSS:

◆ *VSS writer*—An application-aware software component (usually from an application vendor) that ensures the consistency of data to back up

◆ *VSS requester*—A backup tool or command asking for a snapshot to be created

◆ *VSS provider*—A tool that manages the shadow copies after they're created (a software provider comes with Windows Server, but one can also come from a storage subsystem vendor with integrated snapshot capability)

◆ *VSS coordination service*—A part of the operating system that coordinates the cooperation of all necessary VSS components

In order for a VSS-enabled backup to work properly, the VSS requester asks for a backup set to be created. The VSS writer responds by coordinating the queuing of disk writes for the associated application (quiesces the application). This action of halting disk writes to related files allows the VSS provider to create a point-in-time shadow copy of the files used by the application. After the show copy is created, the VSS writer (application) is informed that I/O operations can proceed as normal. When I/O operations are restored to normal, the VSS requester (backup software) has access to the snapshot and can proceed with creating a consistent backup copy of the application's data (see Figure 7.1).

FIGURE 7.1

VSS shadow-copy process

1. Requestor asks VSS for writer details and to prepare for shadow-copy creation.
2. Writer creates a description of the components and the restore method.
3. Writer prepares for shadow-copy creation (completes transactions, flushes caches).
4. Writer tells VSS it's ready.
5. VSS tells the writer to quiesce data (a maximum of 60 seconds) and then flushes and freezes the filesystem.
6. VSS tells the provider to create the shadow copy (a maximum of 10 seconds).
7. VSS thaws the filesystem and releases the writers from quiesce.
8. VSS verifies that I/O was held and that the shadow copy was created.
9. If the copy was successful, VSS tells the requestor where to find the data, and the backup can proceed.

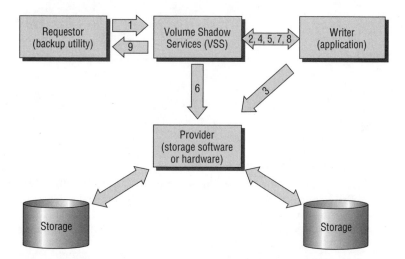

Windows Server 2008 includes a VSS writer for many of the applications and services included with the platform, including file services, Internet Information Services (IIS), Background Intelligent Transfer Service (BITS), and Hyper-V. The Hyper-V VSS writer lets you back up properly enlightened VMs while they're running. You can also do rapid backup of unenlightened VMs (those without installed integration components; more on this later).

Successfully completing a VSS-aware backup is complex and must be done relatively quickly to limit the effect on VSS-aware applications—I/O can't be held indefinitely. If underlying disk performance is slow or is under high load, the VSS snapshot process may take longer than allowable, and the shadow-creation process may fail. A VSS request from a physical host to an enlightened VM needs to not only hold I/O between the VM and the VHD but also ask VSS-aware applications within the VM to quiesce writes (see Figure 7.2). This longer chain of VSS coordination further complicates the VSS process.

Even with the complicated orchestration necessary for VSS-integrated backups, they vastly improve backup and recoverability of Windows-based applications and services, including Hyper-V–based VMs. VSS gives software developers and administrators tools to reduce system downtime and meet recovery objectives.

FIGURE 7.2
VSS process with a
virtual machine

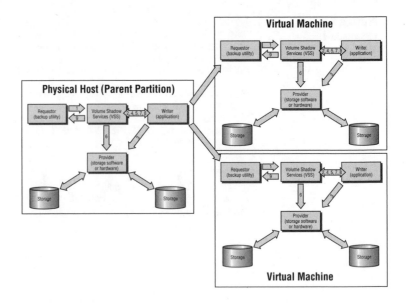

VSS BACKUPS AND SAVING STATE

When you integrate VSS, it allows you to back up VMs with installed ICs without interruption. What happens to VMs without ICs? Rather than pass the VSS request through the ICs to coordinate the queuing of disk writes, the VSS writer for Hyper-V saves the state of a non-enlightened VM. Saving state temporarily halts processing in the VM and writes the contents of memory for the VM to disk (to the associated VSV file) during VSS processing. Although you interrupt processing in the VM, you help ensure that you create a valid backup.

You can also use *saving state* to back up VMs with applications that don't support VSS (no properly functioning VSS writer), even if they have ICs installed. You can force the saving of state during a host-based VSS backup by disabling the Backup Integration Service in the VM settings, accessible via the Hyper-V Manager (see Figure 7.3).

Note that all integration services are enabled by default. This isn't true for all child operating systems, because some enlightened operating systems (Linux, for instance) may not include support for VSS.

A key result of forcing the Saved state of a VM is the VM's restore state. Restoring a backup of a VM in the Saved state means the VM will still be in that state when recovered. You can return the VM to the Running state from Saved and almost instantly begin processing. In contrast, a VM that uses the Backup Integration Service and VSS integration won't be recovered to Saved state; it will be restored as Off and subsequently started.

TIP Disabling the Backup IC capability can be a great way for you to improve the end-to-end recovery time for some VMs, because the VM may not require startup.

Disabling the Backup IC capability can be a great way for you to improve the end-to-end recovery time for some VMs, because the VM may not require startup.

FIGURE 7.3
Virtual machine
settings—
disabling the
Backup Integration
Service

You must consider the interruption in processing during backup, VM recovery state, and data consistency when you employ VSS for VM backup and recovery. Review Table 7.1 to see how VSS Backup Integration is applied.

TABLE 7.1   Volume Shadow Copy Services Backup Integration

BACKUP INTEGRATION SERVICE STATUS	VM STATE DURING BACKUP	SERVICE INTERRUPTION DURING BACKUP?	VM STATE UPON RESTORE
Enabled	Running	No	Off
Missing/Disabled	Saved	Yes	Saved

SNAPSHOTS DO NOT A BACKUP MAKE

With Hyper-V, you can use VSS to make snapshots of running VMs. You can make snapshots from the Hyper-V Manager console or via scripts and programs using the appropriate Windows Management Interface (WMI) APIs. You can repeatedly capture the running state of a VM and quickly roll back to a known state. Snapshots can facilitate common testing scenarios, such as repeated installation or reconfiguration of software. The integrated snapshot capability has only limited production value, because it doesn't in itself provide backup and recovery of a VM, the VM configuration, or the configuration of the physical host. You can back up snapshots via common physical host-based backup solutions and restore them with a VM backup.

Host-Based Backup Approaches

You can take advantage of the benefits of virtualization by creating backups on a Hyper-V physical host. Numerous approaches let you create recoverable images of VMs, including the following:

- Export/Import
- Physical to virtual (P2V) image capture
- Manual VHD backup
- Windows Server Backup (WSB)
- Third-party backup and recovery tools
- System Center Data Protection Manager (DPM)

Each approach includes trade-offs you should consider when you select a solution. Table 7.2 summarizes high-level considerations and issues for each of the backup approaches mentioned.

TABLE 7.2   Subjective Comparison of Backup and Recovery Approaches

	SOFTWARE COST	NETWORK UTILIZATION	STORAGE UTILIZATION	RECOVERY FLEXIBILITY	ADMIN EXPERTISE REQUIRED	OVERALL COST/ VALUE
Export/Import	☺	☺	☹	☺	😐	😐
P2V	😐	😐	☹	☺	☹	☹
Manual Backup	☺	😐	☺	☺	☹	😐
Windows Server Backup	☺	😐	😐	😐	☹	😐
Third-Party Tools	☹	😐	😐	☺	☺	😐
Data Protection Manager	😐	☺	☺	☺	☺	☺

Export/Import

Using the Hyper-V Manager console or WMI APIs to export a VM is a simple, cost-effective way to create a backup instance. Export duplicates the configuration data and associated VHD files for a VM. The process also makes the output transportable so that you can import the VM and start it on a separate Hyper-V host.

You should understand certain drawbacks of the export process:

◆ The export process doesn't work on running VMs. A VM's state must be Off or Saved to initiate an export, limiting the usefulness of export for backup and recovery when VM uptime is required.

◆ An export process must typically write the VM information to locally attached storage— not to a file share. Internet SCSI (iSCSI) attached volumes and removable disks (such as USB) can provide flexible destinations for Hyper-V. During recovery, the storage location housing the export is used to host the VM files. This means if you attach a USB drive to a Hyper-V host and import a previously exported VM, the VHDs will continue to exist on the USB drive and be used by Hyper-V for that VM.

For better performance and stability, you may want to copy the entire export directory to dedicated storage on a physical recovery host before you import it.

Physical to Virtual Conversion

Some administrators consider using physical to VM conversion (P2V) for backup and recovery for physical hosts. If you regularly schedule conversions, you can use a P2V image of a physical server for recovery services on a virtualization host in the event of a failure. This is an important strategy for physical systems enabled by virtualization. You can use the same process and tools for backup and recovery of an existing VM. The process of capturing a VM in this manner is known as a virtual to virtual (V2V) conversion or migration.

You can use P2V and V2V conversion for backup and recovery, but each has limited applicability for VM backup and recovery. With VM information already encapsulated in VHD files, executing the assessment and conversion processes is largely unnecessary. For VMs that use pass-through disk or iSCSI mounted volumes, V2V may be a viable and valuable option to provide backup outside of a child-based (inside the VM) solution.

Manual VHD Backup and Recovery

Because the configuration information for a VM is contained in files, you can move and recover a VM via an entirely manual process. You can duplicate VM data files (VHD), configuration files (XML), and memory files (VSV) and restore them manually and with a high degree of flexibility. We'll review a sample manual backup and recovery process at the end of the chapter.

Windows Server Backup

Windows Server 2008 includes WSB as a replacement for NTBackup, which is no longer available. Like NTBackup, you can access WSB via a graphical interface or through command-line options for automation of repeatable backup and recovery options.

Similar to other Windows Server 2008 backup solutions, WSB is fully VSS-aware and, when properly configured, can minimize VM downtime during the backup process. You'll learn how to use WSB and walk through WSB backup and recovery later in this chapter.

Enterprise Backup Tools and Solutions

All enterprises are invested in an existing backup and recovery process and often rely on dedicated third-party tools. Enterprise-wide, dedicated backup and recovery tools promise to provide the highest level of operational consistency by reducing inconsistent user interfaces for administrators and centralizing hardware and media (tape and disk).

Many traditional enterprise backup solutions do a poor job of exploiting virtualization for better disaster recovery and business continuity. These solutions may be inadequate because of monolithic architectures, components, or vendor-driven economic models. Backup solutions that understand and integrate with storage enhancements such as shadow copies; allow for fast, low-cost disk-based backup; or include tight Hyper-V integration and awareness will provide you the most benefit. System Center DPM is one such tool that will be discussed in detail in Chapter 12, "System Center Data Protection Manager."

Agent Multiplexing

Some organizations may need a single system or technology for compliance reasons, to include all system backups or application data of a certain type. The costs for certain solutions can be driven by expensive backup agents or clients that are application specific. Enterprises with an investment in existing, monolithic backup architectures that don't support Hyper-V, or for which the cost of a Hyper-V agent may be prohibitive, can often still use Hyper-V backup (see Figure 7.4).

Using Windows Server Backup or a manual backup process to create static, restorable file sets of Hyper-V VMs can often enable more flexible backup and recovery scenarios with other backup and recovery technologies. Centralizing backups to a single file share or storage device using WSB, a custom manual process, or a cost-effective commercial solution such as DPM can reduce the per server or per agent licensing expense for other backup and recovery solutions.

FIGURE 7.4
Backup
multiplexing

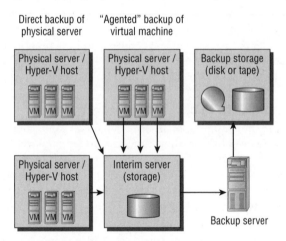

Beware of Bloat in Host (Parent) Backups

Many traditional server-backup tools support backup and recovery of physical systems running Hyper-V, because Hyper-V is a Windows Server 2008 role. By virtue of their support for file-based backup and integration with VSS, they can easily provide the same backup and recovery features to filesystem-based components of a Hyper-V physical host. Note that specific backup and recovery services vary between backup tools, and you should confirm supported scenarios with the particular solution vendor and through testing.

A key benefit of physical host-based backup in a virtual environment is derived from the encapsulation of VM data in VHD files. Applications residing within a VM may not be *backup aware*—they may not be able to integrate with common backup and recovery tools. You can essentially ignore application- or platform-specific backup awareness if you properly manage and replicate a VM's configuration, state, and storage data (save the state of the VM, snapshot the "in flight" configuration and associated VHDs, restart the VM, replicate snapshots to remote storage). By virtue of their installation within VMs, these applications or services can be made more operationally stable. Parent partition backups of VMs may also reduce licensing costs for certain enterprise backup tools, because they facilitate backup and recovery without the need for certain platform- or application-specific agents in a VM instance.

Encapsulation vastly simplifies backup and recovery of VMs, but it has a downside. Many traditional backup and recovery tools manage recoverable objects at a file level. To perform daily host backup of a VM means that all associated VHD files would require replication.

Previously, you might have set up a physical file server with a nightly incremental backup schedule. With 100GB of files and (for the sake of argument) a 2 percent nightly change, the incremental backup volume might have been 2GB. After virtualization, a host-based backup of the same virtual file server with 100GB of associated VHD would generate 50 times the backup traffic, because the entire virtual hard disk would be replicated.

Without any planning, the increased backup traffic that can result from host-based backups can negatively impact not only the enterprise network but also disk and tape drives and media for backups, and it can expand required backup-timing windows. Enterprise backup and recovery tools optimized for virtualization technology, such as System Center DPM 2007 (discussed in Chapter 12), alleviate the detrimental effect of encapsulation. These tools identify and replicate only changed fractions of storage (VHD) files. Additionally, you can complete incremental backup processes within the VM to reduce backup volume, but doing so eliminates the encapsulation benefit of virtualization.

Common backup scenarios for use with Hyper-V are shown in Figure 7.5, including the use of backup processing from within a VM.

FIGURE 7.5
Common backup
scenarios

Child Backup: Backing Up from Within

Traditional backup solutions call for you to initiate a backup process on a computer and replicate data available to that system to a recoverable file set on either disk or tape. Initiating a backup within a VM is a valid approach to backup and recovery of data, and in some instances a child-based backup is necessary. Common scenarios that may mandate a child-based backup include the following:

◆ Use of pass-through disk

◆ iSCSI storage mounted within a VM

◆ Certain applications running within an enlightened VM

Accessing storage within a VM using pass-through disk or via iSCSI (using the iSCSI initiator in the VM to mount a remote volume) means that some data won't be encapsulated within a VHD for a parent partition-based backup. Because the data isn't in a VHD hosted by (or accessible to) the parent, it may not be easily backed up from the physical host. Although you may be able to use Storage Area Network (SAN) hardware snapshot technology to replicate the data on these volumes, the simplest solution for backing up data accessible to a VM is to use backup or replication software from within the VM.

VSS integration/awareness within a VM is important, because a backup process in the parent partition or physical host can make a VSS request that affects a running child VM. Some applications may not be VSS aware or may not properly integrate with a VSS request that comes through the ICs installed in a VM from a physical host. It may seem that you created a good backup of a VM; but without proper end-to-end VSS coordination between the parent partition and applications inside the VM, backup quality can't be guaranteed.

You can perform child-based backups essentially the same way you have always done physical host backups. Common third-party backup tools rely on the installation of an agent component on a backup client system that transmits data to a central backup server. Installing a backup agent within a network-connected VM enables these existing backup solutions—assuming, of course, that the backup software is supported in the VM.

Manually Backing Up and Recovering a Virtual Machine

You can accomplish backup and recovery a number of ways. We'll devote the remainder of the chapter to walking through two low-cost options for parent-based/host-based backup and recovery using Windows Server Backup and a manual process using VSS via the Diskshadow command.

Windows Server Backup

As noted earlier, WSB is the backup and recovery tool integrated into Windows Server 2008. You can easily use WSB to back up and recover Hyper-V hosts and child VMs. WSB requires that you back up all volumes associated with Hyper-V to facilitate a recovery. This means that you must replicate the *entire* volumes housing any VM-related files as part of a single backup. The WSB requirement to capture all data can substantially increase the overall time and storage to complete a backup. However, WSB does offer a vastly simpler backup and recovery experience.

WSB INSTALLATION AND CONFIGURATION

WSB is an installable feature of Windows Server 2008. To add WSB to an existing Windows Server 2008 system, select Features in the bar on the left side of the Server Manager console (see Figure 7.6), and then select Add Features to start the Add Features Wizard.

NOTE The command-line tools aren't installed by default when you install WSB. To install these tools, expand the Windows Server Backup Features selection and select Command-Line Tools, as shown in Figure 7.6.

FIGURE 7.6
Add Features
Wizard

You can also install WSB from the command line using OCSetup:

```
OCSETUP WindowsServerBackup
```

WSB is VSS aware, but Hyper-V doesn't by default register its associated VSS writer with WSB. Without knowledge of the Hyper-V VSS writer (or other application-aware VSS writers) WSB may be unable to successfully complete a VSS snapshot operation for running VMs during a backup. To register the Hyper-V VSS writer with WSB, add appropriate Registry keys by executing the following two commands:

```
reg add "HKLM\Software\Microsoft\windows nt\currentversion\↵
WindowsServerBackup\Application Support\{66841CD4-6DED-4F4B-8F17-FD23F8DDC3DE}"
```

```
reg add "HKLM\Software\Microsoft\windows nt\currentversion\↵
WindowsServerBackup\Application Support\{66841CD4-6DED-4F4B-8F17-FD23F8DDC3DE}" ↵
/v "Application Identifier" /t REG_SZ /d Hyper-v
```

After you complete the Registry changes, you can review them using a graphical Registry tool such as the Registry Editor (RegEdt32), as shown in Figure 7.7.

FIGURE 7.7
Registry entries

You can also check the entry by querying the Registry:

```
reg query "HKLM\Software\Microsoft\windows nt\currentversion\↵
WindowsServerBackup\Application Support\{66841CD4-6DED-4F4B-8F17-FD23F8DDC3DE}" ↵
/sWindows Server Backup Graphical Interface
```

You can access WSB through the Administrative Tools program group on the Start menu (Start ➢ Administrative Tools ➢ Windows Server Backup). The WSB console is a fairly typical MMC 3.0 snap-in and should look familiar. You can access administrative actions either from the menu bar at the top or via the Actions pane on the right (see Figure 7.8).

FIGURE 7.8
Windows Server
Backup console

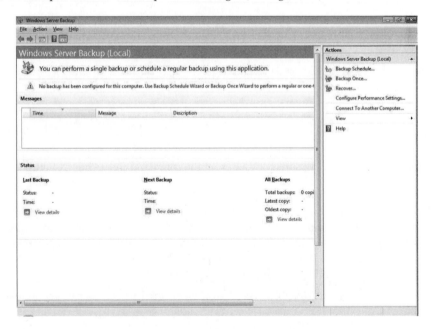

You can configure two types of backup processes through the graphical user interface: a *Backup Once* process and a *Backup Schedule*. The Backup Schedule action must use a locally attached disk as the backup destination, and a volume must be dedicated for use by WSB. The Backup Once action has options similar to those of Backup Schedule, but you can use either locally attached storage or a network share as a backup destination. Local volumes used as a destination for Backup Once don't need to be dedicated to WSB.

NOTE   ISCSI has changed what may constitute a locally attached disk. Mounting volumes across local area network (LAN) and even wide area network (WAN) links as if they were internal to a system with iSCSI lets you easily add remote storage to a system for backup/restore and other needs. Chapter 8, "High Availability," includes iSCSI command examples (using `iscsicli`) that you can use to attach volumes as part of a scheduled backup and recovery process.

BACKUP ONCE

You can start a one-time manual backup by selecting the Backup Once action. The Backup Once Wizard walks you through the configurable options (see Figure 7.9); the first choice is to perform a predefined scheduled backup or to select Different Options.

FIGURE 7.9
Backup Options
dialog

Selecting Different Options lets you create a customized backup set. This may be the only option available if no predefined scheduled backups exist. As you proceed through the wizard, you can select volumes to include within the scope of the backup—typically, all attached volumes or a custom subset (see Figure 7.10).

FIGURE 7.10
Select Backup
Configuration
dialog

You can reduce the size and time of the backup by choosing which volumes to include or exclude. If you plan to use a local volume as the backup destination, you should exclude it from the scope of the backup. Remember that all volumes used for Hyper-V VMs must be selected to be within scope of the backup. In Figure 7.11, all Hyper-V related files are housed on C:, and this is the only volume that will be backed up.

FIGURE 7.11
Select Backup
Items dialog

As mentioned earlier, a one-time backup may use a network share or non-dedicated local volume as a destination (see Figure 7.12).

FIGURE 7.12
Specify
Destination Type
dialog

If you want to use a local volume, you can select eligible volumes from a pull-down menu. You can use removable disks (USB or eSATA) as well as other forms of direct attached storage (see Figure 7.13).

FIGURE 7.13
Select Backup
Destination dialog

Some application backups let you clear/truncate the transaction log files as part of the backup process. The Specify Advanced Option dialog has no affect on Hyper-V backups, and you can ignore it—select either option (see Figure 7.14).

FIGURE 7.14
Specify Advanced
Option dialog

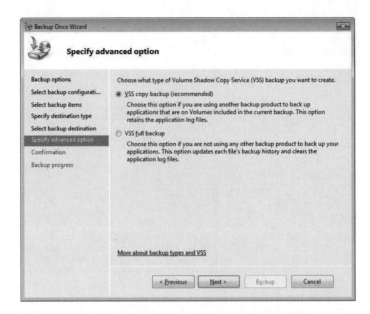

After you choose your configuration options, you must confirm the initiation of a backup (see Figure 7.15).

FIGURE 7.15
Confirmation
dialog

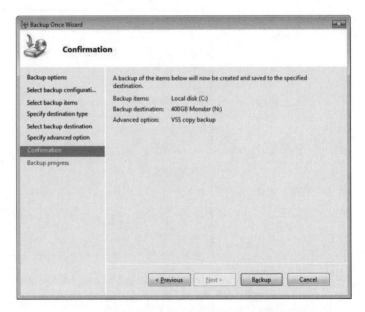

After the backup begins, its status is reflected in the wizard. You may close the wizard at any time while the backup is executing without affecting the backup's progress (see Figure 7.16).

FIGURE 7.16
Backup Progress
dialog

BACKUP SCHEDULE

The process for creating a Backup Schedule is similar to the Backup Once process; we won't include the flow of the schedule wizard here. As the name suggests, this action lets you define backup processes that execute on a regularly scheduled basis—either once a day or more than once a day. Remember that scheduled backups require a dedicated volume, unlike one-time backups. WSB reformats the volume you select as the backup destination, and all data contained on the volume is destroyed (see Figure 7.17).

FIGURE 7.17
Scheduled backup
format warning

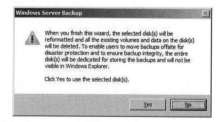

PERFORMING A BACKUP USING THE COMMAND LINE

Extensive command-line support is provided for WSB via the WBadmin command. The command-line tools provide increased flexibility for scheduling and managing backup and recovery processing; we won't cover them here. Documentation of the WSB command-line tools is available online at http://technet.microsoft.com/en-us/library/cc754015.aspx.

RESTORING WITH WSB

Recovering VMs and their configurations is a simple process via the graphical user interface. We won't cover the process to recover the parent partition and physical host, but you can do this easily with WSB. (Often, recovery of the physical host isn't required for a VM recovery.)

To begin the recovery of a VM, launch WSB (Start ➤ Administrative Tools ➤ Windows Server Backup), and select Actions ➤ Recover. The Recovery Wizard walks you through the restore process, beginning with the selection of the recovery server (see Figure 7.18).

FIGURE 7.18
Server selection

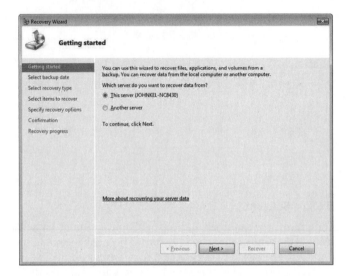

Typically, you'll have multiple backup sets available from which to restore. Available backup sets are displayed with a calendar to help you choose (see Figure 7.19). Note that the most recent backup is selected by default.

FIGURE 7.19
Select Backup Date dialog

You can also choose the type of recovery. You can restore individual files, entire volumes, or applications using WSB. For a Hyper-V recovery, select Applications (see Figure 7.20).

FIGURE 7.20
Select Recovery
Type dialog

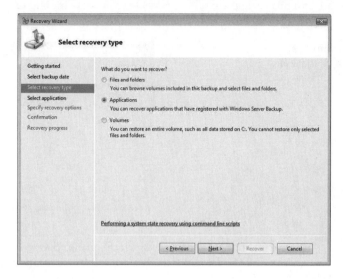

Often, Hyper-V is the only application listed for recovery (see Figure 7.21), because other applications typically aren't loaded in the parent partition.

FIGURE 7.21
Select Application
dialog

The names (in this case, the GUID) of VMs and the Initial Store for the Hyper-V configuration are listed as application components to be restored (see Figure 7.22). Note that *all* VMs that are part of a backup are restored; WSB can't restore individual VMs backed up from the same volume.

FIGURE 7.22
Application components list

You have two options for the restore location of recovered application data. You can direct the recovery of VM-related files to the original source location or to another location (see Figure 7.23).

FIGURE 7.23
Specify Recovery Options dialog

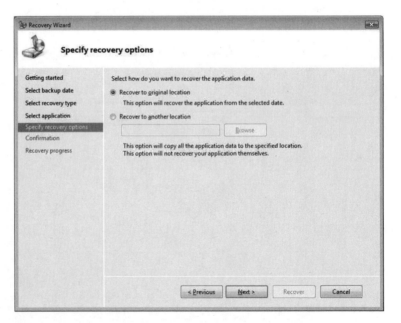

After you select all your options, the Recovery Wizard Confirmation screen appears, and the restore proceeds (see Figure 7.24).

FIGURE 7.24
Confirmation of backup and restore options

Similar to the backup process, you can watch the recovery progress in the wizard (see Figure 7.25). The wizard's progress bar shows the completion percentage for each item you selected for recovery.

FIGURE 7.25
Recovery Progress dialog

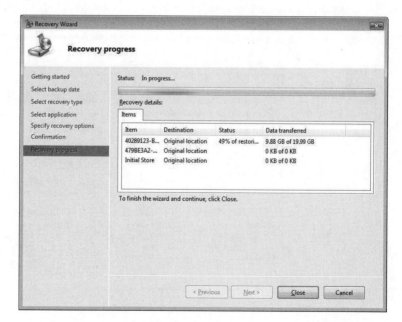

The wizard also displays the final recovery status (success or failure); see Figure 7.26. In the Recovery Details, the wizard lists the total amount of data transferred.

FIGURE 7.26
Recovery complete

As with the backup wizard, you can close the Recovery Wizard before recovery is complete. You can view the status of historic backup and recovery jobs as well as other WSB-related messages in the Messages windows in the main WSB console (see Figure 7.27).

FIGURE 7.27
WSB console with
logged events

Performing a Manual Backup

As we mentioned earlier in the chapter, you can successfully craft and execute a manual backup and restore of Hyper-V VMs and their configurations. Such a process can take advantage of the VSS in a manner similar to WSB. Creating such a process requires substantial testing and tinkering and lacks the vendor support of a more mainstream backup process. To develop and automate this kind of manual backup and restore, you must understand the command line, batch files, scripting, and the relatively new Diskshadow command, and you must have a thorough grasp of Hyper-V. A manual process isn't well suited for all recovery scenarios, and the example we'll explore here won't apply to many situations.

The backup and recovery method outlined in the next section makes numerous unstated assumptions about underlying infrastructure—including hardware performance, software patch levels, and other critical considerations that full-featured, supported backup solutions may more easily and completely address. This process doesn't, for example, back up or recover virtual network switch information defined on the physical host, which would be necessary for proper VM operation. Understanding this process is important in developing a complete understanding of backup and recovery for Hyper-V, but the batch files and scripts aren't supported in any fashion.

THE *DISKSHADOW* COMMAND

Diskshadow is a command-line tool included in Windows Server 2008 that exposes the functions of VSS. It lets you interact with VSS directly in an interactive mode or automate VSS-related tasks via prewritten scripts.

A fantastically useful function of Diskshadow is the ability to request a VSS snapshot and expose the resulting point-in-time copy as a drive letter. This gives you read access to a consistent snapshot for backup purposes. You can automate the coordinating VSS snapshot for required Hyper-V volumes, expose these volumes to the operating system, and copy required files for a recovery of VMs, all from within Diskshadow.

To access Diskshadow, type **Diskshadow** from the command line. Because Diskshadow is its own command shell, you can also start it from the search bar. You can access available commands and options through Help by typing **/?** in the Diskshadow command shell. From within the shell, you can list VSS writers, requestors, and providers; set a variety of VSS-related options; control backup processes; create, expose, and delete shadow copies; and perform other VSS-related tasks.

You can run a prewritten script with Diskshadow by launching the command with the **-s** parameter and specifying the name of the text-based script file:

```
diskshadow -s HyperVBackup.txt
```

The script file should contain the sequence of Diskshadow commands and options to be executed. Follow these high-level steps to automate a Hyper-V backup:

1. Identify the volumes to back up.

2. Verify that the Hyper-V Writer is available and ready.

3. Create shadow copies.

4. Expose the shadow copies for backup.

5. Copy the files.

6. Unexpose the shadow copies.

For the purposes of this example, we'll assume that all required files for backup are housed on two core volumes C: and F:. All VM configurations and VHDs are stored in F:\VHDs, and required pointers to VM configuration files remain in C:\ProgramData\Microsoft\Windows\ Hyper-V\. You need to coordinate a VSS snapshot of both C: and F: to successfully recover VMs in this case. Here is an example Diskshadow script fragment to accomplish this process:

```
begin backup
        add volume C: alias ConfigVolume
        add volume F: alias VHDVolume
        writer verify {66841cd4-6ded-4f4b-8f17-fd23f8ddc3de}
        create
        EXPOSE %VHDVolume% X:
        EXPOSE %ConfigVolume% Y:
        EXEC c:\HypervBackup.bat
        UNEXPOSE X:
        UNEXPOSE Y:
end backup
```

Additional housekeeping commands and options are required to successfully complete the backup process (shown later, in the complete listing). Note the EXEC command in the script segment, which invokes a batch file. It's called after the configuration volume (C:) and the VHD volume (F:) are snapped to create a shadow copy and exposed as drives X: and Y:. This batch file accomplishes the critical task of copying required files to secure storage—either locally attached or elsewhere on the network. You can easily accomplish this task using xcopy. Following are example commands to copy the required data exposed on drives X: and Y: to a local G: drive.

```
:
Xcopy x:\VHDs\*.* g:\HyperVBackup\VHDs\*.* ↵
  /e /s /y /F /O /X /R /H /B

xcopy y:\ProgramData\Microsoft\Windows\Hyper-V\*.* ↵
  g:\HyperVBackup\ProgramData\Microsoft\Windows\Hyper-V\*.* ↵
  /e /s /y /F /O /X /R /H /B
```

A complete VM backup process may require multiple component batch files with robust error checking, a scheduler, and one or more Diskshadow scripts. Ensuring the complete backup of a Hyper-V physical host, all settings, and VM data requires much more than is shown here; components of a complete (and entirely unsupported) backup process for VMs are shown in Figure 7.28.

The commented batch and script files supporting this process appear in Listings 7.1, 7.2, and 7.3. You can start the example backup process by launching Start_backup.bat, which calls Diskshadow using a prewritten script file: HyperVBackup.txt. The script file in turn calls HyperVBackup.bat to replicate (using xcopy) the necessary files for a subsequent recovery of the VMs.

FIGURE 7.28
Example Disk-
shadow backup
process flow

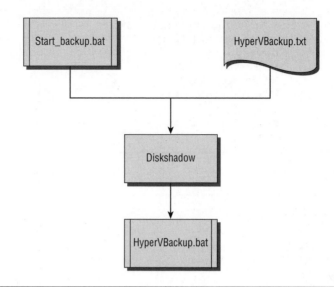

LISTING 7.1   Start_backup.bat

```
@echo off
cls
REM Calls Diskshadow to backup running Hyper-V Virtual Machines
REM
REM This example process assumes all virtual machine files
REM are homed on the F: drive and located in F:\VHDs
REM This includes VM related configuration files
REM
REM Also captures contents of
REM C:\HyperVBackup\ProgramData\Microsoft\Windows\Hyper-V\
REM
REM note the -S option which allows for the use of a pre-configured script
REM
Echo Beginning backup process...
diskshadow -s HyperVBackup.txt > c:\HyperVBackup.log
Echo Completed backup process. Check c:\HyperVBackup.log for results
```

LISTING 7.2   HyperVBackup.txt

```
set context persistent
set metadata C:\backup.cab
set verbose on
begin backup
      add volume C: alias ConfigVolume
      add volume F: alias VHDVolume
```

```
            #The GUID of the Hyper-V Writer is below
            writer verify {66841cd4-6ded-4f4b-8f17-fd23f8ddc3de}
            create
            EXPOSE %VHDVolume% X:
            EXPOSE %ConfigVolume% Y:
            EXEC c:\HypervBackup.bat
            UNEXPOSE X:
            UNEXPOSE Y:
end backup
```

LISTING 7.3   HyperVBackup.bat

```
@Echo off
REM Note that backup could be to any accessible storage local
REM or over the network
REM
REM Also note that running this copy process more than once
REM to the same destination can result in unnecessary files being retained.
REM
REM
REM The destination should be cleared or perhaps renamed before each copy.
REM Renaming the destination folder to reflect a particular backup generation
REM (rename g:\HyperBackup to g:\HyperBackup-OLD for example).
REM
g:
cd \
if exist g:\HyperVBackup-OLD (
      rmdir g:\HyperVBackup-OLD /s /q
)
pause
if exist g:\HyperVBackup (
      rename HyperVBackup HyperVBackup-OLD
)
pause

REM copy centralized VHD files to locally attached USB Drive
Xcopy x:\VHDs\*.* g:\HyperVBackup\VHDs\*.* /e /s /y /F /O /X /R /H
pause

REM copy Hyper-v Configuration files to locally attached USB Drive
xcopy y:\ProgramData\Microsoft\Windows\Hyper-V\*.* ↵
g:\HyperVBackup\ProgramData\Microsoft\Windows\Hyper-V\*.* ↵
      /e /s /y /F /O /X /R /H
```

NOTE   You can copy files captured in this manner to the appropriate locations in the directory hierarchy of a preexisting VM export. Landing VHD, VSV, XML, BIN, and other files in the correct locations with proper security is a complicated process. Swapping files into exported VM configurations is simplified if the VM exported and backup files are all generated while the VM is in an Off state.

RECOVERING FROM A MANUAL BACKUP

The basic purpose of recovering from a manual backup is to put copies of all necessary files back where they were before, which is not as simple as it sounds. The information and files required to recover a Hyper-V host and dependant VMs can be spread widely, with some information residing in the Registry, on the operating system volume, on other local volumes, and across network links.

Many files have critical security attributes (file ownership, for example) that must be preserved as part of the backup and recovery process. Again, using a backup tool engineered specifically for the backup and recovery of Hyper-V may be simpler and more effective in most scenarios than a manual backup process. Recovery of VMs in the following scenario assumes that the Hyper-V physical host didn't fail or that it has already been recovered up to the point where VMs require restore. It also assumes that all VMs will be recovered from the same backup and that existing VMs configured on the host may be overwritten.

The following high-level steps are required to recover VMs and their configuration to the same Hyper-V host:

1. Save state, and shut down the running VMs.

2. Stop Hyper-V services.

3. Restore files.

4. Start Hyper-V services.

5. Start the VMs.

The RestoreVMs.bat batch file in Listing 7.4 controls the restore process from the previously automated backup. It calls the SaveStateAll.vbs script file in Listing 7.5 to request a Save State of configured, running VMs so they won't be negatively affected by the halting of key Hyper-V services. The services are stopped to eliminate the risk of file locking while objects are copied back to the server.

LISTING 7.4   RestoreVMs.bat

```
REM
REM Restore requires that all VMs be off
REM - safest bet is shut down Hyper-V on the host
REM
@echo off
```

```
cls
echo NOTE THIS RESTORE WILL OVERWRITE THE ENTIRE SERVER's HYPER-V CONFIGURATION
pause
Echo .
echo Are you REALLY sure?
echo        ******
pause
echo Stopping all running virtual machines...
REM
REM requires a tiny little VBS script to stop VMs
REM - not always a great idea!
REM
cscript c:\SaveStateAll.vbs
Echo .
Echo Please check to ensure no Virtual Machines are running
Echo before proceeding with restore process
Pause
REM
Echo Stopping Hyper-V Services...
sc \\localhost stop VMMS
sc \\localhost stop VHDSVC
sc \\localhost stop nvspwmi
REM
REM copy centralized VHD files FROM locally attached USB Drive
REM
Xcopy g:\HyperVBackup\VHDs\*.* F:\VHDs\*.* /e /s /y /F /O /X /R /H
REM
REM copy Hyper-v Configuration files FROM locally attached USB Drive
REM
xcopy g:\HyperVBackup\ProgramData\Microsoft\Windows\Hyper-V\*.* ↵
   c:\ProgramData\Microsoft\Windows\Hyper-V\*.* ↵
   /e /s /y /F /O /X /R /H
REM
Echo Starting Hyper-V Services...
sc \\localhost start VMMS
sc \\localhost start VHDSVC
sc \\localhost start nvspwmi
Echo Hyper-V configuration and virtual machine backups should now be restored!
Echo You may now restart your virtual machines
```

LISTING 7.5   SaveStateAll.vbs

```
' Script that saves the state of running VMs on a Hyper-V enabled server
' NOTE:  Must be run as Administrator!
'
```

```
strComputer = "."
Set objWMIService = GetObject("winmgmts:\\" _
& strComputer & "\root\virtualization")
Set vmcollecion = _
    objWMIService.ExecQuery("SELECT * FROM Msvm_ComputerSystem",,48)

' loop through all instances in collection
For each vm in vmcollecion
    VMStateCode = vm.EnabledState
    ' request state change if appropriate
        ' - the host should never be eligible
    if ( vm.EnabledState = 2 or _
              vm.EnabledState = 32768) and _
              vm.Description <> _
              "Microsoft Hosting Computer System" Then
        Wscript.Echo "Saving " & vm.ElementName
        RequestReturn = vm.RequestStateChange(32769)
    End If
Next
Wscript.Echo VbCrLF
```

Comments on the Manual Recovery Process

The majority of required recovery data resides in the VHD files for each VM. Without proper recovery of the XML configuration files, as well as shortcuts to these files (both external to the VHDs), the VMs won't start. Security information tied to these files must be preserved for full recovery of VMs (which is why so many parameters appear at the end of each xcopy command in HyperVBackup.bat and RestoreVMs.bat).

You can successfully recover individual VMs using this manual backup process. Virtual machines may even be restored to alternate hosts, but success may require additional manual configuration. For example, to recover to a physical host with only a single volume (C:), you must manually edit the VM configuration files to reflect the new host drive (C: rather than F:). Configuration shortcuts (found in C:\ProgramData\Microsoft\Windows\Hyper-V\Virtual Machines\) may also require your attention.

Summary

Modern enterprises depend on successful backup and recovery of applications, services, and systems. The encapsulation of software within VMs gives you new scenarios you can use to back up, migrate, and restore server-based services and applications. Virtualization does create disruptions to traditional operational procedures and processes. But with planning and testing, you can exploit these disruptions and use the benefits of virtualization to investigate, construct, and adopt more efficient backup and recovery processes.

Chapter 8

High Availability

Failover clusters typically protect against hardware failure. Overall system failures (system unavailability) often aren't the result of server failures, but are more commonly caused by power outages, network stoppages, security issues, or misconfiguration. A redundant server generally won't protect against an unplanned outage such as lightning striking a power substation, a backhoe cutting a data link, an administrator inadvertently deleting a machine or service account, or the misapplication of a zoning update in a fibre-channel fabric.

Failover clustering protects against certain hardware failures but few of the typical causes of system instability or unavailability.

You can use numerous approaches to maximize system availability, and virtualized operating-system instances can help toward this end. In this chapter, we show you how to leverage Windows failover clustering of Hyper-V (commonly referred to as Quick Migration) as well as Windows failover clustering within virtual machines (application-level cluster).

This chapter will cover the following topics:

◆ Windows Server 2008 failover clustering

◆ Storage considerations for clustering

◆ Building a failover cluster for Hyper-V

◆ Clustered virtual-machine management

Windows Server 2008 Failover Clustering

A *failover cluster* is a group of similar computers (referred to as *nodes*) working in a coordinated fashion to increase the availability of specific services or applications. You typically employ failover clusters to increase availability by protecting against the loss of a single physical server from an unanticipated hardware failure or through proactive maintenance.

If you've worked with a failover cluster (Microsoft Cluster Service [MSCS]) using Windows NT Server, Windows 2000 Server, or Windows Server 2003, you already understand the basics of failover clustering in Windows Server 2008. Like those earlier Windows Server clustering technologies, it uses shared disks in a *shared nothing* model to provide multiple servers one-at-a-time volume access for processing.

But failover clustering in Windows Server 2008 differs from those implementations in several notable ways. Changes introduced for Windows Server 2008 focus on simplifying, securing, and stabilizing installations. Updates include the elimination of the cluster service account, networking enhancements, and support for parallel SCSI.

The most significant difference for administrators is the vastly simplified setup process supported by cluster validation, which we take you through step by step later in this chapter. The cluster-validation process helps to ensure a better cluster experience by identifying and eliminating configuration issues up front. During the validation process, you can check requirements for the creation of a cluster. The automated validation process includes discrete sections and tests that do the following:

♦ Inventory the hardware, software, and configuration of each individual node

♦ Check network-configuration items such as TCP/IP settings and firewall configuration, and validate communication

♦ Investigate the storage infrastructure by listing disks, identifying clusterable storage, and validating failover capability

♦ Examine the configuration, installed software, and settings across systems to ensure a uniform configuration

After successful validation, you can quickly set up nodes to form a failover cluster. You can automate failover configuration for services and applications when you use the High Availability Wizard for common application failover scenarios. This wizard contains more than a dozen preconfigured application and service selections that set up failover capabilities homed on a failover cluster (see Figure 8.1). After a cluster is validated and created, you can select this action for an application or service and test its suitability for clustering. If the application is appropriate, the wizard automatically configures it for high availability (HA).

FIGURE 8.1
Some available
high-availability-
ready services and
applications

The setup and validation changes in Windows Server 2008 enable server generalists (rather than clustering specialists) to quickly and efficiently configure a failover cluster. Determining if your cluster configuration meets support requirements no longer requires checking the Microsoft Hardware Compatibility List (HCL) or Server Catalog for the exact hardware setup.

The specific support requirements for creating a failover cluster are as follows (as per Microsoft):

◆ Successfully passing the Validate test in the Failover Clusters Management snap-in.

◆ All hardware and software components must meet the qualifications to receive a "Certified for Windows Server 2008" logo.

You can build a simple failover cluster with two servers, networking infrastructure, and shared storage, as shown in Figure 8.2. With appropriate physical servers, enough network cards, cables, and suitable shared storage, you can set up and configure a Windows Server 2008–based failover cluster in a matter of hours.

FIGURE 8.2
A simple cluster of
Hyper-V hosts

Quick Migration

When you consolidate systems through virtualization, you raise the potential business impact of a single physical-server failure. Failover clustering can help protect against this risk. Using failover clustering to protect virtual machines (VMs) has been dubbed *Quick Migration* by Microsoft.

Configuring Quick Migration involves validating and creating a failover cluster and then successfully configuring one or more VMs for HA. Clustering is configured within the parent partitions on multiple Hyper-V capable systems and can protect configured child partitions. Beyond the consolidation benefits you can achieve through Hyper-V, the benefit of Quick Migration is that it can make services that aren't cluster-aware highly available by clustering the servers hosting VMs.

After you set up the cluster, it will allow for nearly continuous operation of VMs during planned maintenance of the underlying hardware as well as automated recovery (VM restart) in the event of unplanned node failures. For planned maintenance, you can move VM(s) to another node from within the Failover Cluster Management console (or by using enterprise-management software such as System Center Virtual Machine Manager). At a high level, Quick Migration performs the following actions for VMs that are part of a VM group requested to move to another node:

◆ Saves the VM state: Stops execution, and writes the contents of RAM into the associated .VSV file on shared storage

◆ Unregisters the VM configuration on the current node

◆ Registers the VM configuration on the target node

◆ Resumes the VM: Reads the contents of the associated .VSV file into RAM, and resumes execution

More is going on behind the scenes to facilitate the movement of services (managing access to storage, for example), but this is the basic process as it pertains to the VMs. The VMs are essentially frozen on one system, passed to another system, and thawed. The amount of time the services on a moved VM are unavailable is roughly proportional to the time required to execute this process—the more RAM allocated to and used by a VM, the longer it will take to save and reload the VM on a different cluster node. Because the VM isn't executing at that point, the workload deployed in the VM has no influence on the migration times.

QUICK MIGRATION VERSUS LIVE MIGRATION

Quick Migration as implemented in Windows Server 2008 causes migrated VMs to suspend operations while they are migrated to a new physical host. The next release of Windows Server (Windows Server 2008 R2) includes a capability referred to as Live Migration, which more efficiently migrates running VMs between failover cluster nodes, and nearly eliminates processing interruptions.

Protect the VM or Protect the Application?

As mentioned earlier, with Quick Migration, failover clustering of physical Hyper-V systems can make VMs (child partitions) highly available. It may make sense to create failover clusters *between* VMs—making cluster-aware applications or services inside multiple VMs highly available. By clustering between child VMs, you can consolidate multiple application failover clusters on a single physical server or a group of servers, which can help you meet consolidation and availability goals.

One consideration for clustering within VMs is the lack of access to common types of shared storage from within a VM. VMs don't have direct access to physically attached shared storage (via fibre channel Host Bus Adapters (HBAs) or serial-attached SCSI [SAS] controllers), and pass-through disk isn't supported for clustering applications and services within VMs. For these reasons, you must use storage presented via the network to meet shared storage requirements, such as Internet SCSI (iSCSI), as shown in Figure 8.3.

FIGURE 8.3
Clustering within/
between VMs

Another key consideration is the *cluster awareness* of a particular workload. File services, printing, Domain Name Service (DNS), Dynamic Host Configuration Protocol (DHCP), Windows Internet Naming Service (WINS), Internet Storage Name Service (iSNS), and other common services are failover cluster–aware out of the box in Windows Server 2008. Other applications and services lend themselves to different HA approaches, including using the Network Load Balancing (NLB) feature in Windows Server 2008. NLB enables two or more servers (VM or physical) to combine into a single virtual application cluster—typically for the delivery of stateless services such as Web or FTP applications.

Required Components for Failover Clustering

We'll focus on creating clusters specifically for use with Hyper-V without diving deeply into less common clustering scenarios. Common components are required for successful cluster deployments, including appropriate hardware and the correct software.

SERVER HARDWARE

The same basic hardware is required to cluster Hyper-V as to run Hyper-V on a stand-alone system, but with additional requirements for failover clustering. First, the systems in your cluster (the nodes) should be identical in configuration. Why must your cluster nodes be the same?

The more dissimilar a cluster node is from other systems in a cluster, the less likely it is to successfully assume the operation of an application or service. A simple example is a two-node cluster of servers that are identical except for RAM. What may happen if the active node has 8GB of RAM and the passive, backup server has only 6GB of RAM? If most of the RAM (7GB) on the active node is in use by VMs, how can the passive node take over operations? It can't—and in the event of a failover, some of the VMs will go offline. Your hardware should be identical, from the amount of RAM down to the settings and firmware revisions of interface cards.

The Cluster Validation Wizard does many checks to ensure that you'll have a stable, reliable cluster. It evaluates the CPU manufacture and versions, BIOS settings, the network configuration, network interface card (NIC) settings, the storage configuration, security—a vast array of settings and system parameters to validate that the servers you wish to cluster will work together.

This extensive checking is fantastic. But sometimes you may not want or need all the automated testing. For example, perhaps you'd like to create a simple cluster for training or testing. In such cases, the Validation Wizard lets you create failover clusters that aren't optimal. For example, you can use a single NIC rather than multiple NICs for separate networking functions (iSCSI access, cluster intercommunication, application services, general networking, and so on).

CPUs

If the Validation Wizard will let you off with a warning for loose operational practices, why not use a mix of Intel and AMD processors in your cluster? In short, CPUs differ in their capabilities and characteristics, even if they're from the same manufacturer. How memory is managed and what instructions are available varies by processor family and minor revision. These variations in CPUs become significant in failover clustering because VMs are migrated *in flight* from one node to another.

As noted earlier, the process of proactively migrating VMs from one node to another is similar to hibernating a running laptop, removing the stopped hard drive, installing the drive in another identical laptop, and starting it again in the other laptop. Hardware for cluster nodes should be as similar as possible because Hyper-V nodes with different hardware are unlikely to support the stateful migration of VMs.

NETWORK

Networking is a core function of a failover cluster. It's the manifestation of uptime to other systems, and it lets nodes communicate status and access storage (in the case of iSCSI). Network interfaces should be dedicated to a single purpose (management, storage access, applications/VMs, and so on) to ensure adequate performance, security, and availability of network resources.

SHARED STORAGE

Beyond having multiple networks attached and physical systems to run Hyper-V, you also need shared locations on which to store VMs and their configurations. Failover cluster nodes have traditionally accessed disk volumes presented to the cooperating systems via a fibre-channel Storage Area Network (SAN) or other shared storage subsystem. iSCSI attached storage is increasingly used in addition to traditional fibre-channel SANs for block-level access. iSCSI can often be installed and managed at a lower cost and with less complexity. It is also technically possible to host VMs on traditional Windows file shares (CIFS-based) with additional security and configuration. There is no support at this time for hosting VMs via Network Attached Storage (NAS) using either the CIFS or the NFS protocols.

MAJORITIES, QUORUMS, AND VOTING

Shared storage provides another important function beyond storing the VMs: it can act as a witness in determining which node controls shared resources (the volumes used for data). Although a disk-based witness (also referred to as a quorum disk) isn't required for a cluster, this witness functionality enables a cluster of two nodes to clearly identify which system has access to storage and thus control of the running applications or services (VMs). In the event of a single node failure, the remaining node can vote with the witness to restart a failed application or service.

Without a witness in a two-node Hyper-V cluster, Quick Migration could still function, but restarting a failed VM resulting from a down physical node would require intervention. This *node and disk majority* model included in Windows Server 2008 failover clustering is an enhancement over earlier Windows-based availability clusters: it doesn't require a dedicated disk volume, and it enables the cluster to continue to function even if the disk witness is unavailable (the nodes can vote without the witness to take action).

Traditional block-level storage requires the following elements for cluster volumes:

◆ The style of partitions can be master boot record (MBR) if they're less than 2TB in size or GUID Partition Table (GPT) if they're larger

◆ Basic disk (not dynamic)

◆ Witness disk (*quorum*) formatted NTFS

A similar quorum configuration can rely on a file share as a witness in Windows Server 2008, rather than traditional block-level storage; this model is called *node and file share majority*.

SOFTWARE

Failover clustering for Windows Server 2008 requires either Windows Server 2008 Enterprise Edition or Data Center Edition on the Hyper-V host systems. Although it may be possible to configure nodes with different editions of Windows Server 2008 within a cluster (Enterprise Edition and Data Center Edition), doing so isn't suggested. You can use Server Core or the full installation of Windows Server 2008 for cluster creation, but you can't configure a mixture of nodes using Server Core and full Window Server 2008.

Storage Considerations for Clustering

At the heart of every failover cluster is some type of shared storage to host the application or service being shared between nodes. Quick Migration is no different than other failover cluster solutions in its reliance on storage; however, considerations for clustering VMs are different than for other applications or services.

Using Pass-through Disk to Improve Performance

Virtual machines typically access disk-based information in the form of a virtual hard disk (VHD) file, which contains all the data for a given virtual disk. VHD files, in conjunction with a VM's configuration, define the VM. The portability and versatility of the VHD file enables simplified disaster recovery and facilitates the failover functionality. But in some cases, the VHD file presents limitations that can negatively affect the performance and scalability of a given VM (as noted in Chapter 3, "Configuring Hyper-V").

To alleviate disk-related performance bottlenecks from VHD files, you may configure pass-through disk for disks used by highly available VMs. Configuring highly available VMs to use pass-through disk provides enhanced I/O performance as well as access to larger (than 2TB) disk volumes. Using pass-through disk eliminates the VHD-related benefits of virtualization (simplified backup and recovery, snap shot capability, and more). Combining VHDs with pass-through disk can also be valuable: Housing a VM's boot disk within a VHD while accessing an additional pass-through volume for data may provide an appropriate mix of system performance and recoverability (see Figure 8.4).

FIGURE 8.4
Virtual machines with highly available pass-through disk

Virtual Machines with Highly Available "Pass Through" Disk

Hyper-V Host1 — Pass-through disk — Hyper-V Host2

Clustering with GUIDs and Mount Points

It's possible (and in some situations advisable) to use volumes without assigning drive letters—mounting and using volumes via their GUIDs or as mount points within folders. You may want to use these two methods of accessing volumes (without drive letters) when you require large numbers of volumes and have insufficient driver letters available. Mounting volumes via GUIDs or mount points is supported for failover clusters, but either approach adds a great deal of complexity to the overall configuration.

Configuring Multiple VMs on a Single Physical Volume

Microsoft released an update that increases functionality in the Windows Server 2008 Failover Cluster Management console for Hyper-V (KB951308). One key enhancement lets you configure and manage multiple VMs on a single shared disk from within the cluster-management console.

This capability simplifies storage provisioning and management as well as the VM configuration process.

Before the release of this update, you had to manually configure resources and dependencies to host multiple VMs in this manner. Dedicating a disk for each highly available VM is a common recommended practice. You can move each VM between nodes independently if it's hosted on a dedicated disk/logical unit number (LUN). By hosting multiple VMs on a single disk, the unit of migration (or failure) becomes the disk, meaning that any migration of services or applications from one node to another requires all VMs hosted on that disk to move. In the case of Hyper-V, this increases the overall migration time for VMs hosted on the disk, because multiple VMs must be saved before the disk can be accessed by the target cluster node. You must weigh the cost of labor for storage provision and management against the increased migration time of highly available consolidated VMs.

Using a clustered file system (CFS) provides an alternative to "one VM per disk" while still allowing individual VM movement between nodes. A CFS lets systems lock resources at a level other than the disk level. This enables failover cluster nodes to access files on the same volume at the same time. Sanbolic's Melio FS is an example of an existing cluster filesystem that works with Windows Server 2008 and Hyper-V. Windows Server 2008 R2 will include Cluster Shared Volumes (CSVs), which are disks that can be shared by multiple Hyper-V nodes at the same time.

LIVE MIGRATION IN WINDOWS SERVER 2008 R2 CAN USE EITHER A CFS OR CSV

The nearly transparent migration of VMs from one node to another supported in Windows Server 2008 R2 works best with some sort of cluster file or volume access. The CSV included with Windows Server 2008 R2 is only for use with Hyper-V. You may want to consider a CFS for more complicated clustering or data sharing applications.

Building a Failover Cluster for Hyper-V

As noted earlier, building a failover cluster for Hyper-V Quick Migration is a straightforward process of configuring multiple, similar physical servers with shared networking, shared storage, and Windows Server 2008. At a high level, you follow these steps to build a failover cluster for Hyper-V (see Figure 8.5):

1. Configure the network infrastructure.

2. Install required roles, features, and updates.

3. Provision storage, and prepare the disk.

4. Validate the cluster.

5. Create the cluster.

6. Configure the service or application.

FIGURE 8.5
Step-by-step
sample cluster
configuration

Setting Up a Failover Cluster

In the remainder of this chapter, we'll walk through these high-level steps and the details behind them required to configure a typical two-node Hyper-V failover cluster. We'll include considerations and comments, to help you develop insight into the overall process. The entire procedure used here should take less than a workday, including all required tasks from unpacking and installing hardware through installing and configuring failover clustering.

CONFIGURING THE NETWORK INFRASTRUCTURE

Not to sound casual about infrastructure requirements, but failover clustering requires pretty much the same security and networking infrastructure as most other contemporary Microsoft technologies. If you're reading this, you're probably already aware of the requirements—the cluster nodes need to be attached to a network with DNS, an Active Directory (AD) domain in which each node has a valid machine account, an accessible domain controller (DC), and an account that has administrator rights on the nodes (it can be a domain user account that has been added to the local administrator group on each system). Note that the account needs the right to create computer objects in the domain. Other networking requirements, dependencies, and recommended practices are involved in creating a failover cluster for Hyper-V (multiple network interface cards, for instance), but the foundation of stable DNS, AD, and the proper administrative access are fundamental requirements that you can't overlook.

INSTALLING ROLES, FEATURES, AND UPDATES

To install and configure failover clustering, you must install specific Windows Server 2008 roles and features (see Table 8.1). You must install the Hyper-V role along with the Release to Manufacturing (RTM) update KB950050 of Hyper-V (install the update first, and then add the role). This update is available from `http://update.microsoft.com` as a noncritical optional update. You also need to install the Failover Clustering feature and (depending on your storage requirements) the Multipath I/O feature.

You install features in a manner similar to that used for server roles: Start Server Manager, select Features, and choosing Action ➤ Add Features. Remember that an important update for failover clustering (KB951308) increases the functionality when you work with Hyper-V. Also take care to check for additional Microsoft updates for failover clustering and Windows Server that should be installed. Many key (non–security related) updates aren't distributed via the automated update processes. The best option to locate and obtain noncritical updates for Microsoft products is via `http://support.microsoft.com`, where you can search by product, topic, or knowledge base (KB) article.

TABLE 8.1   Typical Features and Roles Installed for Quick Migration on Physical Nodes

ROLE/FEATURE	NAME
Role	Hyper-V
Feature	Failover Clustering
Feature	Multi-Path I/O

PROVISIONING STORAGE WITH iSCSI

Attaching storage via iSCSI can be a simpler overall process than connecting to storage via traditional fibre channel. Regardless of your storage infrastructure, you should confirm with the manufacturer that it's compatible with failover clustering in Windows Server 2008. A wide variety of iSCSI-capable storage devices (called *targets*) are available on the market, including Windows Server–based Unified Data Storage Server (WUDSS) systems that can present block-level storage to other systems. We won't show the process of provisioning storage on the iSCSI target system, but we'll demonstrate a minimal configuration of the client systems (initiators) common to any iSCSI-based cluster setup. Two volumes have been preconfigured on the iSCSI target for presentation to the demonstration cluster: a 1GB witness and a 60GB VM store.

Open the Control Panel on one of the installed Hyper-V nodes, and double-click the iSCSI Initiator service.

NOTE If you're accessing the iSCSI Initiator service for the first time, you'll be prompted to start the Microsoft iSCSI service (it's off by default) and to enable exceptions in the Windows Firewall.

On the iSCSI Initiator Properties page, you can enter information and configure behavior to locate, log in to, and access iSCSI storage devices. Each iSCSI device (initiator or target) is typically assigned an iSCSI Qualified Name (IQN) that identifies the devices. An IQN is automatically generated for the initiator in the format iqn.*yyyy-mm.<reversed domain name>*. You do have the option to change the IQN, but typically this isn't required.

You locate iSCSI-based storage for your initiator by adding Target Portal information to the Discovery tab or by configuring an Internet Storage Name Service (iSNS) on your network. You can proceed by entering the IP address of the iSCSI target as a target portal, which discovers preconfigured iSCSI targets to which access has been granted.

Switching to the Targets tab shows iSCSI targets that have been preconfigured for use. Click the Log On button to see the Log On To Target dialog. This screen provides configurable options for access to the iSCSI target, including future logon behavior and enablement of multipath support.

After the node is logged onto the target, you must configure the volumes to be used (in this case, we'll assume they're preconfigured for you). Clicking the Autoconfigure button causes the iSCSI Initiator service to automatically configure the devices for use.

When the iSCSI Initiator configuration is complete, you can access the disks; they should be visible in the Disk Management section of Server Manager (although they aren't yet accessible as online, formatted volumes).

You can also use the command line to complete all actions required to configure the iSCSI Initiator. The command line is necessary when using Server Core, since it has no graphical user interface (GUI). Following are example commands that show how to enable and configure the iSCSI Initiator using the command line. First, you must enable the state of the iSCSI Initiator service and start the service using the SC command:

1. Set the iSCSI Initiator service to start automatically:

   ```
   sc \\localhost config msiscsi start= auto
   ```

2. Start the iSCSI Initiator service:

   ```
   sc start msiscsi
   ```

3. Complete the remaining tasks using the iSCSI command-line interface (iscsicli):

   ◆ Add the target portal:

   ```
   iscsicli QAddTargetPortal <IP address of Portal>
   ```

   ◆ Add the target:

   ```
   iscsicli QAddTarget <iqn address of target>
   ```

◆ Log in to the target:

```
iscsicli QloginTarget <iqn address of target>
```

◆ Make Login Persistent

```
iscsicli PersistentLoginTarget <iqn address of target> ↵
T * * * * * * * * * * * * * * * * * 0
```

◆ Bind all persistent volumes:

```
iscsicli BindPersistentVolumes
```

4. Confirm some critical settings by using these two command lines:

```
iscsicli ListPersistentTargets
iscsicli ReportTargetMappings
```

PREPARING THE DISK

After you complete the storage-connectivity work for each node, you must configure the individual disks for use (bring them online, initialize them as MBR or GUID partition table [GPT], create volumes, and format). You can accomplish all these tasks by running Server Manager or Computer Management and accessing Storage\Disk Management *on one of the nodes* sharing the storage (see Figure 8.6).

FIGURE 8.6
Shared disk before configuration

First, right-click each of the new, offline volumes (in the gray Disk block) and bring each disk online. You must also initialize each disk as either MBR or GPT (GPT allows for volumes larger than 2TB) by right-clicking in the same area of the display. After you initialize the disks with drive letters assigned, create new, simple volumes on each device, and format them with the NTFS filesystem. Assign drive letters to your cluster storage that make some sense. For this demonstration, the witness is labeled *Witness* and has the drive letter W:, and the VM store is drive V: and is named *VMs*, as shown in Figure 8.7.

FIGURE 8.7
Shared disk after configuration

Remember that assigning drive letters isn't required for failover clustering; and in some cases, with large number of volumes, it's impractical.

After you complete the storage configuration on the first node, log into the other node, and access the disk configuration. Because the volumes have already been initialized and formatted, you should only need to *on line* each disk (that is, right-click each of the new, offline volumes and bring it on line) and change the assigned drive letters to match those of the other node.

VALIDATING THE CLUSTER

The servers are ready, features and roles are installed, and the storage is configured. The next step in creating your failover cluster is to jump in and validate your configuration using the Failover Cluster Management console, which you can access via Administrative Tools (see Figure 8.8). In the console, click Validate A Configuration.

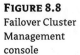

FIGURE 8.8
Failover Cluster
Management
console

As stated earlier, the cluster-validation process eliminates much of the guesswork and manual configuration required by previous implementations of failover clustering, and it's a vast enhancement to the overall cluster setup process. To validate a cluster configuration, enter the names of the nodes to be tested (see Figure 8.9), and click Next.

If the report you receive after validation doesn't show any issues (and your hardware is certified for Windows Server 2008), you have a supportable configuration.

FIGURE 8.9
Validate A
Configuration
Wizard: selecting
systems

You can scroll through the detailed validation report until you see a warning or error, using the familiar and intuitive "green means go, red means stop" paradigm. For the run shown in Figure 8.10, the nodes were found to contain inconsistent levels of software.

FIGURE 8.10

Cluster validation report: system configuration sections

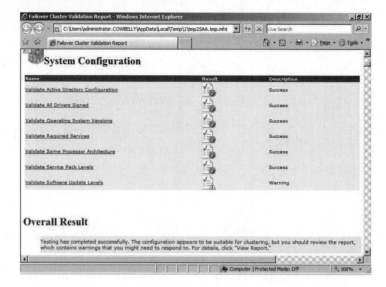

Clicking Validate Software Update Levels—which in this example is flagged by a warning—displays more detailed reporting information that you can act on, as shown in Figure 8.11 (you can install or remove updates).

FIGURE 8.11

Cluster validation report detail

CREATING THE CLUSTER

After you successfully validate your proposed cluster configuration, you're ready to create your cluster. Below Validate A Configuration in the middle of the Failover Cluster Console is the option to Create A Cluster. Creating a cluster is just as simple as validating. At the completion of the cluster-creation process, the nodes are ready to protect cluster-aware applications or services, including Hyper-V.

CONFIGURING HYPER-V

Before you cluster VMs with Hyper-V, you should make the Hyper-V configuration on each node consistent and ready to use the configured shared storage. Ensure that all node-specific settings are identical in the Hyper-V Manager. (As noted in earlier chapters, you can access the Hyper-V Manager by expanding the Hyper-V role in Server Manager or via the Start menu as part of Administrative Tools.) Include the names for all defined virtual networks and default file locations. The Hyper-V role should already be installed on each of the cluster nodes.

In the Hyper-V Manager, review the existing virtual networks defined on each node (select a Hyper-V server at far left, and choose Action ➢ Virtual Network Manager). Ensure that all defined networks that will be used by clustered VMs exist and are identical on all physical Hyper-V nodes. For this cluster, you'll define two virtual networks on each node, as shown in Table 8.2.

TABLE 8.2   Sample Cluster Defined Virtual Networks

NAME	DESCRIPTION	CONNECTION TYPE
External	Bound to physical NIC	External
Internal	Access between VMs and host	Internal only

Changing the default file locations for clustered Hyper-V nodes is also a good practice, but not necessary. VM configuration data and VHD files must be stored on share storage, but this isn't the default setting in Hyper-V. Changing the default on cluster nodes helps to ensure that the configuration for new VMs and their associated VHD files will be created on shared volumes. If you select the appropriate shared storage location each time you provision a new VM, the defaults settings are irrelevant.

Select a Hyper-V server at left in the Hyper-V Manager, and choose Action ➢ Hyper-V Settings. For this cluster, you'll change the default path for both VHDs and VMs to V:\. Note that you can't change both nodes at the same time to point to V:\: Only one Windows Server at a time has access to a shared volume, and the Hyper-V Manager validates access to the paths entered into these fields. To successfully change these settings, the node must be provided exclusive access to the volume. You can accomplish this by a series of reboots of the nodes, save this task for later, or forgo making the change indefinitely after the Hyper-V cluster configuration is complete and VM services (and the volume) can be moved to the node.

NODE-SPECIFIC RESOURCES

You must review one final node-specific resource: each VM's CD/DVD capture setting. Locally captured CD/DVD drives and or ISO images can cause a moved VM to fail to resume, because those resources are typically node specific (an ISO file located on one node on the D: drive won't be accessible on another node after the VM is moved). Be sure that no CD/DVD resources are captured on VMs residing on failover clusters except when in use.

CREATING A VIRTUAL MACHINE

The last step before you complete the cluster configuration is to create a VM to make highly available. You still create (or place and import) VMs using the Hyper-V Manager. Create and configure a VM on the shared storage through Hyper-V Manager using the node that has ownership of the shared storage volume.

To import a VM, copy the export to the shared volume, and import it using the Hyper-V Manager. For this cluster, copy a pre-created (and Syspreped) Windows Server 2008 Enterprise Edition VHD to V:\, using the Hyper-V Manager connected to Node1 (which has access to the drive), and create a new VM configuration.

After you create and configure the VM, shut it down and remove captured CD/DVD resources.

NOTE You should change the Automatic Start Action to Nothing, because the state of the VMs will be managed via the cluster service going forward. The Automatic Start Action setting can be found in the Management section of each VM's Settings.

CONFIGURING FAILOVER FOR A VIRTUAL MACHINE

After you create a VM, you can make it highly available. Return to the Failover Cluster Management console, select the configured cluster at left (in this case, named Hyperv), and expand it by clicking the + next to the cluster name (see Figure 8.12).

Choose Action ➤ Configure A Service Or Application, or right-click Services And Applications and choose Configure A Service Or Application. Doing so starts the High Availability Wizard, which automates the configuration of HA services for common applications including Hyper-V.

Scroll down the list of services and applications, choose Virtual Machine, and click Next. Select the VM to be made highly available (more than one may be listed if you have multiple VMs available). After you complete the wizard, the VM will be configured to be highly available and can execute on any of the configured cluster nodes.

Clustered Virtual Machine Management

After you make a VM highly available, you can proactively move it between nodes by accessing the Failover Cluster Management console, selecting the appropriate VM instance below Services And Applications, and moving it to another node. Before the VMs can perform any useful work, however, you must turn them on.

To start the VM, expand Services And Applications, and click the VM instance to be started (see Figure 8.13). Select the VM to be managed in the center pane, right-click, and select Start.

FIGURE 8.12
Services and applications before VM configuration

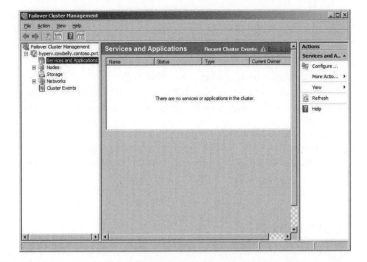

FIGURE 8.13
Virtual machine online and highly available

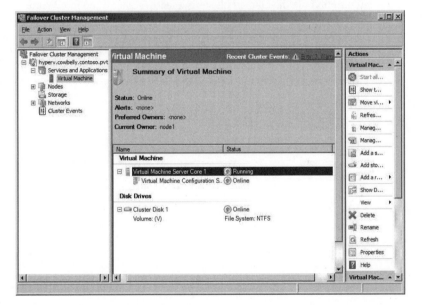

As noted earlier, the state of highly available VMs is controlled by the cluster service. Because the Hyper-V Manager isn't completely integrated with failover clustering, it doesn't communicate with the cluster service to coordinate the status of a VM. To illustrate this point, try using the Hyper-V Manager to save state for a clustered VM.

When the cluster service detects that the VM isn't running, it will try to restart the VM. Depending on timing and other factors, it may restart the VM, mark it as "failed" with a restart attempt later (the default in Server 2008 is up to 15 minutes), or attempt to move the VM to another node in the cluster.

You should make VM state changes (Save, Shutdown, Turn Off) in the Failover Cluster Management console to ensure proper cluster-service integration. To change the state of a VM, select the appropriate VM instance below Services And Applications, highlight the VM you want to modify, and choose the appropriate action.

VM configuration changes other than state are still commonly accomplished via the Hyper-V Manager, which you can launch from within the Failover Cluster Management console. Select the appropriate VM instance below Services And Applications, and choose the action Manage VM.

NOTE   System Center Virtual Machine Manager 2008 (see Chapter 11, "System Center Virtual Machine Manager") is tightly integrated with failover clustering and provides a virtualization management infrastructure and console that you can use to manage VM configuration, state, and cluster capacity.

Summary

The configuration of highly available VMs has been vastly simplified by carefully constructed automation via the failover clustering feature integrated into Windows Server 2008. You can create a simple failover cluster of Hyper-V–ready hosts in a matter of hours with proper preparation; doing so can help you meet the ever-increasing demands for robust computing infrastructure. With additional planning and testing, you can also create complex configurations with varied availability requirements, but such configurations will probably require a higher investment in properly trained people, good processes, and the right technology to meet availability goals.

Chapter 9

Understanding WMI, Scripting, and Hyper-V

It's fortunate that the technology underpinnings exist in Windows and Hyper-V to customize access to virtual machines for users, easily automate processes, and collect information about a virtualization environment. You can use command-line tools, batch files, and scripting languages to tailor solutions in Windows Server 2008 and Hyper-V to meet nearly any virtualization requirements.

This chapter examines many of the scenarios you may encounter that require more than standard tools and looks at some of the automation techniques you can use with Hyper-V. We'll look at the role of Windows Management Instrumentation (WMI) for managing Hyper-V and how you can use WMI from both VBScript and Windows PowerShell. Only a basic understanding of programming concepts is expected, and the chapter introduces PowerShell. Detailed scripting examples are shown in Chapter 10, "Automating Tasks."

We'll cover the following topics in this chapter:

- ◆ Common management tasks
- ◆ WMI overview
- ◆ Scripting technology overview
- ◆ PowerShell for newcomers
- ◆ Common elements of WMI scripts
- ◆ WMI Virtualization classes

Common Management Tasks

Virtualization administrators everywhere perform similar tasks in their environments that can be categorized into common groups:

- ◆ Provisioning
- ◆ Configuration management

- ◆ Access management

- ◆ Migration

- ◆ Backup and recovery

- ◆ Data collection and monitoring

You can use interactive tools such as the Hyper-V Manager, Task Manager, and System Center Virtual Machine Manager (SCVMM) for these administrative tasks. Interacting directly with these tools provides flexibility but not always the highest efficiency.

System provisioning provides a great example of flexibility with less efficiency. Many organizations have a mature process for acquiring, installing, and operating new systems. In these enterprises, an end user may need to complete an electronic form to request a new server. In the past, this request would trigger the purchase of a new physical system that might be online and available weeks or months later. With the advent of virtualization, you can create a new virtual machine (VM) in a matter of minutes, provided sufficient capacity exists in the environment. With VM provisioning, you can set up an automated system where users can submit a request for a new VM; a server is then created without an administrator intervening.

Data-collection tasks demonstrate the value of automation as well. You can display the individual Media Access Control (MAC) address of each virtual network adapter in the Hyper-V Manager by viewing each VM's settings individually (see Figure 9.1).

FIGURE 9.1
MAC address in the
Hyper-V Manager

What if you need an audit of MAC addresses and their associated virtual local area networks (VLANs)? Clicking though the settings for each network interface card (NIC) on each VM and recording the addresses manually can take a lot of time and may not provide an accurate accounting due to errors or bad handwriting. You can easily retrieve this information through a script-based query of the parent partition (see Figure 9.2), so why not create a time-saving automated report that you can use repeatedly?

FIGURE 9.2

MAC address listing using Power-Shell Library

```
PS C:\> get-vm | list-vmnic | ft -auto

VM                         MACAddress   Type                              Network
--                         ----------   ----                              -------
P2V Demo                   00155D48302E Microsoft Emulated Ethernet Port
Scratchy SLES 10 x64       00155D48301C Microsoft Synthetic Ethernet Port Public
Scratchy SLES 10 x86       00155D48301B Microsoft Synthetic Ethernet Port Public
XP Client 1                00155D48302B Microsoft Synthetic Ethernet Port Private
SCO 507                    00155D48302D Microsoft Emulated Ethernet Port  Public
SLES 10                    00155D48301D Microsoft Synthetic Ethernet Port Public
Greenwich core             00155D48302F Microsoft Synthetic Ethernet Port Public
Server 2003 #1             00155D483015 Microsoft Synthetic Ethernet Port

PS C:\>
```

Time and quality pressures commonly drive administrators to automate tasks. You can follows two basic paths to automation and reporting with Hyper-V: customized scripts and commercial management tools.

Hyper-V was designed for optimal integration with Microsoft management tools (as well as third-party tools). Microsoft System Center Operations Manager (SCOM) and SCVMM together provide a fantastic management infrastructure to automate and collect data for physical and virtual systems that isn't available with the Hyper-V console alone. SCVMM includes capabilities for virtualization automation beyond what is available from custom scripts, including the following:

◆ Virtualization-specific task orientation

◆ Specialized PowerShell *cmdlets* (pronounced "commandlets") for virtualization management

◆ Script generation

◆ Heterogeneous virtualization platform management (Hyper-V, Virtual Server, and VMware)

System Center tools allow you to meet enterprise response metrics for all aspects of system management. To maximize value, all enterprises using Windows should aim to use System Center tools.

In some situations, System Center tools are unavailable. In such cases, you may need other tools or custom scripts. Hyper-V has a rich interface through a virtualization WMI provider, accessible via scripts and numerous tools. This provider lets you control and monitor VMs and the physical host on which they run. Creating custom scripts via the WMI provider can give you more flexibility and portability than SCVMM. However, custom scripts are often more complex and lack the detailed error handling and high-quality code that comes with commercial software tools.

WMI Overview

The preferred method of administering Hyper-V is by leveraging the WMI-based APIs provided. WMI is Microsoft's implementation of an industry-wide initiative called Web-Based Enterprise Management (WBEM) that involves accessing and managing systems in an enterprise environment. WMI uses the Common Information Model (CIM) standard to represent system components. The CIM is maintained by the Distributed Management Task Force (DMTF), of which Microsoft is a member.

Some administrators consider WMI to be Microsoft's primary management-enabling technology for Windows. WMI enables access to many system components—from hardware all the way up to installed applications. You can use WMI to access event logs, operating system attributes, processes, installed applications, and much more. You can use it to easily start or stop processes on local or remote systems, reboot a system, inventory installed applications and patches, and even check the internal temperature of a server. Nearly everything you need to manage Hyper-V is available through WMI. More complex HyperCall APIs let developers implement integration components between VMs and the host OS, for example, but they aren't intended for use by administrators.

Nearly all Windows development tools and scripting languages can access WMI and use it to simplify the creation of tools and code for managing Hyper-V. Common scripting languages that you can use include Windows PowerShell, VBScript, JScript, and Perl. You can also use C/C++, C#, Visual Basic, and other compilable programming languages to create WMI-based tools. You can even access WMI from the command line using the WMI command-line interface (WMIC), which is included in Windows XP, Windows Server 2003, Windows Vista, and Windows Server 2008 (see Figure 9.3). WMI namespaces may be accessed remotely, enabling remote data-collection management.

NOTE Because WMI has been an integral part of Windows for many years, you can create tools and scripts to manage Hyper-V that you can execute from earlier versions of Windows. It's possible for WMI-based Hyper-V management scripts to run from Windows 2000 and newer systems to manage remote Hyper-V hosts.

The hypervisor is managed by a service running in the parent partition and has no other connection to the outside world. This virtualization provider is the service that is the target for WMI calls for anything wanting to give instructions to the hypervisor (see Figure 9.4). The hypervisor itself has no access to network services and no understanding of user accounts—it's the management service that validates that the user is trying to perform a task.

FIGURE 9.3
Using WMIC to
access Hyper-V
from Windows XP

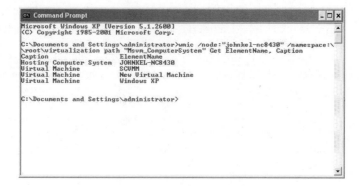

FIGURE 9.4
WMI virtualiza-
tion provider

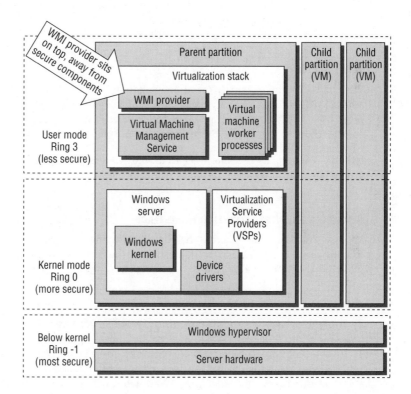

Accessing WMI

The key to unlocking the value of WMI is to understand where relevant information may lie.
Windows offers more than 100 providers to access system components, including the event log,
the Registry, performance counters, and so on. Software developers—including Microsoft—can

add new providers, and that is what has been done for Hyper-V. The virtualization WMI provider exposes a rich interface that lets you monitor and control Hyper-V and the virtual environment.

WMI organizes information on a given computer into namespaces. Information about the computer's hard disk, operating system, hotfixes, and so on, are found in the root\cimV2 namespace. Hyper-V uses the root\virtualization namespace.

Properties of objects that are accessible through WMI (like a VM name) are organized into groups called *classes*. Hotfixes have a class, processors have a class, and VMs have a class named MSVM_ComputerSystem. There may be one or more instances of an object class. For example, on a system with four VMs, there are four instances of the MSVM_ComputerSystem object, one for each VM (and a fifth for the parent partition).

WMI classes for a provider are commonly accessed via the corresponding namespace. The namespace that corresponds to the classes made available by the virtualization provider is \root\virtualization. Scripting tools access WMI through a WMI scripting library. The WMI scripting library provides the set of script-enabling objects to access the WMI infrastructure.

WMI Security

WMI uses Windows security to validate logon information on local computers and for remote access. WMI enforces security for resources at the level of individual namespaces. For the purposes of all WMI-related examples in this book, it's assumed that you'll execute them with full administrative access to the parent partition and the underlying WMI namespaces.

NOTE   The security check for WMI occurs only when a user logs in. Changes to user access (including access revocation) take effect the next time a user logs on.

Accessing the Virtualization Namespace

You use similar syntax to access the virtualization namespace for nearly any tool or language. Establishing a connection to the namespace is the first step and generally requires referencing or selecting \root\virtualization.

WMI Scripting Tools and Resources

By knowing what tools and resources are available, you can simplify the process of creating custom scripts and tools with WMI. The first and most important resource is the online Microsoft TechNet Script Center (http://www.microsoft.com/technet/scriptcenter/). The Script Center contains valuable samples and guides for Microsoft-focused administrative scripting in a variety of scripting languages including Windows PowerShell and VBScript.

If you have little scripting experience, you can access online scripting tutorials. The Script Center also has several tools that can speed the creation of WMI-centric scripts and tools. Scriptomatic 2.0, PowerShell Scriptomatic, and WMI Code Creator let you browse available WMI namespaces and generate simple code examples to access data and execute methods.

Browsing the Virtualization Namespace

Accessing and browsing the elements of the virtualization namespace is an excellent hands-on approach to understanding how to use it. You can use the WMI Code Creator for this purpose.

It's available from the TechNet Script Center at (www.microsoft.com/downloads/details.aspx ?FamilyID=2cc30a64-ea15-4661-8da4-55bbc145c30e&DisplayLang=en). Follow these steps:

1. To access the namespace, first download, unpack, and run the tool WMICodeCreator.exe. The WMI Code Creator provides several capabilities, including the ability to generate code that you can use to do the following:

    ◆ Query for WMI data

    ◆ Execute a method in WMI

    ◆ Receive an event

    ◆ Browse WMI namespaces

2. When the WMI Code Creator starts, it enumerates available WMI namespaces and classes on the local computer. By default, it starts on the Query For Data From A WMI Class tab, displaying the commonly used namespace root\CIMV2 (see Figure 9.5).

FIGURE 9.5
WMI Code Creator default screen

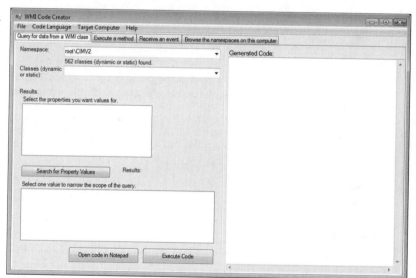

TIP   Root\CIMV2 is a fantastically useful WMI namespace that enables access to a host of system properties worthy of additional investigation.

3. You can access available WMI namespaces in WMI Code Creator using the Namespace pull-down menu. Select the root\virtualization namespace and choose the Msvm_ ComputerSystem class in the pull-down menu to display the properties of the class (see Figure 9.6).

FIGURE 9.6
Virtualization provider and the Msvm_ComputerSystem class

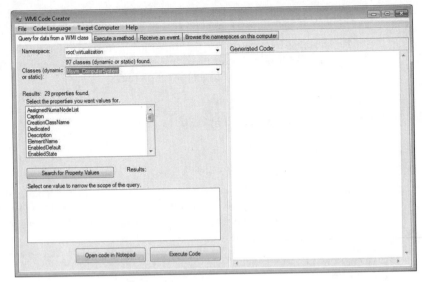

Msvm_ComputerSystem represents the parent partition/hosting Hyper-V system in the namespace. Using this class, you can discover and alter general information about VMs, such as their name and state.

4. To show the friendly name for a VM (for example), select ElementName in the Results box, and click the Search For Property Values button. The names of each VM on the local system are displayed (see Figure 9.7).

FIGURE 9.7
ElementName = friendly virtual machine name

Note that the parent partition (JOHNKEL-NC8430) is also listed as a VM. This is because it runs on top of the hypervisor just as other VMs do (remember that the parent partition is a special class of VM). Changing the selection of properties to include both ElementName and Caption shows both sets of values (you can multiselect by holding the Ctrl key while clicking additional properties, as shown in Figure 9.8).

FIGURE 9.8
Caption and
ElementName

Browsing the WMI virtualization namespace can help you develop an understanding of which classes and elements contain useful information, but WMI Code Creator does a great deal more. On the right side of the screen, you can see example generated code, which you can save and use to create more complicated scripts or tools that use the properties you select. Here's an example:

```
strComputer = "."
Set objWMIService = GetObject _
    ("winmgmts:\\" & strComputer & "\root\virtualization")
Set colItems = objWMIService.ExecQuery( _
    "SELECT * FROM Msvm_ComputerSystem",,48)
For Each objItem in colItems
    Wscript.Echo "----------------------------------"
    Wscript.Echo "Msvm_ComputerSystem instance"
    Wscript.Echo "----------------------------------"
    Wscript.Echo "Caption: " & objItem.Caption
    Wscript.Echo "ElementName: " & objItem.ElementName
Next
```

Clicking the Execute Code button executes the sample code (in this case, VBScript) using the Windows Script Host (see Figure 9.9).

FIGURE 9.9

Sample script output

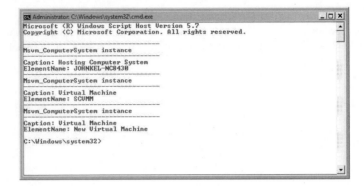

WMI Code Creator can generate example code for VBScript, Visual Basic .NET, and C#. As noted, it has additional capabilities that we won't discuss further. To generate sample code for other languages, you can use The Scriptomatic 2.0 from the TechNet site. The Scriptomatic has similar WMI code-generating capabilities for VBScript, Perl, Jscript, and Python. The PowerShell Scriptomatic has similar capabilities and generates code in Windows PowerShell. The Scriptomatic tools lack element search/browsing as well as method execution and event handling found in the WMI Code Creator.

Scripting Technology Overview

Before diving further into what you can accomplish with scripting, let's take a step back and review scripting in general. A *scripting language* is a programming language used to control applications or other system components. In this way, scripts are different from other programs: they're sets of instructions to a computer that run tasks implemented in other programs. Scripting languages have many of the features found in full-scale programming languages—storing results in variables, running commands only if conditions are met, and so on.

Common Scripting Languages for Windows

Windows administrators commonly use batch files (.BAT or .CMD) to string together commands that can be entered at the command prompt. VBScript or other Windows Script Host (WSH) dependant scripting languages have been available for years to perform complex administrative automation that can more flexibly interact with systems and applications.

Microsoft released Windows PowerShell in 2006 to provide a more extensible and script-able command-line shell for administrators. Windows PowerShell includes integration with the Microsoft .NET Framework. Although older scripting technologies may not include all the bells and whistles of PowerShell, they're still useful for automating tasks with Hyper-V.

VISUAL BASIC SCRIPT

Microsoft launched Visual Basic Script (also called VBScript or VBS) in the mid-1990s. It initially targeted web developers for *Active Scripting* (formerly known as *Active-X* scripting) along with JScript and third-party Active Scripting tools. It lets you automate routine tasks using the WSH. VBScript examples for administration are common and relatively easy to find on the Internet.

New versions of VBScript and other Active Scripting tools aren't planned. Contemporary tools that use the .NET Framework (PowerShell and Visual Basic .NET) will replace VBScript and other WSH-dependant languages.

NOTE VBScript, JScript, Perl, and other scripting tools without a dependency on the .NET Framework still have value. A Server Core installation of Windows Server 2008 doesn't include the .NET Framework, and thus PowerShell is unavailable for automation tasks (this will change with future versions of Server Core). Active Scripting tools continue to be used because of their portability and widespread compatibility. VBScript and PowerShell automation scripts are the focus of Chapter 10.

JSCRIPT

JScript is the Microsoft dialect of ECMAScript (originally JavaScript). It uses the WSH in the same fashion as VBScript, and you can use it in a similar way to automate administrative tasks. JScript seems to be used less frequently by administrators than VBScript, and scripting examples for Hyper-V automation aren't included in this book. If you desire, you should be able to adapt WMI-intensive VBScript code samples easily to JScript.

PERL, PYTHON, AND OTHERS

The WSH can use scripting engines other than VBScript and JScript—including Perl and Python. It's not uncommon to see administrators taking advantage of Active State Perl for automation; but again, we won't cover WSH samples other than VBScript.

COMMAND-LINE TOOLS

Sadly, few traditional command-line tools ship with Hyper-V to automate common administrative tasks. You can use WMIC to interrogate and affect Hyper-V. A brief WMIC command-line example with functionality similar to that of the WMI Code Creator sample case is shown here, and the results appear in Figure 9.10:

```
WMIC /namespace:\\root\virtualization PATH "Msvm_ComputerSystem" ↵
  Get ElementName, Caption
```

FIGURE 9.10
WMIC accessing Hyper-V information

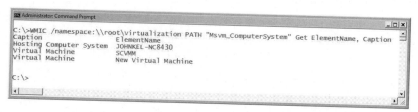

WMIC includes an interactive shell that you can invoke by typing **WMIC** from a command prompt. You can access integrated help for WMIC by typing **/?** from within the shell. WMIC doesn't have the flexibility of other scripting tools, but it does enable command-line access to

Hyper-V via WMI. Combined with batch files (a form of scripting), WMIC can provide the required WMI connection to Hyper-V and automation support.

TIP   WMIC is the predecessor to PowerShell, and it's an underutilized administrative tool included in Windows XP through Windows Server 2008—including Server Core. WMIC defaults to the root\CIMV2 namespace, which includes access to all manner of system information.

WINDOWS POWERSHELL

Windows PowerShell is a scripting language and interactive shell designed especially for system administration. Introduced by Microsoft in 2006, it's customizable with complete access to the .NET Framework. Task-focused *cmdlets* allow you to manage systems from the command line as well as access key data stores, including the Registry and WMI, using a single, consistent syntax.

You can manage event logs, services, processes, and applications with PowerShell. The extensible interface lets you create integrated custom tools and utilities, such as the powerful virtualization-management cmdlets included with SCVMM 2008 (covered in Chapter 11, "System Center Virtual Machine Manager").

PowerShell is an installable feature that's included in Windows Server 2008 and available as a separate download for Windows XP (SP2 or later), Windows Server 2003 (SP1 or later), and Windows Vista.

PowerShell for Newcomers

Windows PowerShell Version 1.0 is part of an effort to provide a comprehensive and rational command-line environment for administration within Microsoft Windows. It can be argued that the command shell within Windows (cmd.exe) has changed little since the introduction of DOS. Although cmd.exe has in fact progressed, it still lacks features common to advanced shells in UNIX, Linux, and other operating systems.

PowerShell addresses many of the shortcomings of the "heritage" Windows command shell while maintaining a reasonable level of consistency and compatibility with it. You can execute existing, familiar stand-alone programs (chkdsk.exe, ping.exe, regedt32.exe, shutdown.exe, and others) from within Windows PowerShell; this command compatibility means you can largely abandon the Windows cmd.exe shell and use Windows PowerShell instead.

NOTE   PowerShell uses the term *command* to mean any single instruction—which can include cmdlets, script files, blocks of script stored as functions, aliases, external programs, or combinations of these grouped together into a pipeline using the vertical bar or pipe character (|).

Windows PowerShell includes new *cmdlets* (pronounced "commandlets"). Cmdlets are small commands named in a consistent way that you can string together into pipelines to create more complex commands that produce customized results. These modular cmdlets with their pipeline "glue" are the real value of PowerShell to you. Cmdlet pipelines can be short and simple or long and complex depending on the results desired. Saving complex collections of cmdlets as scripts to execute from the command line is common (similar to saving collections of cmd.exe commands in a .BAT or .CMD file). Windows PowerShell scripts are typically named with a .PS1 extension.

This section of the chapter is an effort to shed light on the basic items you need to be a functional administrator in an increasingly PowerShell world. PowerShell's flexibility gives you multiple ways to perform the same task (as you may notice). We won't present different approaches to using PowerShell in many cases—we'll leave alternate (and sometimes more concise) coding examples to more comprehensive PowerShell resources outside of this book. Our goal in this section is to enable you to be functional, not to strive for mastery. If you're already familiar with Windows PowerShell, you can skip ahead to the "Common Elements of WMI Scripts" section of the chapter.

PowerShell Installation and Setup

PowerShell ships in the box with Windows Server 2008 and can be added as a feature through Server Manager. You install features in a similar manner to server roles by starting Server Manager, selecting Features, and select the Add Features option from the Action menu (see Figure 9.11).

FIGURE 9.11
Selecting
PowerShell in
Server Manager

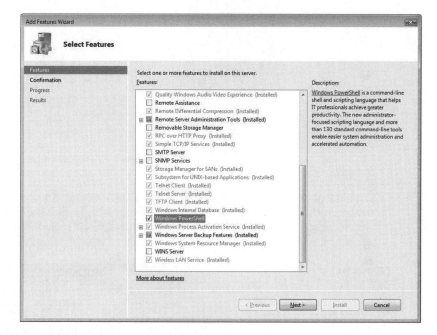

After you install PowerShell, you can start it either by opening a command window and typing **PowerShell** or by selecting Windows PowerShell from the Start menu.

NOTE   Version 2.0 of Windows PowerShell is available as a community technology preview but isn't included in Windows Server 2008 (it will ship with Windows Server 2008 R2). Both versions require the .NET Framework version 2.0, but some features of PowerShell version 2.0 rely on the .NET Framework 3.0, including the Graphical PowerShell feature and the Out-GridView cmdlet. PowerShell Versions 1.0 scripts should run unmodified in Version 2.0.

PowerShell is integrated with Windows security features included in Windows Server 2008 and Windows Vista, including User Account Control (UAC). UAC is intended to improve system security by limiting the privileges of applications. If you enable UAC, you may find that when you run PowerShell (or the cmd.exe shell) you don't have sufficient rights to complete many common tasks. Disabling UAC eliminates this security block but isn't advisable in many environments. You can disable UAC through the Control Panel by clicking the User Accounts icon (see Figure 9.12).

FIGURE 9.12
Disabling UAC

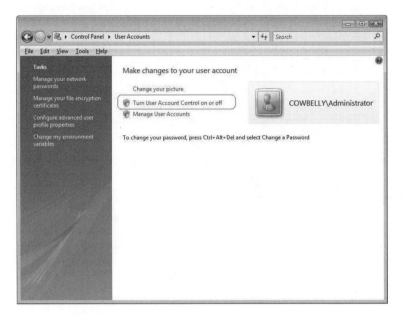

Note that turning UAC on or off requires a system reboot. An alternative to disabling UAC is to start PowerShell with elevated privileges. To do so, right-click the Windows PowerShell selection on the Start menu to reveal additional startup options, including Run As Administrator (see Figure 9.13).

FIGURE 9.13
Right-clicking
to Run As
Administrator

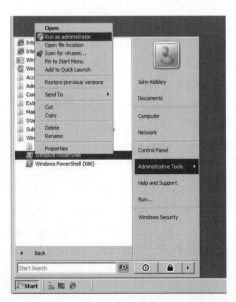

After you start PowerShell, you're greeted with a DOS-like window with a slightly altered prompt that starts with PS (see Figure 9.14).

FIGURE 9.14

PowerShell upon starting

Numerous startup options are available for PowerShell, including parameters to display help (PowerShell Help), suppress the logo, specify the data input and output formats, and other options.

Integration with UAC is only one example of the secure design of PowerShell. The execution of stand-alone scripts is blocked as part of the initial installation (see Figure 9.15).

FIGURE 9.15

Restricted execution of scripts

To enable scripts, you must change the execution policy using the set-executionpolicy cmdlet:

```
Set-executionpolicy -ExecutionPolicy "RemoteSigned"
```

This cmdlet allows saved scripts (.PS1 files) to be executed without having been digitally signed.

Finding Your Way Around PowerShell

Rights are escalated, scripts can run, the shell is up and ready to go—now what? Understanding how to investigate the secrets of PowerShell and use cmdlets is the core of being a functional PowerShell user.

VERB-NOUN FORMAT FOR CMDLETS

The names of cmdlets native to PowerShell are constructed using an easy-to-remember verb-noun format. A cmdlet that retrieves information commonly starts with the word *get* and a dash, and ends with a description of the information desired. Typing **get-process** returns information about running processes, and **get-service** returns information about configured services. For Hyper-V, **get-WMIObject** is critical because it retrieves information using WMI. Commonly used PowerShell verbs include add, clear, convert, export, format get, import, invoke, join, measure, move, new, out, remove, select, set, start, update, where, and write.

ASKING POWERSHELL FOR HELP

PowerShell has integrated, flexible help that you can access by using the same verb-noun format and typing **get-help**. Typing **get-help** by itself displays general help information for using PowerShell. Following the cmdlet with another cmdlet (`get-help get-WMIObject`, for example) displays help information specific to that cmdlet (see Figure 9.16).

FIGURE 9.16
get-help get-
WMIObject

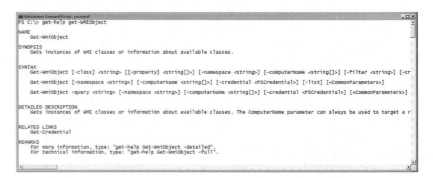

Detailed examples for how to use each cmdlet are available by specifying the `-examples` parameter with `get-help` (for example, `get-help get-WMIobject -examples`). You can retrieve more information by using other parameters or by following a cmdlet with `-?` (for example, `get-WMIobject -?`).

NOTE This is an example of PowerShell's consistency. All cmdlets use `-?` to provide help information. There is no question of whether to use /H, -help, or -?.

Often, help information is too extensive to fit on a single screen. Following a request for help with a pipe to `more` can make information more usable (`get-WMIobject -? | more` or `get-help get-WMIobject -full | more`). The `help` function is available and equivalent to `get-help`, except it already includes logic for paging. Typing **help** followed by a cmdlet name pages through help information (`help get-WMIobject` is the same as `Get-Help Get-WMIObject | more`).

The integrated help is extensive and not limited to individual cmdlets. To access a list of help topics, type **get-help about***.

NOTE But wait. Didn't we say PowerShell uses a verb-noun format? What about `help` and `more`? They don't use that format. PowerShell uses aliases (and some functions like `more`) to let you use commands that are familiar in CMD or UNIX shells. The `Set-Location` cmdlet has an alias of CD. More is slightly more complicated.

FINDING COMMANDS, ALIASES, AND MEMBERS

The consistent verb-noun format isn't always enough magic to help you find or remember the right cmdlet to complete a task. Finding cmdlets is simplified with the `get-command` cmdlet. Available cmdlets can be filtered, listed, and sorted in a number of convenient ways including by verb, noun, command type, and other criteria. Perhaps you need to understand all the cmdlets available for manipulating services. Typing **get-command -noun service** creates such a list (see Figure 9.17).

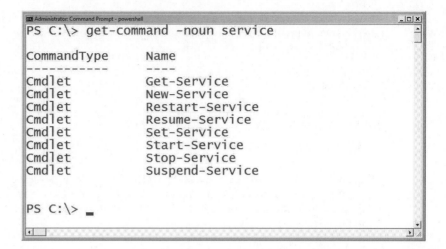

```
PS C:\> get-command -noun service

CommandType        Name
-----------        ----
Cmdlet             Get-Service
Cmdlet             New-Service
Cmdlet             Restart-Service
Cmdlet             Resume-Service
Cmdlet             Set-Service
Cmdlet             Start-Service
Cmdlet             Stop-Service
Cmdlet             Suspend-Service


PS C:\>
```

But knowing the proper cmdlets isn't enough: Understanding the information they expose is key as well. Everything passed to or returned by any PowerShell command is an object. With CMD, if you store text in an environment variable, the text is all there is. In PowerShell, if you store text, it's a .NET string object with a collection of properties such as `length` and methods such as `PadRight()`. You can expose the information accessible through a cmdlet or other object by using `get-member`. Piping any cmdlet to `get-member` lists the component information available. Typing **get-service | get-member** shows the methods and properties associated with the cmdlet.

Aliases are abbreviations or alternate names for running cmdlets in PowerShell to save typing. The `sort-object` cmdlet, for example, has the `sort` alias defined. GWMI is an alias for Get-WMIObject, which is used extensively to manage Hyper-V. You can generate a listing of aliases by typing **get-alias** or **get-command -commandtype alias**.

NOTE   Aliases can reduce typing, but PowerShell also includes a tab-completion feature so you can avoid typing long cmdlet names and parameters. For example, typing **get-h** followed by the Tab key completes the typing of **get-help**.

Making Things Work in PowerShell

PowerShell includes commands and functions to perform all the familiar programming tasks: accepting input, creating output, evaluating information, looping, and navigating through data stores (including filesystems, the Registry, variables, and more). Keep in mind while you're using PowerShell that it's insensitive to case (unless you ask it to differentiate)—uppercase and lowercase are treated the same.

RUNNING EXISTING COMMANDS

As noted earlier, you can execute existing Windows commands from within PowerShell. You can enter multiple independent commands on the same line if you separate them with a semicolon (;). With `cmd.exe`, individual commands you type into the same shell windows can also be entered on the same line but are separated by an ampersand (&). This means that typing commands one after the other like this

```
C:
cd \logs
Dir
```

has the same result in PowerShell as the following:

```
C:; cd \logs; dir
```

WARNING   Caution! Some commands have been "replaced" in PowerShell by roughly equivalent aliases or cmdlets. `Del`, for example is an alias for the `Remove-Item` cmdlet, which does a great deal more than delete files and behaves differently (including deleting directories, Registry items, certificates, and other objects).

COMMON CMDLET PARAMETERS

Different cmdlets are intended to perform different functions, but the standard syntax for PowerShell cmdlets means they often have common options. Parameters common to all cmdlets are listed in Table 9.1.

TABLE 9.1   Common PowerShell Cmdlet Parameters

PARAMETER	DESCRIPTION
`-Verbose`	Asks the cmdlet for more detailed execution information than the default provides
`-Debug`	Asks the cmdlet to provide debugging information
`-ErrorAction`	Specifies how to handle errors: `Continue` (default), `Stop`, `SilentlyContinue`, `Inquire`
`-ErrorVariable`	Specifies the variable to contain error information (beyond the standard `$error`)
`-OutVariable`	Specifies the variable that contains output
`-OutBuffer`	Specifies the number of objects to buffer before calling the next cmdlet in a pipeline
`-WhatIf`	Shows what happens if the cmdlet is executed, without actually executing the cmdlet (only for cmdlets that alter system state)
`-Confirm`	Prompts you before the cmdlet executes (only for cmdlets that alter system state)

PowerShell: `Get-Help about_CommonParameters`

Not all common parameters affect all cmdlets. -WhatIf and -Confirm are useful only for cmdlets that make changes to a system. -Verbose works only for cmdlets that support increased detailed.

PIPELINES

A *pipeline* is a string of cmdlets executed in sequence where objects are passed for processing. Objects resulting from the execution of the first command in the pipeline become the input for the next command. Nearly every useful task completed in PowerShell uses pipelines. As mentioned earlier, commands in the pipeline are separate by a vertical bar (|) also sometimes referred to as a *pipe*.

Pipes are also used in the cmd.exe shell (type *<filename>* | **more** to display a file one screen at a time), but they're less useful. Piping output in the cmd.exe shell is limited to text and doesn't include the benefits of an object model as with PowerShell. get-service | get-member, mentioned earlier, helps to illustrate this point. get-service has specific member components that are part of a model that get-member understands and can consume. By calling get-service and passing the object created by the call to get-member as input, get-member can consume information that is part of the object.

FILTERING WITH *WHERE-OBJECT*

Administrative tasks commonly require that the cmdlet process only a subset of information returned. You may need to apply filtering to tasks such as starting or stopping particular services or finding processes that use large amounts of RAM. The where-object cmdlet enables filtering of information. Including where-object as part of a pipeline can create useful filters by testing the values of objects. For example, you can use get-service to list all services on a system. Adding a filter for services that include "Hyper-V" in the display name yields a much shorter list (see Figure 9.18):

```
get-service | where-object {$_.displayname -match "Hyper-V"}
```

TIP   Where-Object has an alias of Where; they can be used interchangeably.

FIGURE 9.18
Services found
via filter

```
PS C:\> get-service | where {$_.displayname -match "Hyper-V"}

Status    Name                 DisplayName
------    ----                 -----------
Running   nvspwmi              Hyper-V Networking Management Service
Running   vhdsvc               Hyper-V Image Management Service
Running   vmms                 Hyper-V Virtual Machine Management

PS C:\>
```

NOTE $_ is *a* variable that represents the current pipeline object. It's commonly seen and used for filtering with where-object, looping with foreach-object, and making decisions with switch.

Showing filtered information from a cmdlet is only part of what you may need to accomplish. You can pass filtered output to yet another cmdlet for action to be taken. You can make the previous example more functional by extending the pipeline:

```
get-service |
where {$_.displayname -match "Hyper-V"} | Start-Service
```

NOTE As mentioned earlier, Where is the associated alias for the Where-Object cmdlet and can be used to shorten filter statements.

The numerous comparison operators you can use with Where and Where-Object are listed in Table 9.2.

TABLE 9.2 Comparison Operators

OPERATOR	DESCRIPTION	EXAMPLE	TRUE/FALSE
-eq	Equal	10 -eq 10	True
-ne	Not equal	10 -ne 10	False
-gt	Greater than	10 -gt 10	False
-ge	Greater than or equal to	10 -ge 10	True
-lt	Less than	10 -lt 10	False
-le	Less than or equal to	10 -le 10	True
-like	Wildcard comparison	"one" -like "o*"	True
-notlike	Wildcard comparison	"one" -notlike "o*"	False
-match	Regular expression comparison	"book" -match "oo"	True
-notmatch	Regular expression comparison	"book" -notmatch "oo"	False

PowerShell: Get-help about_comparison_operators

NOTE Remember that PowerShell isn't case sensitive, so comparison by default disregards case. Adding the letter c to the front of a comparison operator (-cmatch instead of -match) enforces case sensitivity.

DECISION MAKING

PowerShell includes common comparison tools like `if` and `switch` (case statement). You can use comparison operators (already shown) with `if`. Later in the chapter, we'll cover the numeric codes representing the execution state of a VM. Following is an example of how to evaluate state using `if`:

```
if ($state_num -ne 2)
{
    Write-Host "Virtual Machine is not in the Running State"
}
else
{
    Write-Host " Virtual Machine is running"
}
```

More than one VM execution state exists; and although you can nest `if` statements, the code may be hard to read. You can use `switch` to simplify decision-making:

```
switch ($state_num)
{
        2         {$State_text = "Running"}
        3         {$State_text = "PowerOff"}
        4         {$State_text = "ShuttingDown"}
        10        {$State_text = "Reset"}
        32768     {$State_text = "Paused"}
        32769     {$State_text = "Saved"}
        32770     {$State_text = "Starting"}
        32771     {$State_text = "SnapshotInProgress"}
        32772     {$State_text = "Migrating"}
        32773     {$State_text = "Saving"}
        32774     {$State_text = "Stopping"}
        32776     {$State_text = "Pausing"}
        32777     {$State_text = "Resuming"}
        Default   {$State_text = "Unknown"}
}
```

USING VARIABLES

PowerShell allows for the use of variables like other languages. Variables are preceded by the dollar sign ($), and you can assign values using the familiar equal sign (=):

```
$i = 1
```

A variable can contain a simple object—1 in the previous example is an integer—or complex objects. A single property of an object can be assigned to a variable, and multiple objects—the output from a cmdlet, for example—can be stored in a single variable. You can assign a list of the processes on a system (for instance) and access it later:

```
$Processes = Get-Process
```

Cmdlets commonly return a collection, or *array*, of objects. The variable $Processes holds multiple entries—one for each process returned by Get-Process (and accessible by an array index or subscript):

```
write-host $Processes[0]
```

NOTE The write-host cmdlet isn't necessary here, but we include it to make a point. You could type **$Processes[0]**, and the contents of the variable would be displayed.

Each instance of a process within $Processes contains accessible member properties. You can access these elements by using the member name as shown in Figure 9.19, which displays the service name of one instance:

```
write-host $Processes[0].Name
```

FIGURE 9.19

Accessing
Information in
a collection

```
PS C:\> $Processes = Get-Process
PS C:\>
PS C:\> write-host $Processes[0]
System.Diagnostics.Process (Ati2evxx)
PS C:\>
PS C:\> write-host $Processes[0].Name
Ati2evxx
PS C:\>
```

PowerShell sets numerous important predefined variables. You can find information for these by typing **help about_automatic_variables** in the shell. One valuable predefined variable is $_,which represents the current pipeline object. $_is often used in pipelines or other code with where-object, switch, and foreach-object, as in this example (shown previously):

```
get-service | where-object {$_.displayname -match "Hyper-V"}
```

LOOPING

As in other coding languages, the cmdlets for, foreach, while and do/while let you iterate through data or repeat an operation until a condition is met:

For *Loop*

You use for to create a loop that runs commands in a script block while a specified condition evaluates to true. The format of a for loop is as follows:

```
for (<init>; <condition>; <repeat>) {<script_block>}
```

The following sample shows a simple for loop that prints out a sequence of numbers:

```
for ($i = 10; $i -ge 0; $i--)
{
   write-host "Countdown: $i"
}
```

Foreach *Loop*

The foreach statement provides for loop functionality for stepping through a series of values in a collection of items (array). Foreach can be more useful than for in PowerShell given its object-focused nature. Looping through a collection that is assigned to a variable is common and made simple by foreach:

```
foreach ($<item> in $<collection>){<command_block>}
```

Examples later in the chapter demonstrate how to use foreach to change the state of VMs. The following sample is adapted from that code:

```
$VMs = Get-WMIObject -Namespace root\virtualization ↵
-Class Msvm_ComputerSystem
foreach ($VM in $VMs)
{
   write-host "VM Name:"   $VM.ElementName
}
```

In this example, the output of the Get-WMIObject cmdlet is assigned to $VMs, which becomes the set of information to be processed. You don't need to first assign the output of a cmdlet to a variable in order to use foreach. The collection or array to be processed may be included as part of the foreach statement:

```
foreach ($VM in Get-WMIObject -Namespace root\virtualization ↵
-Class Msvm_ComputerSystem)
{
   write-host "VM Name:"   $VM.ElementName
}
```

In either case, the output is identical.

NOTE   There is also a foreach-object cmdlet (with an associated foreach alias) that is different from the foreach statement. foreach-object allows you to loop through each instance of an object as part of a pipeline. You can learn more about foreach-object on your own, or check out the examples in Chapter 10.

While *and* do/while

While and do/while are loops that execute while a condition is true. The difference between them is the point at which the condition is evaluated. While checks a condition before entering the loop and may not enter the loop:

```
while (<condition>){<command_block>}
```

do/while executes the loop first and then evaluates the condition. A do/while loop always executes at least once:

```
do {<command_block>} while (<condition>)
```

You can see the difference between while and do/while in the following sample code. In each case, the variable $i is initialized to 10 before entering the loop. Because the value of $i is already 10, the while loop doesn't execute:

```
$i = 10
while($i -lt 10) {
    write-host "The value is " $i
    $i++
}
```

The check for the do loop is at the end, so the loop is executed once, even though the condition is false:

```
$i = 10
do {
    write-host "The value is " $i
    $i++
} while($i -lt 10)
```

While and do/while can be useful in managing various aspects of VM configuration (waiting for the VM to be in a specific state, for instance).

CREATING FUNCTIONS

You can group pieces of PowerShell code into blocks as functions. You call functions similarly to cmdlets by typing the name of the function. Functions can accept input as arguments or values passed through a pipeline. Unlike functions in other languages, PowerShell functions return all output to the caller of the function (VBScript and C programmers may expect only specifically designated values to be returned). Functions must be defined before being called, so they're typically first in PowerShell script files.

To create a function, you wrap and name a block of code as follows:

```
Function Say_Hi
{
    write-host "Hello World"
}
```

You can then call the function Say_Hi from within PowerShell (see Figure 9.20).

FIGURE 9.20
Calling a pre-defined script function

```
PS C:\> Function Say_Hi
>> {
>>      write-host "Hello World"
>> }
>>
PS C:\> Say_Hi
Hello World
PS C:\>
```

A more useful (Hyper-V related) example creates a function to show the state of VMs running on the local system (it's based on a code example shown later in the chapter):

```
Function Show-VM
{
write-host ""
write-host "Name                    Description↵
                State"
write-host "------------------- -----------↵
--------------------- -------------"
foreach ($VM in Gwmi -Namespace root\virtualization ↵
-Query "Select * from Msvm_ComputerSystem")
{   $name = $VM.Elementname.PadRight(19," ")
    $desc = $VM.Description.PadRight(33," ")
    $state_num = $VM.EnabledState
    switch ($state_num)
    {
        2         {$State_text = "Running"}
        3         {$State_text = "PowerOff"}
        4         {$State_text = "ShuttingDown"}
        10        {$State_text = "Reset"}
        32768     {$State_text = "Paused"}
        32769     {$State_text = "Saved"}
        32770     {$State_text = "Starting"}
        32771     {$State_text = "SnapshotInProgress"}
        32773     {$State_text = "Saving"}
        32774     {$State_text = "Stopping"}
        32776     {$State_text = "Pausing"}
        32777     {$State_text = "Resuming"}
        default   {$State_text = "Unknown"}
    }
    Write-host "$name $desc $State_text ($State_num)"
}write-host ""
}
```

After the function is loaded, you can type **Show_VM** in PowerShell to list the friendly name, description, and state of each VM (see Figure 9.21).

FIGURE 9.21
Calling a useful function

```
PS C:\HyperV> Show-VM

Name                Description                             State
------------------- --------------------------------------- -------------
JOHNKEL-NC8430      Microsoft Hosting Computer System       Running (2)
SCVMM               Microsoft Virtual Machine               Saved (32769)
New Virtual Machine Microsoft Virtual Machine               PowerOff (3)
Windows XP          Microsoft Virtual Machine               Running (2)

PS C:\HyperV>
```

LOADING SCRIPTS AND FUNCTION LIBRARIES

You can save predefined groups of commands in script files for later use. (The preceding function example was loaded from a file and executed.) As mentioned earlier, PowerShell code is typically saved in files with a .PS1 extension. The call to load and run a prewritten script file must include the explicit path to the file, or it won't execute.

NOTE PowerShell searches for files in directories listed in the Path environment variable; but unlike in CMD, the current folder isn't considered for such searches.

Typing just the name of the script file generates an error, as shown in Figure 9.22.

FIGURE 9.22
Calling a script incorrectly

FIGURE 9.23
Successfully calling a script

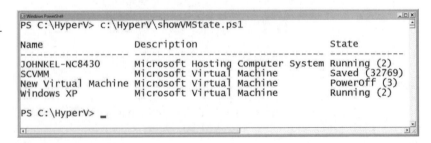

As mentioned, you can execute a script using the full path (see Figure 9.23).

To execute a script from the current directory, precede its name with a period and a backslash (.\ or <period><backslash>, as shown in Figure 9.24).

You can also save prewritten libraries of functions in .PS1 files and load them for use in PowerShell. Loading a library of functions is similar to running a script (using the path), except that the call to the library must be by preceded by an additional period and space before the path (see Figure 9.25).

FIGURE 9.24
Calling a script
in the current
directory

```
PS C:\HyperV> .\showVMState.ps1

Name                   Description                         State
----                   -----------                         -----
JOHNKEL-NC8430         Microsoft Hosting Computer System   Running (2)
SCVMM                  Microsoft Virtual Machine           Saved (32769)
New Virtual Machine    Microsoft Virtual Machine           PowerOff (3)
Windows XP             Microsoft Virtual Machine           Running (2)

PS C:\HyperV>
```

FIGURE 9.25
Loading a library
of functions

```
PS C:\> . c:\hyperv\showVMState-Func.ps1
PS C:\> show-VM

Name                   Description                         State
----                   -----------                         -----
JOHNKEL-NC8430         Microsoft Hosting Computer System   Running (2)
SCVMM                  Microsoft Virtual Machine           Saved (32769)
New Virtual Machine    Microsoft Virtual Machine           PowerOff (3)
Windows XP             Microsoft Virtual Machine           Running (2)

PS C:\>
```

TIP   Remember that the execution of unsigned scripts is blocked by default in PowerShell. You
can use the set-executionpolicy cmdlet to allow for the execution of scripts.

Common Elements of WMI Scripts

WMI scripts have some common elements regardless of the language used. Short scripts (like
the one generated in the previous section) frequently have three core sections:

◆   Connect: Access WMI

◆   Collect: Request and receive WMI data

◆   Project: Act on or display the WMI data

A brief walkthrough demonstrating the basics of accessing the WMI virtualization
namespace using VBScript and PowerShell follows. This walkthrough provides a foundation
only; you'll find more advanced information about automation and scripting in Chapter 10.

WMI and VBScript

A listing of the VBScript created earlier by the WMI Code Creator is shown in Figure 9.26,
divided into its three core sections.

FIGURE 9.26

VBScript sample, in sections

Connect

```
strComputer = "."
Set objWMIService = GetObject("winmgmts:\\" & strComputer & "\root\virtualization")
```

Collect

```
Set colItems = objWMIService.ExecQuery(
    "SELECT * FROM Msvm_ComputerSystem",,48)
```

Project

```
For Each objItem in colItems
    Wscript.Echo "----------------------------------"
    Wscript.Echo "Msvm_ComputerSystem instance"
    Wscript.Echo "----------------------------------"
    Wscript.Echo "Caption: " & objItem.Caption
    Wscript.Echo "ElementName: " & objItem.ElementName
Next
```

Walking through the sample script provides examples of each of the required elements of WMI scripting. The first step in any WMI script is to connect to the WMI Service on the intended target computer. The first two lines of the script accomplish this by specifying the moniker for the WMI scripting library (`winmgmts`), the local system, and the WMI namespace. An object reference is returned, which enables access to WMI on the target system. A simplified one-line version of this VBScript code is as follows:

```
Set objWMIService = GetObject("winmgmts:\\.\root\virtualization")
```

As noted earlier, you can access WMI from a remote computer. Replacing the `.` in the `strComputer` variable (or the `.` between the slashes in the simplified example) with the resolvable name of a remote system returns an object reference for WMI on the remote system.

After you establish a connection to WMI, the cmdlet typically retrieves information. In the example, all resource instances that are exposed as part of `MSVM_ComputerSystem` are requested and (we hope) returned. The resources in this case are VM instances:

```
Set colItems = objWMIService.ExecQuery _
  ("SELECT * FROM Msvm_ComputerSystem",,48)
```

NOTE The SELECT verb may appear familiar. Windows Management Instrumentation Query Language (WQL) is a great deal like Structured Query Language (SQL) and lets you query the CIM repository using similar syntax.

The information returned by this query is in the form of a collection (`colItems`), which is a group of related objects (VMs). You can access the collection using a simple `for` loop to display the desired information for each VM. A simpler version of the sample code is shown here:

```
For Each objItem in colItems
    Wscript.Echo "-----------------------------------"
  Wscript.Echo "VM Name:" & objItem.ElementName
  Wscript.Echo "  Type:" & objItem.Caption
Next
```

The complete, simplified VBScript is as follows, and the improved output is shown in Figure 9.27:

```
Set objWMIService = GetObject _
  ("winmgmts:\\.\root\virtualization")

Set colItems = objWMIService.ExecQuery _
  ("SELECT * FROM Msvm_ComputerSystem",,48)

For Each objItem in colItems
    Wscript.Echo "-----------------------------------"
  Wscript.Echo "VM Name:" & objItem.ElementName
  Wscript.Echo "  Type:" & objItem.Caption
Next
```

FIGURE 9.27
Improved sample
script output

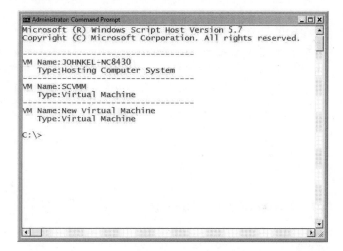

TIP   WSH runs VBScript (.VBS) using WScript as the default host. Setting the default script host tells Windows how to handle the output of scripts you run. With WScript as the default, output from a VBScript creates a pop-up message box every time it writes output to the screen, unless it was called directly using CScript (from the command prompt—cscript <script.vbs>). Using CScript, output is displayed in a command-prompt window. You can change the default script host to avoid this situation by typing **cscript //h:cscript** at a command prompt.

WMI and PowerShell

PowerShell's task-focused design simplifies the process of connecting to WMI, retrieving data from Hyper-V, and putting that data to use. The PowerShell code snippet necessary to access the same information from Hyper-V as the VBScript sample is much shorter while generating similar output (see Figure 9.28):

```
Get-WMIObject -namespace root\virtualization -class Msvm_ComputerSystem |
Format-Table ElementName, Caption -autosize
```

FIGURE 9.28

PowerShell output

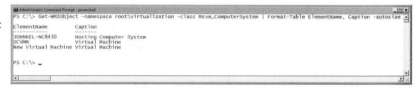

PowerShell version 1.0 does can't remotely access other systems. That being said, `Get-WMIObject` is unlike other cmdlets in that you can use it to target remote systems because it relies on WMI. In a way similar to the VBScript sample, you can specify a remote system by adding an option to specify the target:

```
Get-WMIObject -computername node1 -namespace root\virtualization ↵
-class Msvm_ComputerSystem | Format-Table ElementName, Caption
```

Aliases, which we mentioned earlier, illustrate PowerShell's task-focused design. Shortcuts for commonly typed cmdlets are built in, including one for the `Get-WMIObject` cmdlet: `gwmi`. Using `gwmi` and other aliases shortens the input:

```
gwmi -namespace root\virtualization -class Msvm_ComputerSystem |
ft ElementName, Caption
```

Virtualization Classes

The virtualization provider includes more than 100 associated classes for managing and monitoring Hyper-V. These classes are well documented on Microsoft's MSDN website (`http://msdn.microsoft.com/en-us/library/cc136992(VS.85).aspx`). The MSDN reference provides great insight for scripting access to Hyper-V, including limited scripting examples.

NOTE   The number of classes associated with the virtualization provider is much larger than 100. Some classes aren't specific to the provider/namespace or aren't intended for common use. These classes typically aren't accessed for script-based automation, but they may be visible, depending on the tools used to access the provider/namespace.

Useful WMI Virtualization Classes to Know

Each class (and its associated methods) was created with at least one purpose in mind. You may not find each class as useful for day-to-day automation tasks. Classes that have been found useful repeatedly for automation are listed in Table 9.3, including brief descriptions.

TABLE 9.3   Frequently Used WMI Virtualization Classes

FUNCTIONAL GROUP	VIRTUALIZATION CLASS	PROPERTY COUNT	COMMENT/ DESCRIPTION
Virtual System	Msvm_ComputerSystem	29	Parent or child computer system (VM); core to many automations
Virtual System	Msvm_VirtualSystemGlobalSettingData	13	Global settings for a VM
Virtual System	Msvm_VirtualSystemSettingData	21	Virtualization-specific settings for a VM
Management	Msvm_VirtualSystemManagementService	21	Virtualization service on the parent (host)
Management	Msvm_ VirtualSystemManagementServiceSettingData	12	Setting for the virtualization service on the parent (host)
Resource Mgmt	Msvm_AllocationCapabilities	11	Means by which a client can discover the valid range of default settings for a virtual resource; useful for adding storage resources
Resource Mgmt	Msvm_ResourceAllocationSettingData	21	Current and recorded allocation states of a virtual resource; useful for storage-related tasks
Integration	Msvm_KvpExchangeComponent	34	State of the key/value pair exchange component that enables data exchange between child and parent (shutdown, timesync, other); dependant on ICs

TABLE 9.3 Frequently Used WMI Virtualization Classes *(CONTINUED)*

FUNCTIONAL GROUP	VIRTUALIZATION CLASS	PROPERTY COUNT	COMMENT/ DESCRIPTION
Integration	Msvm_ShutdownComponent	32	State of the shutdown component; enables request for a clean shutdown; dependant in ICs
Processor	Msvm_Processor	47	Virtual processor in a VM
Processor	Msvm_ProcessorPool	19	Aggregation of processor resources allocated to a VM
Processor	Msvm_ProcessorSettingData	28	Virtual processor settings for a VM
Memory	Msvm_Memory	66	Memory allocated to a VM
Memory	Msvm_MemorySettingData	24	Configured state of memory on a VM
Storage	Msvm_DiskDrive	56	Hard disk inside a VM
Storage	Msvm_DVDDrive	56	DVD drive inside a VM
Storage	Msvm_IDEController	36	IDE controller attached to a VM
Storage	Msvm_ImageManagementService	21	Virtual media controller for a VM (.vhd, .iso, and .vfd files)
Storage	Msvm_MountedStorageImage	15	Details for manually mounted storage image
Storage	Msvm_StorageJob	39	Image operation created by Image Management Service

TABLE 9.3   Frequently Used WMI Virtualization Classes *(CONTINUED)*

FUNCTIONAL GROUP	VIRTUALIZATION CLASS	PROPERTY COUNT	COMMENT/ DESCRIPTION
Storage	Msvm_VirtualHardDiskInfo	6	Details about the existing VHD image (.vhd file)
Network	Msvm_EmulatedEthernetPort	53	Emulated Ethernet adapter (legacy network adapter)
Network	Msvm_EmulatedEthernetPortSettingData	22	Configured state of an emulated Ethernet adapter (legacy network adapter)
Network	Msvm_ExternalEthernetPort	54	External Ethernet port (physical network adapter on the parent)
Network	Msvm_InternalEthernetPort	53	Internal Ethernet port (internal network adapter on the parent)
Network	Msvm_SwitchLANEndpoint	30	LAN endpoint connected to an Ethernet port (internal or external)
Network	Msvm_SwitchPort	24	Port on a virtual network switch
Network	Msvm_SyntheticEthernetPort	53	Synthetic Ethernet adapter
Network	Msvm_SyntheticEthernetPortSettingData	23	Configured state of a synthetic Ethernet adapter
Network	Msvm_VirtualSwitch	27	Virtual network switch

TABLE 9.3   Frequently Used WMI Virtualization Classes *(CONTINUED)*

FUNCTIONAL GROUP	VIRTUALIZATION CLASS	PROPERTY COUNT	COMMENT/ DESCRIPTION
Network	Msvm_VirtualSwitchManagementService	21	Controller for global networking resources including switches, switch ports, and internal Ethernet ports

Understanding how these classes interrelate to automate common tasks is important. Walking through some examples should help you begin to develop value-added automation tools.

THE MSVM_COMPUTERSYSTEM CLASS

Global/general settings and information for VMs are accessible using the various virtual system classes. Msvm_ComputerSystem was used for the earlier sample code examples because it's central to many automation tasks. Looping through a collection of VMs is one of the most fundamentally useful management or data-collection tasks. As demonstrated, Msvm_ComputerSystem supplies a list of all VMs (including the parent partition) as well as general information about each VM. Important properties of the class include those listed in Table 9.4.

TABLE 9.4   Important Properties of Msvm_ComputerSystem

PROPERTY NAME	COMMENT
ElementName	Display name of a VM (friendly)
Name	Unique name of a VM object (unfriendly, but useful)
Caption	Instance type: VM or host
Description	Instance type: VM or host (verbose)
EnabledState	VM state: turned off, running, or in between
HealthState	Heath indicator: 5=healthy, 25=critical error
InstallDate	Installation date and time (valuable for sprawl control)
TimeOfLastConfigurationChange	Configuration-change date and time
TimeOfLastStateChange	State-change date and time

Properties exposed in Msvm_ComputerSystem are the key to coordinated data collection and system-wide management. For example, if you want to save the state of all running VMs on a given host, you can use Msvm_ComputerSystem. You may need to save (for example) the state of all VMs in order to restart the physical system for maintenance. To accomplish this task, you check the state of each child partition and, if necessary, make a request to change the state to Saved:

```
foreach ($VM in gwmi -Namespace root\virtualization -Query ↵
 "Select * from Msvm_ComputerSystem ↵
Where Description='Microsoft Virtual Machine'")
{
  # request state change if appropriate
   if (($VM.EnabledState -eq 2) -or ($VM.EnabledState -eq 32768))
   {
    write-host "Saving ",$VM.Elementname
    $RequestReturn = $VM.RequestStateChange(32769)
  }
}
```

You can accomplish the same result using the following single-line example:

```
gwmi -namespace root\virtualization -query ↵
"Select * from MSVM_computerSystem where ↵
((Caption like 'Virtual%') and ↵
(enabledState=2) or (enabledState=32768))" | ↵
foreach {$_.requestStateChange(32769) }
```

The enabledState property contains a numeric value that describes the execution state of each machine. The requestStateChange method understands these same values for changing the state of a VM. The known values are shown in Table 9.5.

TABLE 9.5   Virtual Machine States

STATE DESCRIPTION	STATE CODE
Unknown	0
Enabled (Running)	2
Disabled (PowerOff)	3
Shutting Down	4
Paused	32768
Suspended (Saved)	32769
Starting	32770
Snapshotting	32771

TABLE 9.5   Virtual Machine States *(CONTINUED)*

STATE DESCRIPTION	STATE CODE
Migrating	32772
Saving	32773
Stopping	32774
Deleted	32775
Pausing	32776
Resuming	32777

The ability to both decode and request state codes is important. Adding the status descriptions to screen output and diagnostic logs is handy and relatively simple with a switch (case) statement. Output from a function containing the PowerShell code sample below can be seen in Figure 9.29:

```
write-host ""
write-host "Name                    Description↵
                State"
write-host "------------------- -----------↵
---------------------- -------------"
foreach ($VM in gwmi -Namespace root\virtualization ↵
-query "Select * from MSVM_Computersystem")
{   $name = $VM.Elementname.PadRight(19," ")
  $desc = $VM.Description.PadRight(33," ")
  $state_num = $VM.EnabledState
  switch ($state_num)
  {
          2         {$State_text = "Running"}
          3         {$State_text = "PowerOff"}
          4         {$State_text = "ShuttingDown"}
          10        {$State_text = "Reset"}
          32768     {$State_text = "Paused"}
          32769     {$State_text = "Saved"}
          32770     {$State_text = "Starting"}
          32771     {$State_text = "SnapshotInProgress"}
          32772     {$State_text = "Migrating"}
          32773     {$State_text = "Saving"}
          32774     {$State_text = "Stopping"}
          32776     {$State_text = "Pausing"}
          32777     {$State_text = "Resuming"}
          Default   {$State_text = "Unknown"}
  }
  write-host "$name $desc $State_text ($State_num)"
}write-host ""
```

FIGURE 9.29
Friendly show-
state output

```
PS C:\Scripts> .\showvmstatenicer.ps1

Name                  Description                              State
--------------------  ---------------------------------------  ---------------
JOHNKEL-NC8430        Microsoft Hosting Computer System        Running (2)
SCVMM                 Microsoft Virtual Machine                Saved (32769)
New Virtual Machine   Microsoft Virtual Machine                PowerOff (3)

PS C:\Scripts>
```

Knowing the VM state is critical for some operations. Many resources can't be added or altered while a VM is running, saved, or paused, including memory, disk, CPU, and network cards.

VM system state is one example of critical information required to successfully automate Hyper-V, which you can access and alter through `Msvm_ComputerSystem`. `Msvm_ComputerSystem` is also the home for the display name for VMs. Querying WMI for an individual VM by the friendly name is a simple process, using the `ElementName` property:

```
$VM = gwmi -namespace root\virtualization -query ↵
"select * from Msvm_ComputerSystem where ElementName='Windows XP'"
```

`$VM` is assigned an object describing the VM "Windows XP," which includes the less friendly Name element (see Figure 9.30).

FIGURE 9.30
Elements of "Win-
dows XP"

```
PS C:\> $VM = gwmi -namespace root\virtualization -query "select * from Msvm_computersystem where
P'"
PS C:\> $VM


__GENUS                    : 2
__CLASS                    : Msvm_ComputerSystem
__SUPERCLASS               : CIM_ComputerSystem
__DYNASTY                  : CIM_ManagedElement
__RELPATH                  : Msvm_ComputerSystem.CreationClassName="Msvm_ComputerSystem",Name="
                             A6-5C544BBE7B3E"

__PROPERTY_COUNT           : 29
__DERIVATION               : {CIM_ComputerSystem, CIM_System, CIM_EnabledLogicalElement, CIM_Lo
__SERVER                   : JOHNKEL-NC8430
__NAMESPACE                : root\virtualization
__PATH                     : \\JOHNKEL-NC8430\root\virtualization:Msvm_ComputerSystem.CreationC
                             erSystem",Name="48C16CF1-D57B-4774-9BA6-5C544BBE7B3E"
AssignedNumaNodeList       : {}
Caption                    : Virtual Machine
CreationClassName          : Msvm_ComputerSystem
Dedicated                  :
Description                : Microsoft Virtual Machine
ElementName                : Windows XP
EnabledDefault             : 2
EnabledState               : 3
HealthState                : 5
IdentifyingDescriptions    :
InstallDate                : 20081108200557.000000-000
Name                       : 48C16CF1-D57B-4774-9BA6-5C544BBE7B3E
NameFormat                 :
OnTimeInMilliseconds       : 0
OperationalStatus          : {10}
```

The `Name` element is the common thread tying much of the information about a VM together between the various virtualization classes. `Name` contains the unique identifier for a VM. Unlike the friendly `ElementName`, this unique name is maintained (and searchable) in virtually all the virtualization classes containing information and resources about a VM and its components. Amazingly, it isn't exposed in the Hyper-V Manager console. Expanding the use of classes is simple when you understand this relationship. For example, the amount of RAM assigned to a VM isn't accessible via `Msvm_ComputerSystem` but is exposed by `Msvm_Memory`. You can find the unfriendly (but useful) Name first and use it to request information about RAM from Msvm_Memory (see Figure 9.31):

NOTE Nothing is returned by Msvm_memory if the VM isn't running, because no memory is allocated.

```
$VM = GWMI -Namespace root\virtualization -Query ↵
"Select * from Msvm_ComputerSystem Where ElementName='Windows XP'"
GWMI -Namespace root\virtualization -Query ↵
("Select * from Msvm_Memory Where SystemName= '$($VM.name)'") | ↵
format-table blocksize, numberofblocks -autosize
```

FIGURE 9.31
Using Name to access other classes

```
PS F:\> $VM = GWMI -Namespace root\virtualization -Query "Select *
>> from Msvm_ComputerSystem Where ElementName='Windows XP'"
>>
PS F:\> GWMI -Namespace root\virtualization -Query ("Select *
>> from Msvm_Memory Where SystemName= '$($VM.name)'") |
>> format-table blocksize, numberofblocks -autosize
>>

blocksize numberofblocks
--------- --------------
  1048576            512


PS F:\> _
```

The VM name isn't always accessible as a stand-alone element. For some operations, you must search for it as part of a larger element—such as instanceID in the following example, where you change the amount of RAM allocated to a VM:

NOTE Allocated memory can't be changed for a running VM.

```
$VM = GWMI -Namespace root\virtualization -Query ↵
"Select * from Msvm_ComputerSystem Where ElementName='Windows XP'"

$MemoryDesired = 348
$Memory=GWMI -NameSpace "root\virtualization" -Query ↵
"select * from Msvm_MemorySettingData where ↵
instanceId Like 'Microsoft:$($vm.name)%'"
$Memory.Limit          =   $MemoryDesired
$Memory.Reservation    =   $MemoryDesired
$Memory.VirtualQuantity =   $MemoryDesired
$SettingArguments=@($VM.__Path, @($Memory.psbase.GetText↵
([System.Management.TextFormat]::WmiDtd20)) , $null)

$ManagementData = GWMI -NameSpace "root\virtualization" ↵
-Class "MsVM_virtualSystemManagementService"
$ManagementData.psbase.invokeMethod(↵
"ModifyVirtualSystemResources",$SettingArguments)
```

Many unforeseen circumstances can affect the execution of scripts. For efficient production use of your scripts, you should incorporate effective error handling to address common scenarios.

Summary

The virtualization WMI provider is a flexible and useful tool for manipulating and interrogating Hyper-V. Much as a chisel would be useless without a hammer or the hands of a craftsman, the provider requires additional tools and expertise to demonstrate value. You can access the virtualization namespace through tools including the command line (WMIC), flexible scripting languages (VBScript, PowerShell, and others), and WMI browsers and code generators. WMI lets you manage Hyper-V from platforms that can't accommodate the Hyper-V Manager, including Server Core and older versions of Windows. Windows PowerShell provides a consistent syntax and command model for Hyper-V automation that we'll explore in greater detail in Chapter 10.

Chapter 10

Automating Tasks

In the previous chapter, you were introduced to Windows Management Instrumentation (WMI) and scripting concepts that are important to understanding how to effectively automate Hyper-V administrative tasks. The chapter used some relatively simple automation tasks and code examples.

The focus of this chapter is to show you how to accomplish more complex automation tasks for managing a Hyper-V virtualization environment. The examples in this chapter are exclusive to Hyper-V, unlike the Windows PowerShell code generated by (and used with) System Center Virtual Machine Manager (SCVMM) discussed in Chapter 11, "System Center Virtual Machine Manager 2008."

This chapter will discuss common administrative areas as well as automation and scripting examples. Scripting samples are primarily written in Windows PowerShell and rely heavily on a prewritten library of functions available on the Internet.

Common administrative tasks are often categorized in the following groups, which are the topics we'll cover in this chapter:

- Provisioning
- Configuration management
- Access management
- Migration
- Backup and recovery
- Data collection and monitoring

Building on the Work of Others

In Chapter 9, "Understanding WMI, Scripting, and Hyper-V," you were introduced to the Hyper-V WMI provider and namespace. The script examples in Chapter 9 were fairly simple. Although they're useful, they don't accomplish much. Writing useful scripts can take a great deal of time and effort. Developing an understanding of the right WMI classes to access and how best to use them can be laborious. Using the insights of others and building on their efforts is an attractive approach to efficient Hyper-V automation. SCVMM is the best way to benefit from the expertise of others (to be covered in Chapter 12), but you can also use other approaches.

Many of the examples in this chapter use an evolving, prewritten library of Windows PowerShell Hyper-V functions. The library was created by James O'Neill and is available from CodePlex (http://www.codeplex.com).

TIP James O'Neill has a wonderful blog at http://blogs.technet.com/jamesone/ where he goes into great detail about Windows, virtualization, motor racing, and other topics.

CodePlex is Microsoft's website for open source project hosting, and it's home to numerous useful development projects. You can find code for other Hyper-V focused initiatives on CodePlex, but James' library is among the most complete currently available anywhere; it's used widely for Hyper-V automation. His HyperV.PS1 management library uses all the same WMI calls discussed in Chapter 9. The difference is that the calls in the library are surrounded by carefully written Windows PowerShell code. You can access the library for Hyper-V by navigating to www.codeplex.com/PSHyperv. It's bundled up in a .zip file that you can find by clicking the page's Releases tab. Inside the .zip file you'll find HyperV.PS1, which is the library of functions James has created.

NOTE Remember that you load prewritten Windows PowerShell libraries of functions in a similar way to running a script (specifying the path), except that the call to the library must be by proceeded with an additional period. Also recall that you must set the execution policy in Windows PowerShell to allow for the execution of scripts. See Chapter 9 for more information.

Loading James' HyperV.PS1 library is straightforward, assuming the execution policy is set and you follow proper calling conventions (see Figure 10.1).

FIGURE 10.1
Calling the library

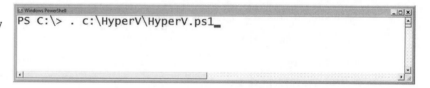

```
PS C:\> . c:\HyperV\HyperV.ps1_
```

When the library loads, it lists the functions available for use (see Figure 10.2).

These predefined Windows PowerShell functions are the underpinning of the useful scripts in this chapter.

NOTE Nearly every function or filter in the library includes helpful examples within the library source code to demonstrate its value. James also included useful testing routines to assist with the complexities of error handling and virtual machine management (examples include Choose-VM and Test-WMIJob). Browsing through the source can provide you with a wealth of ideas about how to use the library, as well as fantastic examples of how to write great Windows PowerShell code.

FIGURE 10.2
Functions in the library

```
Windows PowerShell
New-VMInternalSwitch
New-VMPrivateSwitch
New-VMRasd
New-VMSnapshot
New-VMSwitchPort
Ping-VM
Remove-VM
Remove-VMdrive
Remove-VMNIC
Remove-VMSCSIcontroller
Remove-VMSnapshot
Set-VM
Set-VMCPUCount
Set-VMDisk
Set-VMMemory
Set-VMNICAddress
Set-VMNICConnection
Set-VMState
Shutdown-VM
Start-VM
Stop-VM
Suspend-VM
Test-VHD
UnMount-VHD


PS C:\> _
```

Provisioning

Creating new virtual machine (VM) instances is the first big, useful automation task to conquer. With a good VM provisioning process, you can quickly and reliably create new VMs in minutes.

Creating a Bare-Bones VM

We'll use the provisioning process to help make the point about creating your own scripts versus using James O'Neill's library of functions. The following Windows PowerShell code creates a new VM instance on the local server with the display name of New VM:

```
# Set the display name of the VM
$New_VM_Name = "New VM"
$VM_Service = GWMI -namespace root\virtualization ↵
Msvm_VirtualSystemManagementService
$NewVM = $VM_Service.DefineVirtualSystem()

# Parse the result and find the created VM
$resultID = $NewVM.DefinedSystem.Split('=')[2]
$resultID = $resultid.split('"')[1]
$VM = GWMI -namespace root\virtualization Msvm_ComputerSystem |
  where {$_.Name -match "$resultID"}

$VMSettingData = GWMI -namespace root\virtualization ↵
Msvm_VirtualSystemSettingData -filter "SystemName = `'$($VM.Name)`'"
```

```
# Set the display name of the VM
$VMSettingData.ElementName = $New_VM_Name
$VM_Service.ModifyVirtualSystem($VM.__PATH, $VMSettingData.psbase.getText(1))
```

Not all that much code is shown, but then again, it doesn't do much. You create a new VM on the local physical system and give it the intended display name. By contrast, the following single line of code accomplishes the same task using HyperV.PS1:

```
$myVM = (New-VM "New VM")
```

Using the library vastly simplifies VM management tasks by reducing the amount of code you need to write. In either case, you set defaults for the number of processors (one) and the amount of RAM (512MB), but you do little else. The VM defined at this point is similar to a bare-bones PC kit (see Figure 10.3): It has only a virtual case, a power supply, a motherboard, limited RAM, and a single processor. The VM has no hard disks, no CD/DVD, and no network interface cards (NICs). You must attach and configure all these resources before you can use the VM.

FIGURE 10.3
Virtual settings after creating a basic VM

Defining a usable VM means more effort. You must write additional code to perform the following actions:

- Change the amount of RAM
- Alter the number of virtual CPUs
- Add NICs
- Connect NICs to a particular virtual switch

- Create a virtual hard disk (VHD) file

- Add hard drive(s) attached to VHD file(s) or pass-through disk

- Add CD/DVD drive(s)

- Mount CD/DVD(s)

- All other provisioning tasks (you get the point—changing startup actions, BIOS boot order, and so on)

Each of these actions requires you to weave more code into the basic provisioning process. The complexity of a script that must be hand crafted and maintained to handle all provisioning processes can be substantial. Writing a script of this magnitude is similar to running a marathon—not everyone has the capacity or even wants the challenge (especially if a free ride is available, like James' library!). The following Windows PowerShell sample (using the library) completes the common VM provisioning tasks mentioned and starts the new VM, with the execution shown in Figure 10.4:

```
$New_VM_Name  = "New VM"
$New_VHD_Name = "c:\VHDs\$($New_VM_Name).VHD"


$myVM = (New-VM $New_VM_Name)
Set-VMMemory    $myVM 1024MB
Set-VMCPUCount $myVM 2
Add-VMDrive     $myVM 0 0
New-VHD         $New_VHD_Name 20GB -wait
Add-VMDisk      $myVM 0 0 $New_VHD_Name
Add-VMDrive     $myVM 1 0 -dvd
Add-VMDisk      $myVM 1 0 "C:\ISOs\Server2008.iso" -dvd
Add-VMNIC       $myVM -virtualSwitch "Public"


Start-VM $myVM
```

FIGURE 10.4
Script execution

```
Administrator: Command Prompt - powershell
PS C:\> $New_VM_Name   = "New VM"
PS C:\> $New_VHD_Name = "c:\VHDs\" + $New_VM_Name + ".VHD"
PS C:\>
PS C:\> $myVM = (New-VM $New_VM_Name)
Created VM
Set VM Name
PS C:\> Set-VMMemory    $myVM 1024MB
Set memory for 'New VM' to 1024MB.
PS C:\> Set-VMCPUCount $myVM 2
Set CPU Count for 'New VM' to 2.
PS C:\> Add-VMDrive     $myVM 0 0
Added drive to 'New VM'.
PS C:\> New-VHD         $New_VHD_Name 20GB -wait
VHD Creation of c:\VHDs\New VM.VHD : Completed
OK
PS C:\> Add-VMDisk      $myVM 0 0 $New_VHD_Name
Added disk to 'New VM'.
PS C:\> Add-VMDrive     $myVM 1 0 -dvd
Added drive to 'New VM'.
PS C:\> Add-VMDisk      $myVM 1 0 "C:\ISOs\Server2008.iso" -dvd
Failed to add disk to 'New VM', result code: 4096.
PS C:\> add-vmnic       $myVM -virtualSwitch "Public"
Added NIC to 'New VM'.
PS C:\>
PS C:\> Start-VM $myVM
Changing state of New VM: Job Started.
\\DQUAD\root\virtualization:Msvm_ConcreteJob.InstanceID="82964178-EB42-42C1-93F
1-1E90767CF13A"
PS C:\>
```

You can immediately see the results of this compact and complete script in the Hyper-V console. Each customized element of the VM's settings are reflected in the settings (see Figure 10.5).

FIGURE 10.5
VM settings after creating a complete VM

NOTE You can also set BIOS options (such as boot order) and startup/shutdown actions for a VM using the Set-VM function:

```
Set-vm $myVM -bootorder @(3,2,0,1)
```

You can find friendly names for boot media (rather than numbers) in the definition of the $BootMedia global variable in HyperV.ps1. Additional global variables exist to clarify the codes behind VM state as well as startup, shutdown, and recovery actions. To set the default startup action for a VM to always start, use either of the following lines:

```
set-vm -$myVM -autoStart $StartupAction["AlwaysStartup"]
set-vm -$myVM -autoStart 2
```

You can add error handling and management to the earlier basic provisioning script (checks to ensure the ISO file exists, disk space is sufficient, the Public network switch is defined, and each step of the process completes successfully), but it may not be necessary in all situations.

NOTE You may notice that we call all the useful tools in HyperV.PS1 functions, when in actuality many of them are defined as filters. Functions and filters are essentially the same thing (filters are a subset of functions). They're both blocks of code that process data. The difference is in how they process data that is piped into them from other functions. Through the evolution of the library, many functions have been converted to filters to add support for piped input, and some filters have changed to functions. Rather than split hairs and keep track, we'll continue to call everything a function.

Remote Virtual-Machine Provisioning

It hasn't been explicitly mentioned in the chapter yet, but most functions in the library have been constructed to be executed against a remote server by specifying the `-server <hostname>` argument. Remotely managing servers is key, because Windows PowerShell doesn't run on the more compact Core installations of Windows Server 2008. Calling the New-VM function and specifying a remote host (if successful) populates $myVM with information about a new VM created on that remote host:

```
$myVM = (New-VM $New_VM_Name -server "RemoteHost")
```

Any code in the examples that uses $myVM to set VM settings (Set-VMMemory, Set-VMCPUCount), add resources (Add-VMDrive, Add-VMDisk, Add-VMNIC), or in other ways affect the VM (Start-VM) should work properly remotely.

NOTE   When a variable containing the description of a VM is passed to any of the functions that affect the VM, the function automatically contacts the remote server. If no VM parameter is passed to a function, or convenience dictates that you access the VM by name, you need to specify the –Server parameter.

Some functions don't rely on the VM information found in $myVM, such as New-VHD (called to create a new VHD to be later attached to the VM). Calls to these functions must also include the -Server argument:

```
$New_VM_Name  = "New VM"
$New_VHD_Name = "c:\VHDs\$($New_VM_Name).VHD"
$Target_Host = "RemoteHost"

$myVM = (New-VM $New_VM_Name -server $Target_Host)
Set-VMMemory   $myVM 1024MB
Set-VMCPUCount $myVM 2
Add-VMDrive    $myVM 0 0
New-VHD        $New_VHD_Name 20GB -wait -Server $Target_Host
Add-VMDisk     $myVM 0 0 $New_VHD_Name
Add-VMDrive    $myVM 1 0 -dvd
Add-VMDisk     $myVM 1 0 "C:\ISOs\SC07.iso" -dvd
Add-VMNIC      $myVM -virtualSwitch "Public"

Start-VM $myVM
```

Precreating Generic VHDs

In the previous provisioning example, the VM created has an ISO image file *inserted* in its virtual CD/DVD drive from which you can install Windows Server 2008. Automating the insertion of an installation disk for a vanilla operating system is a convenient way to build VMs, but installation still requires considerable time and manual intervention (clicking through).

Creating a generic VM for a given operating system instance is a more efficient way to create multiple VMs. Installing a particular operating system version/edition once completely (the x64 full installation of Windows Server 2008 Enterprise Edition, for instance) followed by properly executing SysPrep.exe can save time and effort for repeated installations. SysPrep.exe is Microsoft's system-preparation utility, which you can use to *depersonalize* a configured operating system instance for widespread deployment (commonly using an imaging tool such as ImageX and/or an automated deployment tool like Windows Deployment Services). When you correctly execute the command, you reset key system elements, such as name and security identifier (SID), so that you can configure them again to ensure uniqueness in your environment.

TIP SysPrep.exe is specific to each edition of Windows. For Windows Vista and Windows Server 2008, it ships with the product and can be found in the C:\Windows\system32\sysprep directory.

You can run SysPrep.exe either by passing it various command-line arguments to guide behavior (see Figure 10.6) or via a graphical interface (see Figure 10.7).

FIGURE 10.6
Sysprep arguments

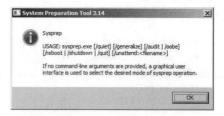

FIGURE 10.7
Sysprep graphical
interface

You should keep in mind that not all software can be preinstalled and configured before you run SysPrep.exe. The following list includes items that you can configure and tasks you can set before executing SysPrep.exe:

◆ Installing updated integration components (ICs), if not already included in the installation media

◆ Setting the time zone

◆ Configuring the patching option

◆ Applying patches from Windows Update

◆ Adding common features (PowerShell, for example)

The manual installation of Windows Server 2008 Enterprise Edition typically takes more than 50 minutes when you apply patches and complete common configuration tasks. Duplicating a VHD file that has been Syspreped and re-personalizing should take a small fraction of this time (80% to 90% less time is common, depending on system performance).

Automated installation (using answer files and scripts) can further reduce the install effort by automating domain joining, system renaming, and license activation, as well as the installation and configuration of application software and server roles.

TIP   You can find detailed information and guidance about how to automate these tasks using SysPrep.exe online at TechNet.Microsoft.com and other websites.

Here's a modified version of the VM provisioning script, including code to copy and register a preconfigured VHD file without an installation ISO or a new, blank VHD:

```
$New_VM_Name  = "New VM"
$New_VHD_Name = "c:\VHDs\$($New_VM_Name).VHD"
Copy "c:\SYSPREPed\Windows Server 2008.VHD" $New_VHD_Name

$myVM = (New-VM $New_VM_Name)
Set-VMMemory    $myVM 1024MB
Set-VMCPUCount $myVM 2
Add-VMDrive     $myVM 0 0
Add-VMDisk      $myVM 0 0 $New_VHD_Name
Add-VMDrive     $myVM 1 0 -dvd
Add-VMNIC       $myVM -virtualSwitch "Public"

Start-VM $myVM
```

De-provisioning

You can automate the removal of VMs as well. You may think twice about creating scripts to remove VMs, because (operationally) simplifying the deletion of a VM presents risks. As with the Hyper-V Manager, removing a VM programmatically requires that the VM not be in a running state (stopped or saved). Only the configuration of the VM is removed; associated VHD files are left behind and may also need to be deleted. You can remove a VM with one line of code that uses the function library:

```
Remove-VM "New VM"
```

You may also remove resources attached to a VM using functions included in HyperV.PS1. Table 10.1 lists these destructive functions.

TABLE 10.1   HyperV.PS1 Remove Functions

FUNCTION NAME	DESCRIPTION
Remove-VM	Delete the VM configuration
Remove-VMDrive	Detach a disk (VHD or pass-through)
Remove-VMNIC	Remove a virtual NIC
Remove-VMSCSIcontroller	Remove a virtual SCSI controller
Remove-VMSnapshot	Delete snapshot

Physical Server Setup

Jumping ahead to show basic VM creation (as we did here) may seem like putting the cart before the horse. You want to ensure that the physical server is ready to accommodate VMs before you set up VMs. You have some common tasks to perform on a physical host, all of which you can automate for consistency. There is more value in automating some configuration tasks than others: For example, changing the default path for new VHDs and configuration files can be important, but may not be entirely useful. If you configure failover clustering on a series of hosts, default-ing the settings to a particular volume may be useless, because these settings are typically ignored (VM configuration information and VHDs are often on unique shared storage unless a common file share or cluster file system is used). Automating the creation of virtual network switches may be more important in a clustered environment, because virtual network switches across clusters nodes must be named consistently to ensure smooth operation.

Functions are available to create each of the three kinds of virtual network switches: *private*, *internal*, and *external*. Creating private and internal virtual switches programmatically is a rela-tively straightforward process:

```
New-VMInternalSwitch "VM and Host Network"
New-VMPrivateSwitch "VM ONLY Network"
```

Creating a virtual switch with external connectivity is a bit more complicated, because you must specify a physical network card:

```
New-VMExternalSwitch -virtualSwitchNameName "Wired Network" ↵
-ext "Intel GigE 1"
```

Knowing the name ahead of time for the desired physical NIC is important but not always practical. To simplify virtual-switch creation, use the `choose-VMExternalEthernet` function. This function queries the host operating system to discover Ethernet connections not already in use by Hyper-V. If more than one connection is found, you're prompted to select one, which is returned as the result:

```
choose-VMExternalEthernet |
New-VMExternalSwitch -virtualSwitchNameName "Wired Network"
```

Configuration Management

Discovering, managing, and maintaining the configurations of systems are core tasks in any well-managed infrastructure. Locating virtual hosts and VMs is a first step. Accessing and decoding configuration information for hosts and VMs is key to sustaining the health of the overall environment.

Discovery

The ease with which you can create VMs is both a blessing and a curse. The ability to create entire new virtual system instances with a few lines of code or clicks of a mouse means tra-ditional barriers to server deployment have dramatically changed. No longer do you need to purchase a new server for each new project. Now, a primary goal of server virtualization is often to reduce costs through server consolidation.

Once users begin to understand the speed with which you can create new servers, expectations for new servers increase. As you realize the promise of virtualization, enterprising users will create their own VMs in their own ways. Sometimes, they will create systems without triggering processes to ensure that appropriate software licenses are ordered, backup capacity is reserved, or security audits are performed. The impact and cost implications of an unmanaged virtual environment can be enormous.

NOTE More than once, innovative users have built their own virtual test infrastructures, exposing (for example) Dynamic Host Configuration Protocol (DHCP) servers to production networks and interrupting business.

DETECTING VIRTUALIZATION HOSTS

You can locate installed Hyper-V hosts in a number of ways, including searching servers for running services (vhdsvc, nvspwmi, vmms), scanning volumes for files (including .VHD and .VSV), enumerating WMI namespaces, and using the power and efficiency of Active Directory (AD). You may not know that properly configured virtualization servers (those running Hyper-V and Virtual Server 2005) publish their binding information in AD as Service Connection Point (SCP) objects.

TIP For more information about Service Connection Points, go to the MSDN website at http://msdn.microsoft.com/en-us/library/ms677950(VS.85).aspx.

Querying AD for Hyper-V hosts is a great starting point toward a bounty of information about virtualization in an enterprise environment. The following sample VBScript generates a list and a count of Hyper-V hosts from the current domain:

```
' Adapted from Alex A. Kibkalo -
' (his is more complete) available from
' http://blogs.technet.com/vm/attachment/3048135.ashx

Set objSystemInfo = CreateObject("ADSystemInfo")
Set objRootDSE = GetObject("LDAP://rootDSE")
szDomainShortName = objSystemInfo.DomainShortName
szDomainDN = objRootDSE.Get("defaultNamingContext")

Set oConnection = CreateObject("ADODB.Connection")
Set oCommand = CreateObject("ADODB.Command")
oConnection.Provider = ("ADsDSOObject")
oConnection.Open "Ads Provider"
oCommand.ActiveConnection = oConnection
oCommand.Properties("Page Size") = 99
oCommand.Properties("Searchscope") = &H2 'ADS_SCOPE_SUBTREE
oCommand.Properties("Chase Referrals") = &H60 'ADS_CHASE_REFERRALS_ALWAYS
```

```
oCommand.CommandText = "select distinguishedName from 'LDAP://" _
  & szDomainDN & "' " & _
  "where objectCategory='serviceConnectionPoint' and cn='Microsoft Hyper-V'"
Set oRecordSet = oCommand.Execute
oRecordSet.MoveFirst
Do Until oRecordSet.EOF
    szNodeName = oRecordSet.Fields("distinguishedName")
    ' Trim "CN=<szSCP>,CN="
    szNodeName = Mid(szNodeName, InStr(szNodeName, ",CN=") + 4)
    ' Trim the domain DN
    szNodeName = Left(szNodeName, InStr(szNodeName, ",") - 1)
    wscript.echo szNodeName
    oRecordSet.MoveNext
Loop
wscript.echo "Domain: " & szDomainShortName & _
": " & oRecordSet.RecordCount & " hosts"
```

TIP John Howard posted a similar script on his virtualization blog at http://blogs.technet .com/jhoward/archive/2008/06/30/hyper-v-locate-hyper-v-enabled-servers-in-your-domain.aspx.

Once again, the hyperv.ps1 library demonstrates its value by simplifying the task of searching AD for Hyper-V hosts. Using the Get-VMHost function returns a list of registered Hyper-V servers in the current domain.

ENUMERATING VIRTUAL MACHINES

Creating a list of VMs on a particular host is a relatively simple process, as shown in Chapter 9. Creating such a list is even simpler using the functions included in HyperV.PS1 (see Figure 10.8):

```
get-vm | format-table elementname
```

FIGURE 10.8
List of local VMs

You can access all the externally viewable properties of a VM via the information available from get-vm | FL *.

NOTE   PowerShell allows you to set the default output format for different classes of objects using an XML file. The early versions of the library didn't use this facility, so Get-VM (for example) output a list of all the object properties, and the companion function List-VM provided formatted output. The newer versions of HyperV.ps1 has an associated Hyperv.Format.PS1XML file that defines the default output format. In some cases, the XML file processes a property of an object and displays something that isn't available as a property—for example, translating 2 in the EnabledState property to the text "running."

With the newer versions, if you want to see all the available properties from Get-VM, you can pipe its output into Format-List -Property *; this can be shortened to FL *.

If you want to display output that is different from the default, you can either pipe the output of the function into Format-Table (which can be abbreviated to FT) or customize the PS1.XML file.

Wrapping a call to get-vm with a loop that can access a list of virtualization hosts provides a useful building block for later automation. A simple text file with the name of each server on a single line can be the input (perhaps created from a query of Active Directory). For our purposes, we've created a file named serverlist.txt, which contains two server names:

```
hypernode1
hypernode2
```

Iterating through the text file using get-content and foreach-object can generate a list of configured VMs (see Figure 10.9):

```
get-content .\serverlist.txt |
foreach-object {get-VM -server $_ |
format-table __SERVER, elementname, enabledstate -auto}
```

FIGURE 10.9
List of VMs using host input

NOTE Yes, you could pipeline the output from Get-VMHost to foreach-object, but not all Hyper-V hosts may be online or accessible to you. In that case, exceptions are generated and/or additional error handling is required. You could also call Get-VM and pass it all the host names (Get-VM -server hypernode1, hypernode2 | FT __SERVER, elementname, enabledstate -auto) to achieve a similar result, but we're trying to make some points about looping.

You can extend or alter this basic *host loop* to gather additional useful information beyond those pieces of data exposed by get-VM (which uses the MSVM_ComputerSystem class shown in Chapter 9). Other VM interrogation functions like get-VMState can access additional information and handle common formatting tasks (see Figure 10.10).

```
get-content .\serverlist.txt | foreach-object {get-VMState -server $_}
```

FIGURE 10.10
Using
Get-VMState with
a host input file

Get-VMState decodes the numeric VM state and displays it in a more understandable manner. The function also attempts to display the fully qualified domain name (FQDN) of running VMs with installed ICs. Fully *enlightened* VMs (those with installed ICs) *that are running* can communicate key information about the installed operating system to the parent partition via the ICs. The Get-VMKVP function exposes more of these available attributes (see Figure 10.11):

```
get-vmkvp "Windows XP"
```

FIGURE 10.11
Get-VMKVP output

NOTE HyperV.PS1 is a work in progress and continues to evolve. The output from Get-VMKVP is a great example. Figure 10.11 shows the output of a version of the library available on www.CodePlex.com from August 2008. A newer version of the library returns more information, as shown in Figure 10.12. Additional functions have been added and updates have been made. Be sure to periodically check CodePlex for updates, to get the most value from the library.

FIGURE 10.12
New Get-VMKVP output

Collecting information such as the operating system version, service pack level, and FQDN without directly accessing a VM can be valuable when you're troubleshooting or auditing your environment. Combining the server loop with get-vmkvp is fairly straightforward (see Figure 10.13):

```
get-content .\serverlist.txt |
foreach-object {get-VM -server $_ | get-VMKVP} |
format-table FullyQualifiedDomainName, OSName, CSDVersion -auto
```

FIGURE 10.13
Looping with Get-VMKVP

```
PS C:\> get-content .\serverlist.txt | foreach-object {get-VM -server $_ | get-V
MKVP} | format-table FullyQualifiedDomainName, OSName, CSDVersion -auto

FullyQualifiedDomainName  OSName                                   CSDVersion
------------------------  ------                                   ----------
BTE-SCOM.DHVirt.local     Windows Server (R) 2008 Enterprise Service Pack 1
SCCMDemo.DHVirt.local     Windows Server (R) 2008 Enterprise Service Pack 1
dhvirt-DC.DHVirt.local    Windows Server (R) 2008 Enterprise Service Pack 1
2008R2SERVER.DHVirt.local Windows Server 7 Enterprise


PS C:\>
```

Windows PowerShell allows you to create output in a great many formats besides standard text, including comma-separated (CSV) and XML. Altering the format of your output can make the information easier for other tools and applications to use. You can create a CSV file of the information shown in Figure 10.13 by calling the **export-CSV** cmdlet:

```
get-content .\serverlist.txt |
foreach-object {get-VM -server $_ | get-VMKVP} |
export-csv -path c:\VMInfo.csv
```

TIP   CSV and XML files are handy formats for producing output to pass to other applications. Windows PowerShell Version 2 includes a useful Out-GridView cmdlet that you can use to view and manipulate data interactively. The graphical interface lets you sort, search, and group data. Figure 10.14 shows output similar to Figure 10.13, but sent to Out-GridView and grouped by operating system name.

FIGURE 10.14
Get-VMKVM set to
Out-GridView

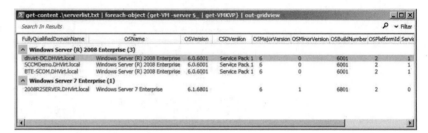

COLLECTING OTHER VIRTUAL MACHINE DETAILS

HyperV.PS1 includes numerous get functions (and one list function). Table 10.2 provides a complete list of these functions and their results.

TABLE 10.2   HyperV.PS1 Get Functions

FUNCTION NAME	DESCRIPTION
Get-VhdDefaultPath	Retrieve the default VHD path (parent specific)
Get-VHDInfo	Retrieve info about a VHD file
Get-VM	Access general VM information
Get-VMBackupScript	Create a DiskShadow backup script
Get-VMByMACaddress	Retrieve VM info by Media Access Control (MAC) address
Get-VMCPUCount	Retrieve the CPU count
Get-VMDisk	Display VM disk controller and drive information
Get-VMDiskByDrive	Access a VM disk by drive
Get-VMDiskController	Access a VM disk by controller

TABLE 10.2   HyperV.PS1 Get Functions *(CONTINUED)*

FUNCTION NAME	DESCRIPTION
Get-VMDriveByController	Access a VM drive by controller
Get-VMFloppyDisk	Display VM floppy disks
Get-VMHost	Query AD for Hyper-V hosts
Get-VMJPEG	Retrieve a JPEG image of a VM display
Get-VMKVP	Return key/value pairs for running VMs
Get-VMMemory	Display the RAM allocated to a VM
Get-VMNic	Retrieve NIC information for a VM
Get-VMNicport	Access network port information
Get-VMnicSwitch	Show the switch connected to a virtual NIC
Get-VMSettingData	Get active settings for a VM (BIOS, asset tag, other)
Get-VMSnapshot	Access VM snapshot information
Get-VMSnapshotTree	Access VM snapshot information and show it as a tree
Get-VMState	Retrieve/decode the VM state and FQDN
List-VMNIC	**Replaced by Get-VMNic—may be eliminated from library**

Get to know these functions. Experiment with them and read the examples included in Hyperv.PS1, and you'll gain a wealth of configuration knowledge.

TIP   Real-life, useful examples abound for get and list functions. For example, only one VM at a time can access a physical CD/DVD resource. A stopped VM may expect access to a drive when it starts and will fail to start if the drive is already being used. Adding a filter to the Get-VMDisk function can help you find VMs that are using the physical CD/DVD: Get-VMDisk * | where {$_.diskpath -match "^IDE"}.

Creating Simple Reports

Windows PowerShell enables nearly limitless options for report generation. You may not have time or the PowerShell savvy to construct the ideal report. The supplied get functions do a fantastic job of exposing the components of Hyper-V and VMs, but sometimes the output is missing important information. List-VMNIC provides a great example of this point. List-VMNIC retrieves a list of configured VMs and their corresponding NICs with MAC address and the connected virtual network switch (see Figure 10.15):

```
get-vm -server hypernode1 | list-vmnic
```

FIGURE 10.15

List-VMNIC output

```
PS C:\> get-vm -server hypernode1 | list-vmnic

VM                  MACAddress       Type              Network
--                  ----------       ----              -------
6 Test Full         00155D485509     Microsoft Emulat... Public
7142 Test           00155D48550B     Microsoft Emulat... Public
7141 Test           00155D48550A     Microsoft Emulat... Public
5 Test Empty        00155D48550C     Microsoft Emulat... Public


PS C:\> _
```

This function can be useful for collecting the MAC addresses for all VMs in your environment, but the output lacks the name of the physical host.

NOTE James has enhanced the Get-VMNIC function, which can for the most part be used in place of List-VMNIC (and includes the physical host name). Note that List-VMNIC may be eliminated from future versions of the library. You should experiment with both and see which makes the most sense for you.

Because the host name doesn't make it to the end of the pipeline, it can't be displayed. Windows PowerShell professionals can modify the function or filter to output the missing information.

NOTE You can modify the function by adding __Server to the selected output (altering HyperV.PS1). This may require a change not only to List-VMNIC but also to other functions it relies on. By altering the base source, you may cause a later change-management challenge for yourself when HyperV.PS1 is revised in CodePlex.

A simpler (better) way to get the desired output and add the missing information is to preserve the information just long enough for it to be useful. Adding a single variable to the loop wrapper to hold the server name from earlier in the pipeline does this. You can create an audit report with a usable administrative MAC address without too much extra code (see Figure 10.16):

```
get-content c:\serverlist.txt | foreach-object {
  $Server = $_;
  get-vm -server $Server | list-vmnic;
  write-host "    Above instances found on Server:" $Server; Write-host
}
```

FIGURE 10.16

Looping
List-VMNIC

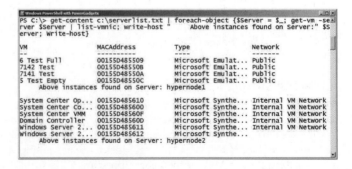

```
PS C:\> get-content c:\serverlist.txt | foreach-object {$Server = $_; get-vm -se
rver $Server | list-vmnic; write-host "    Above instances found on Server:" $S
erver; Write-host}

VM                  MACAddress       Type              Network
--                  ----------       ----              -------
6 Test Full         00155D485509     Microsoft Emulat... Public
7142 Test           00155D48550B     Microsoft Emulat... Public
7141 Test           00155D48550A     Microsoft Emulat... Public
5 Test Empty        00155D48550C     Microsoft Emulat... Public
    Above instances found on Server: hypernode1

System Center Op... 00155D485610     Microsoft Synthe... Internal VM Network
System Center Co... 00155D485600     Microsoft Synthe... Internal VM Network
System Center VMM   00155D48560F     Microsoft Synthe... Internal VM Network
Domain Controller   00155D48560D     Microsoft Synthe... Internal VM Network
Windows Server 2... 00155D485611     Microsoft Synthe... Internal VM Network
Windows Server 2... 00155D485612     Microsoft Synthe...
    Above instances found on Server: hypernode2
```

Although the output clearly shows the NICs homed on each host, it isn't optimal. Mixing implicit output (what comes from the functions) with the explicit write-host is ugly and can present other challenges (if the output is redirected, for example). It would be more useable if the physical server name was listed in a unique column. You can do this a few different ways (without rewriting the source function). Adding the server name to each NIC returned is also fairly easy (see Figure 10.17):

```
get-content c:\serverlist.txt | foreach-object {
    $server=$_;
    get-vm -server $_| list-vmnic|
    add-member -passthru noteproperty "server" $server
} | format-table -auto
```

FIGURE 10.17
Better List-VMNIC

You can achieve similar results by writing more compact code with aliases:

```
gc c:\serverlist.txt |
% {$s=$_;get-vm -server $_|list-vmnic|
add-member -passthru noteproperty "server" $s} |
ft -auto
```

You can also create a function using **foreach** rather than **foreach-object**, which can be called and pipelined to **format-table** (see Figure 10.18):

```
function List-LotsOfNics
{
    foreach ($s in (gc c:\serverlist.txt))
    {
        list-vmnic (get-vm -server $s)|
        add-member -passthru noteproperty "Server" $s
    }
}
```

FIGURE 10.18
Function
List-VMNIC

Regardless of your approach for creating usable scripts and reports, using HyperV.PS1 will save you the time and effort of creating custom code. To make this point again, following is Windows PowerShell code that is roughly equivalent to the previous loop but does *not* use HyperV.PS1:

```
foreach ($s in (gc c:\serverlist.txt)) {
  $vms=gwmi -computer $s -namespace "root\virtualization" ↵
msvm_computersystem -filter "name <> '$s'"
  foreach ($vm in $vms) {
    gwmi -computer $s -NameSpace "root\virtualization"↵
-query "Select * From MsVM_EmulatedEthernetPortSettingData ↵
Where instanceId Like 'Microsoft:$($vm.name)%'"|
    select-object ↵
@{name="VM";expression={$vm.elementname}},↵
@{name="MACAddress";expression={$_.address}},↵
@{name="Server";expression={$_.__SERVER}},↵
@{name="Type";expression={$_.ResourceSubType}},↵
@{name="Network";expression={(gwmi -computer $s ↵
-NameSpace "root\virtualization" -Query "ASSOCIATORS OF ↵
{$(gwmi -computer $s -NameSpace ""root\virtualization"" ↵
-Query ""Select * From Msvm_SwitchPort where __Path='$($_.connection[0].
replace("""\""","""\\"""))'"")} ↵
where resultclass = Msvm_VirtualSwitch").elementname}}
    gwmi -computer $s -NameSpace "root\virtualization" ↵
-query "Select * From MsVM_SyntheticEthernetPortSettingData ↵
Where instanceId Like 'Microsoft:$($vm.name)%'"|select-object @
{name="VM";expression={$vm.elementname}},↵
@{name="MACAddress";expression={$_.address}},↵
@{name="Server";expression={$_.__SERVER}},↵
@{name="Type";expression={$_.ResourceSubType}},↵
@{name="Network";expression={(gwmi -computer $s ↵
-NameSpace "root\virtualization" -Query "ASSOCIATORS OF ↵
{$(gwmi -computer $s -NameSpace ""root\virtualization"" ↵
-Query ""Select * From Msvm_SwitchPort where __Path='$($_.connection[0].
replace("""\""","""\\"""))'"")} ↵
where resultclass = Msvm_VirtualSwitch").elementname}}
  }
}
```

Managing the Virtual Environment

Creating VMs and collecting configuration information about your environment is only a first step. Managing your virtual environment is critical to realizing the benefits of virtualization. You should strive to use enterprise system management tools if at all possible. The Microsoft

System Center family of products provides comprehensive tools to manage physical and virtual environments and is covered in Chapters 11 through 13.

System management can mean many different things, such as managing system configuration, provisioning, performance, security policies, hardware configuration, storage, and even the power state of a system. For our purposes, we'll only discuss managing system state (power state) for VMs and management tasks for VHD files. Scripts shown earlier for provisioning VMs demonstrated how to alter the configuration of a VM (add/set resources). We'll review additional VM configuration tasks later, in the "Maintaining Virtual Systems" section of this chapter.

MANAGING STATE

Chapter 9 included verbose examples of how to show and alter the system state of VMs. In this chapter, Figures 10.9 and 10.10 illustrate accessing and viewing the state of all VMs on a group of hosts to demonstrate information discovery. The system/power state of a VM is represented by an integer value, discussed and shown in Table 9.5 in Chapter 9. You may not need to care much about this table, because the HyperV.PS1 library understands the friendly names of these states. The codes and decodes are contained in the $VMState global variable, found near the beginning of the library. Calling Get-VMState shows the state of all VMs on the local host (see Figure 10.19):

```
Get-VMState
```

FIGURE 10.19
Get-VMState

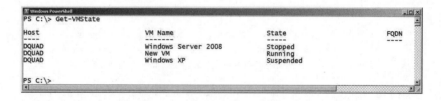

To access the state of a single VM, use the Get-VMState function and specify the friendly name of the VM (see Figure 10.20):

```
Get-VMState "New VM"
```

FIGURE 10.20
Get-VMState for
one VM

NOTE   Depending on the version of Get-VMState you run, you'll see an error if a paused VM is found. A fix for this and other enhancements should be in the latest version of the library. Check www.codeplex.com/psHyperV periodically to discover updates.

Changing the state of a VM is just as simple as retrieving it. Table 10.3 shows state-management functions.

TABLE 10.3   HyperV.PS1 State-Management Functions

FUNCTION NAME	DESCRIPTION
Get-State	Show the state of VMs
Start-VM	Turn on/resume VMs
Stop-VM	Turn off VMs
Suspend-VM	Suspend VMs (pause)
Shutdown-VM	Shut down VMs via ICs
Set-VMState	Specify the desired VM state

You use Start-VM, Stop-VM, Suspend-VM, and Shutdown-VM the same way. To call each of these functions, specify the name of the target VM:

```
Start-VM "New VM"
```

As with many functions in the library, you may also specify a remote physical host:

```
Start-VM "New VM" -server HyperNode1
```

It's important to know the state a VM is in before you make a change request. For example, you can't transition from a saved (suspended) state to paused state. If a VM is already running, a request to start it will fail (see Figure 10.21).

FIGURE 10.21
Trying to start a running VM

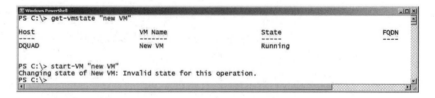

You can change the state of all VMs on a host at once. For example, it could be valuable to put all VMs on a given host into a saved state for backup or while you perform maintenance on the physical system. Using an asterisk instead of the individual VM name with Suspend-VM saves the state of all running or paused VMs (see Figure 10.22):

```
suspend-vm *
```

FIGURE 10.22
Suspending all running VMs

```
Windows PowerShell
PS C:\> get-vmstate

Host                    VM Name                 State                   FQDN
----                    -------                 -----                   ----
DQUAD                   Windows Server 2008     Suspended
DQUAD                   New VM                  Running
DQUAD                   Windows XP              Running                 XPVM


PS C:\> suspend-vm *
Changing state of Windows Server 2008: Invalid state for this operation.
Changing state of New VM: Job Started.
Changing state of Windows XP: Job Started.
\\DQUAD\root\virtualization:Msvm_ConcreteJob.InstanceID="5812D1B4-3A53-4720-A089-E9FA5300DBD8"
\\DQUAD\root\virtualization:Msvm_ConcreteJob.InstanceID="0BF33ED8-045D-49F0-B05B-BE01B1053859"
PS C:\>
```

Understanding the role of ICs is also important. They allow for a coordinated shutdown of a VM. You can facilitate an orderly power-down a VM with installed ICs by using Shutdown-VM (see Figure 10.23):

```
shutdown-VM "Windows XP"
```

FIGURE 10.23

Shutting down a VM with ICs

```
Windows PowerShell
PS C:\> shutdown-VM "Windows XP"
Shutdown of 'Windows XP ' started.
PS C:\> _
```

A VM without installed, running ICs can't take advantage of shutdown integration. An unenlightened VM must be shut down from within the VM or via another means (perhaps simply turned off). Currently, only supported versions of Windows with installed ICs support integrated shutdown. For the example in Figure 10.24, New-VM is a VM with no operating system (or ICs) installed:

```
shutdown-VM "New VM"
```

FIGURE 10.24

Failed shutdown request

```
Windows PowerShell
PS C:\> shutdown-VM "New VM"
Attempt to shutdown 'New VM' failed with code 32768.
PS C:\> _
```

You can't shut down VMs with ICs if the ICs aren't available. For example, if VMs are in a saved (suspended) state, the ICs are unavailable (see Figure 10.25).

FIGURE 10.25

Failed shutdown— all VMs are suspended

```
Windows PowerShell
PS C:\> shutdown-vm *
Could not get shutdown component for 'Windows Server 2008'.
Could not get shutdown component for 'New VM'.
Could not get shutdown component for 'Windows XP'.
PS C:\>
```

MANAGING VHDS

The common container for storing a VM-accessible disk is the VHD file. You can create, change, test, and compact these disks while they aren't in use by a VM. VHD management functions are shown in Table 10.4.

TABLE 10.4   HyperV.PS1 Storage-Management Functions

FUNCTION NAME	DESCRIPTION
New-VHD	Create a new VHD file
Compact-VHD	Show the state of VMs
Convert-VHD	Change to/from fixed or dynamic; create new VHD
Expand-VHD	Increase the size of a VHD
Get-VHDInfo	Retrieve information about a VHD
Merge-VHD	Merge a child with a parent disk (untested at time of writing)
Mount-VHD	Mount a VHD on a host for access
Unmount-VHD	Unmount a VHD from a host
Test-VHD	Validate the integrity of a VHD file

You learned how to create a new VHD file using New-VHD earlier in the chapter as part of VM provisioning. As you're likely aware, you can create VHD files with either a static (fixed) or dynamic size; dynamic is the default. To create a new VHD file, you must supply a name and the desired size (see Figure 10.26):

```
new-vhd tiny 2gb
```

FIGURE 10.26
New-VHD

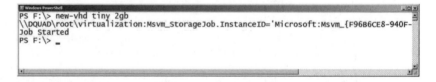

You may notice that the call to New-VHD spawns a job that runs in the background. Some Hyper-V administrative tasks (like VHD creation) can take a long time. In the case of New-VHD, you can opt to have your script wait for the task to complete by using the -wait parameter:

```
New-VHD "big" 20GB -fixed -wait
```

It can take a long time to create a fixed-size VHD file (or perform other VHD-related maintenance tasks). You can save the job ID information to a variable and periodically check the status of the WMI job by using the included Test-WMIJob function (see Figure 10.27):

```
$DiskJob = new-vhd Big 20gb -fixed
Test-WMIJob $Diskjob
```

FIGURE 10.27
Test-WMIJob

```
Windows PowerShell
PS F:\> $DiskJob = new-vhd Big 20gb -fixed
Job Started
PS F:\> Test-WMIjob $Diskjob
Job: Running 3%
OK
PS F:\> Test-WMIjob $Diskjob
Job: Running 47%
OK
PS F:\> Test-WMIjob $Diskjob
Job: Completed
OK
PS F:\>
```

Get-VHDInfo can provide basic information about a VHD file, including the actual file size, the maximum internal size, the type, and whether it's in use at a given time (see Figure 10.28):

```
get-vhdinfo f:\VHds\big.vhd
```

FIGURE 10.28
Get-VHDInfo
retrieves basic
information.

```
Windows PowerShell
PS F:\> get-vhdinfo f:\VHds\big.vhd


Path            : f:\VHds\big.vhd
FileSize        : 21474836992
InSavedState    : FALSE
InUse           : FALSE
MaxInternalSize : 21474836480
ParentPath      :
Type            : 2


PS F:\>
```

Monitoring storage used by VHDs can be a critical management function, particularly when you're using dynamic VHDs. Unexpected VHD growth on a shared physical disk can lead to performance issues for all VMs homed there. You can create a tiny and useful VHD storage report by stringing together the default VHD path and additional formatting options (see Figure 10.29):

```
dir ((get-VHDDefaultPath) + "\*.vhd") |
get-vhdinfo |
format-table path, filesize,MaxInternalSize -auto
```

FIGURE 10.29
VHD size report

```
Windows PowerShell                                                    _ □ x
PS F:\> dir ((get-VHDDefaultPath) + "\*.vhd") | get-vhdinfo |

Path                                      FileSize    MaxInternalSize
----                                      --------    ---------------
F:\VHDs\Big.vhd                           21474836992 21474836480
F:\VHDs\tiny.vhd                          18432       2147483648
F:\VHDs\Windows Server 2008.vhd           10584159232 136365211648


PS F:\>
```

It's useful to access the contents of a VHD file from the virtualization host as if it were a locally attached drive. Being able to add files to or remove files from a VHD without starting a VM can save you time and can facilitate offline maintenance. You can use Mount-VHD and UnMount-VHD to simplify the mounting of local VHD files (see Figure 10.30):

```
Mount-VHD "f:\VHDs\Windows Server 2008.vhd"
```

FIGURE 10.30
Mount-VHD

```
Windows PowerShell                                                    _ □ x
PS F:\> Mount-VHD "f:\VHDs\Windows Server 2008.vhd"
Disk mount: Completed
D:
Disk ID... 2
PS F:\>
```

The function returns the disk ID rather than a drive letter. Typically, the operating system assigns a drive letter, but not every VHD contains a volume that can be mounted and assigned a drive letter. For example, consider the 20GB fixed-size big.vhd created earlier. The VHD wasn't formatted as part of the creation process (it hadn't yet been exposed to an operating system installation process). After mounting, you can use the disk ID to locate the VHD on the host either in the Computer Management console (see Figure 10.31) or using diskpart (see Figure 10.32). You can then perform additional storage tasks from the host.

Compact-VHD, Convert-VHD, Expand-VHD, Test-VHD, and Merge-VHD all help you alter your VHDs in ways consistent with their names. For more information about how to use them, you can review the examples contained in HyperV.PS1.

Maintaining Virtual Systems

Your virtual systems depend on you to keep them properly maintained. Automating required configuration changes, installing software updates, and sometimes rolling back changes are all tasks necessary to keep physical systems and VMs running efficiently.

FIGURE 10.31
Disk management

FIGURE 10.32
Diskpart get disk

CONFIGURATION CHANGES

Business and technical pressures may require you to alter the configurations of existing VMs. Perhaps the applications on a given VM require more RAM or CPU resources. Maybe a physical NIC is experiencing a high network load and some VM traffic must be offloaded to a new interface. Earlier in the chapter, we reviewed functions for automating configuration changes for VMs. Table 10.5 lists functions commonly used from HyperV.PS1 to define or alter the configuration of a VM.

TABLE 10.5   HyperV.PS1 VM Configuration Management Functions

FUNCTION NAME	DESCRIPTION
Add-VMDISK	Add a disk (VHD or ISO) to a defined drive
Add-VMDRIVE	Add a drive to a defined controller
Add-VMFloppyDisk	Add a floppy disk
Add-VMNewHardDisk	Create a new VHD and attach it to a VM
Add-VMNIC	Add a NIC to a VM
Add-VMSCSIController	Add a synthetic SCSI controller
New-VHD	Create a new VHD file
New-VM	Create a new VM
New-VMSwitchPort	Create a new virtual switch port
Set-VM	Set the BIOS boot order and startup/shutdown actions
Set-VMCPUCount	Set the CPU count (1–4)
Set-VMDisk	Change the configuration of an existing disk
Set-VMMemory	Set the amount of RAM
Set-VMNICAddress	Set the MAC address for a virtual NIC
Set-VMNICConnection	Change the config (switch) for an existing NIC

PATCHING

You can update the software components of a running VM the same way you do for a physical system. You can also patch VMs while they're offline using the Offline Virtual Machine Servicing Tool, discussed briefly in Chapter 4, "Virtualization Best Practices." Mount-VHD can be used to access the disk for offline VMs and prestage software for later installation.

SNAPSHOTS

Hyper-V can create point-in-time VM snapshots. You can use retained snapshot information to revert a VM to a known state in the past. Table 10.6 lists the snapshot-related functions found in HyperV.PS1.

TABLE 10.6 HyperV.PS1 Snapshot-Management Functions

FUNCTION NAME	DESCRIPTION
Apply-VMSnapshot	Revert to a previous snapshot
Choose-VMSnapshot	Select a snapshot
Get-VMSnapshot	Access VM snapshot information
Get-VMSnapshotTree	Access VM snapshot information and show it as a tree
New-VMSnapshot	Create a new snapshot
Remove-VMSnapshot	Delete a snapshot
Rename-VMsnapshot	Change the name of an existing snapshot
Update-VMSnapshot	Create a new snapshot using an existing name

NOTE Snapshots aren't backups. You should rarely consider them for use in production. They can provide huge value for development testing purposes (to roll back changes), but they aren't suitable for all situations.

Creating a snapshot is a straightforward process of calling New-VMSnaphot and specifying or passing the target VMs to be snapped (see Figure 10.33):

```
new-vmsnapshot "SLES 10" -wait
```

FIGURE 10.33
New snapshot

```
PS C:\> new-vmsnapshot "SLES 10" -wait
Snapshoting VM 'SLES 10': Job Started
Job: Completed

PS C:\> _
```

A more useful function for creating new snapshots may be Update-VMSnapshot. This function creates a new snapshot and alters the displayed name to something of your choosing (see Figure 10.34):

```
Update-VMSnapshot "SLES 10" "Before Scary Update"
```

FIGURE 10.34
New snapshot with
specified name

```
PS C:\> Update-VMSnapshot "SLES 10" "Before Scary Update"
Snapshoting VM 'SLES 10': Job Started
Job: Completed

Renaming snapshot 'SLES 10 - (12/8/2008 - 2:07:01 PM)' to 'Before Scary
OK
PS C:\>
```

Reverting and applying snapshots is also simplified with the library when you use Choose-VMSnapshot in conjunction with Apply-VMSnapshot (see Figure 10.35):

```
choose-vmsnapshot "SLES 10" | Apply-VMSnapshot
```

FIGURE 10.35
Reverting and
applying snapshots

```
Administrator: Command Prompt - powershell                           _|□|x|
PS C:\> choose-vmsnapshot "SLES 10" | Apply-vmsnapshot
0     +Before Update
1     |--Before Scary Update
Which one ?: 1
OK
PS C:\>
PS C:\> _
```

Managing Access

Controlling access to VMs is an important task for IT managers. When you encapsulate an entire system into a single file, you run into new security challenges. Poorly secured network links to a physical host or shaky backup processes can quickly bypass locked data-center doors. If you have bad security practices, entire virtual systems can be pilfered without detection.

Virtualization enables a new mechanism for system access: remote desktop interaction. You can remotely view and interact with the console of a VM. Before virtualization, server consoles could be secured in a datacenter or computer room unless remote-access tools (IP-based Keyboard/Video/Mouse (KVM) or lights-out/remote console hardware) were employed. Virtualization can create a security opportunity for these formerly inaccessible system consoles.

Securing access to VM consoles is just as important as other means of securing virtual systems. Virtual hosting of desktops also requires careful access-control management for VMs. Chapter 5, "Hyper-V Security," discusses access management for individual VMs. After you set up proper security for user or administrative access, you can start remote display sessions to a particular VM by calling VMConnect.exe. The VMConnect client is typically found in C:\Program Files\Hyper-V, and it has its own set of command-line options, which are shown in Figure 10.36.

FIGURE 10.36
VMConnect
parameters

You can create a remote access session without calling VMConnect.exe directly by using the New-VMConnectSession function.

Migration

In many situations, you need to migrate a VM from one physical server to another. Hardware failures, capacity limitations, and maintenance are all reasons to relocate a VM. You can automate the move of a VM between systems in a number of ways. Common methods include importing/exporting (discussed in Chapter 6), using failover clustering (covered in Chapter 8), performing a simple file copy, or undertaking a virtual to virtual (V2V) migration. SCVMM 2008 supports the automation of VM migration better than any other solution; we'll cover it in Chapter 11.

Simple File Copy

VM information lives in files. Why not copy or move the files that define a VM from one host to another? Finding all the necessary files and ensuring they're properly migrated can be a complicated task. Guaranteeing the VM is in a movable state (off or saved) is important, as is handling host-specific dependencies such as the migration of virtual network resources and security settings.

Copying all the files from one host to another doesn't work without careful coordination. The export and import capabilities exposed through the Hyper-V Manager handle these checks fairly well, and they're a supported way to migrate VMs. SCVMM also has a supported move process as well as V2V capability.

Still, you may find want to move a VM using an entirely unsupported copy process. For more information about how to do this, review the `diskshadow` backup and recovery process detailed in Chapter 7, "Backup and Recovery." Using `xcopy` parameters can address the specifics of file security issues, but you're still likely to run into issues.

Export/Import

Exporting a VM from one host and importing it on another is perhaps the simplest and cleanest migration method to automate without SCVMM. Exporting requires that a VM be either off or in a saved state. `HyperV.PS1` supports the exporting and importing of VMs by using the `Export-VM` and `Import-VM` functions. Calling `Export-VM` requires a reference to the VM to be exported as well as the export path, with optional parameters that include the name of the physical server and the ability to wait for the process to complete (see Figure 10.37):

```
export-VM "New VM" c:\exports -server localhost -wait
```

FIGURE 10.37
Export-VM

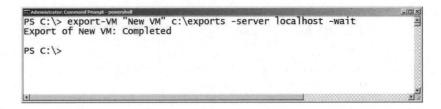

Import-VM only requires the path to the exported VM as a parameter, with optional parameters similar to those of `Export-VM`:

```
import-VM . -wait
```

NOTE Automating export and import can be tricky, and the functions in HyperV.PS1 may not work for you in every instance. Exporting over a network path requires proper security. Import-VM is very picky about the path specified and may work best if you execute it while in the export destination directory, as shown in Figure 10.38.

FIGURE 10.38
Import-VM

SCVMM's ability to move VMs between hosts masks you from the storage and security dependency of Hyper-V export and is a more suitable approach for automate migrations in many environments.

Failover Clustering

Failover clustering facilitates the migration of VMs from one physical host to another with limited down time, but it requires preconfiguration. Hyper-V clusters are presented in Chapter 8, "High Availability." Hyper-V failover clustering (Quick Migration and in the future Live Migration) requires identically configured physical hosts as well as shared storage. You typically automate cluster-management tasks—creation, configuration, and workload migration—using cluster.exe. Clustering tasks that can be performed using the command-line tool can also be completed with the failover-clustering WMI provider (root\MSCluster). SCVMM provides cluster-management capabilities for Hyper-V that you can automate using its set of Windows PowerShell cmdlets.

Virtual to Virtual Migration

Virtual to virtual (V2V) migrations are similar to physical to virtual (P2V) migrations; they're discussed in Chapter 6, "Virtual Machine Migration." Automating V2V migrations is a tricky process and is largely unnecessary if you're moving a VM from one host to another. You can also automate V2V migrations with SCVMM cmdlets.

Backup and Recovery

In Chapter 7, we covered backup and recovery without the use of enterprise tools. System Center Data Protection Manager (DPM) is the best option for enterprise-class backup with Hyper-V; that process is discussed in Chapter 12.

Creating and executing diskshadow script-based backups is simplified using the Get-VMBackupScript (another gift from James O'Neill found in HyperV.PS1). Calling the function generates a diskshadow script similar to the one used in Chapter 7. This script uses the intelligence of other functions in the library to detect the location of VM-related files and back them up. The process created here is elegant, but it may be difficult to follow and a challenge to use and debug in production. You may prefer to use DPM or the processes outlined in Chapter 7.

Collecting and Monitoring Data

Monitoring how your virtual environment performs is key to ensuring smooth operation. You've seen how to locate virtual hosts, enumerate their child VMs, and access configuration information. Visibility into the health and performance of each VM is also important.

Enterprise tools like those found in the Microsoft System Center family are the best solution for collecting, analyzing, and monitoring health and performance. System Center Operations Manager (SCOM), which can be connected to SCVMM, can serve as a repository for historical performance data for your entire Microsoft-centric computing environment. It is challenging to do comprehensive monitoring if you don't have access to System Center tools.

Viewing the Desktop

Before you go too far down the path of data collection, you have to please corporate management. Data centers and operations rooms often have banks of monitors filled with color images including graphs, charts, maps, and system consoles. A dirty little secret of many of these rooms is that certain screens are simply for show—some of the big, blinky displays exist only to create the appearance of a well-monitored environment.

Another truth of large data centers is that operators (personnel who work regularly in the computer room) often need to see what is on the screen of a particular system. It's also a reality that these employees aren't always trusted to interact with these same systems for regulatory reasons or by management mandate.

The virtualization provider allows you to request a JPEG format picture of a VM's desktop. You can capture and display these images in any number of ways, and they can be useful to operators and administrators for auditing/monitoring purposes (or handy to show on a large display). The Get-VMJPEG function creates a JPEG file with a name based on the VM's display (element) name and writes it to the current directory:

```
Get-VM | Get-VMJPEG
```

You can post the generated image files to a Website, save them into SharePoint, or easily view them using Windows Explorer. Regularly capturing an image of the desktop can be useful for troubleshooting or compliance purposes.

Testing for Service

Ping is often the first monitoring tool most administrators use to check the health of a system. It's not a comprehensive test, but it can show that a particular system's TCP/IP stack is accessible under normal circumstances, as well as point out environmental issues on a network (name resolution, routing, firewall settings, or latency challenges). The Ping-VM function makes it convenient to ping configured VMs (see Figure 10.39):

```
get-vm | ping-VM |format-table VMName, FullyQualifiedDomainName, Status -auto
```

FIGURE 10.39
Ping-VM

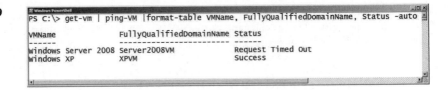

TIP Firewall status for contemporary versions of Microsoft Windows may not allow a response from ping, so this function may not provide much value in a secure environment.

You can also use Test-VMHeartbeat and Get-VMKVP to verify that a VM is running and functioning (Get-VMKVP was discussed earlier in the chapter). You can think of Test-VMHeartbeat as a sort of a ping to the ICs running in a VM. If the heartbeat component included in the ICs is functioning, the test is successful. James has included a timeout parameter for managing the startup sequence of VMs. Using Test-VMHeartbeat, you can stagger an environment's power-up until key network services are ready:

```
start-vm "TestDC"
Test-vmheartBeat "TestDC" -Timeout 300
start-vm "TestExchange"
```

TIP Staggering/delaying the startup of a VM is such a common need that James recently added more options to the Start-VM function. You can alternately use Start-VM "Test-DC" - wait -Heartbeat 300 to achieve the same result.

Accessing Processor Performance Data

You may have noticed that the memory used by VMs is reflected on the Windows Task Manager Performance tab. Every time you start a VM, the amount of memory used by the physical system increases, which is reflected by the Windows Task Manager. This isn't true for processor (CPU) utilization: The CPU load of child VMs isn't reflected in the Windows Task Manager of the host/parent. Figure 10.40 shows the CPU and Memory usage history of a quad-core system.

FIGURE 10.40
Host task manager:
low load

The Task Manager reflects relatively low CPU usage. But the system is the host for a two-processor Server 2003 VM running at over 90% processor load (Figure 10.41 is the Task Manager from within the VM).

FIGURE 10.41
VM: high CPU load

You could query each individual VM remotely to access and retrieve the CPU load, but that wouldn't give you an accurate view of the actual load on the host. It would also require network access to the VM as well as an appropriate level of security.

You can access information about the performance of individual VM virtual processors through the parent using the virtualization provider and the MSVM_Processor class, as reflected by the WMI query in Figure 10.42:

```
GWMI –Class MSVM_Processor –Namespace root\virtualization |
    ft SystemName,LoadPercentage -auto
```

FIGURE 10.42
CPU load-
percentage query

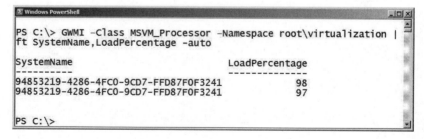

The query shows the CPU load percentage and the unfriendly name of the associated VM. HyperV.PS1 doesn't (at this time) include any processor performance-related functions.

NOTE James has been working on a Get-VMProcessor function that includes processor performance information. Be on the lookout for this new function in an update to the library.

Following is a sample Windows PowerShell function that collects the virtual processor information from a local host and ties in the VM name:

```
function List-VMCPULoad
{Param ($server=".")
   $Procs= GWMI -computerName $server -Namespace ↵
root\virtualization -Class MSVM_Processor
   foreach ($Proc in $Procs) {
      GWMI -computerName $server -Namespace ↵
root\virtualization -Query ↵
"Select * From MSVM_ComputerSystem Where Name = '$($Proc.SystemName)'" |
      add-member -passthru noteproperty "Load%" $Proc.LoadPercentage |
      add-member -passthru noteproperty "CPUID" $Proc.deviceid.split("\")[-1]
   }
}

list-vmcpuload | ft elementname, CPUID, Load% -auto
```

This function gives you a list of all individual running virtual processors on a system, showing each VM name. This may not be entirely useful in developing a clear picture of processor performance, because other processes on the physical host (including other VMs) can reduce the available compute cycles. This interference can artificially reduce the LoadPercentage retrieved from MSVM_Proccessor. For example, both the VMs listed in Figure 10.43 are using about as much CPU as they're allowed (the six virtual cores are running on a host with only four cores). The individual LoadPercentage for each virtual CPU can appear to be low (55% for one) due to the sharing of resources. The VMs themselves believe they're running at full steam, but LoadPercentage doesn't clearly reflect this. Adding an additional four-core VM under extreme CPU load makes this point more clearly, as shown in Figure 10.44.

FIGURE 10.43
Nice CPU load percentage query

```
Windows PowerShell
PS C:\> list-vmcpuload | ft elementname, CPUID, LoadPercentage -auto

elementname             CPUID LoadPercentage
-----------             ----- --------------
Windows Server 2008 0                     85
Windows Server 2008 1                     55
Windows Server 2008 2                     58
Windows Server 2008 3                     55
Windows XP              0                  61
Windows XP              1                  55


PS C:\>
```

With 10 virtual cores all taxed and competing for the power of the 4 physical cores (along with processes on the parent partition), the LoadPercentage is reduced. Looking solely at the LoadPercentage of a single VM can mislead you into believing that a VM isn't low on processing power. To get the actual utilization of each physical processor, it's recommended that you don't use the virtualization provider but instead use the tried-and-true Common Information Model (CIM) version 2.

FIGURE 10.44

More load, lower percentage

```
Windows PowerShell                                                    _ □ ×
PS C:\> list-vmcpuload | ft elementname, CPUID, Loa

elementname                        CPUID LoadPercentage
-----------                        ----- --------------
Windows Server 2008                0                 47
Windows Server 2008                1                 32
Windows Server 2008                2                 44
Windows Server 2008                3                 38
Windows Server 2008 #2             0                 46
Windows Server 2008 #2             1                 37
Windows Server 2008 #2             2                 43
Windows Server 2008 #2             3                 33
Windows XP                         0                 31
Windows XP                         1                 33
```

TIP Several good performance resources describe how to access counters and troubleshoot performance issues for Hyper-V, including "Measuring Performance on Hyper-V" (http://msdn .microsoft.com/en-us/library/cc768535.aspx) and an "All Topics Performance" post titled "How to Get Processor Utilization for Hyper-V via WMI" (http://blogs.msdn.com/tvoellm/ archive/2008/07/14/how-to-get-processor-utilization-for-hyper-v-via-wmi.aspx). They're both informative and can help you create a comprehensive and accurate view of CPU utilization. They also have too much math and too many formulas for day-to-day use.

Accessing the WMI CIMv2 class Win32_PerfRawData_HVStats_HyperVHypervisorLogicalProcessor is the recommended approach, but the formulas to derive processor utilization are a hassle. You can approximate the overall utilization by adding together the loadPercentage values from each virtual processor and dividing the total by the number of physical cores. The following function creates a useful CPU utilization report with color coding to connote high CPU load on individual virtual CPUs, as well as on the host system (see Figure 10.45):

```
function Report-VMCPU
{Param ($server=".")
   $LoadSum = 0
   $PCores = 0
   $VProcs= GWMI -computerName $server –Namespace ↵
root\virtualization -Class MSVM_Processor
   write-host "`n                                CPU  Load"
   write-host "VM Name                           #    %"
   write-host "----------------------------------- ---- -----"
   foreach ($VProc in $VProcs) {
      $VM = GWMI -computerName $server -Namespace ↵
root\virtualization -Query ↵
"Select * From MSVM_ComputerSystem Where Name = '$($VProc.SystemName)'"
      $VMname = $VM.Elementname.PadRight(39," ")
      $VMCPU  = $VProc.deviceid.split("\")[-1]
      $VMCPULOAD = $VProc.LoadPercentage
      Write-Host "$VMname $VMCPU    "  -nonewline
      if ($VMCPULOAD -lt 30) {
```

```
      write-host $VMCPULOAD -backgroundcolor green
   }
   elseif ($VMCPULOAD -gt 80) {
      write-host $VMCPULOAD -backgroundcolor red
   }
   else {write-host $VMCPULOAD}
   $LoadSum = $LoadSum + $VMCPULOAD
}
$PProcs= GWMI -computerName $server –Namespace ↵
root\CIMV2 -Class Win32_Processor
   foreach ($PProc in $PProcs) {
      $PCores = $PCores + $PProc.NumberOfCores }
   $VLoad =  $LoadSum / $PCores
   write-host "`n-----------------------------------------------"
   Write-Host "Physical Host Virtual CPU Perf Summary" -nonewline
   if($Server -ne ".") {
      write-host " for $Server"} else {write-host " "}
   Write-Host "`n       Total Physical Cores: " $PCores
   Write-Host "Approx. Virt. CPU Utilization: " -nonewline
   if ($VLoad -lt 30) {write-host $VLoad -backgroundcolor green}
   elseif ($VLoad -gt 80) {write-host $VLoad -backgroundcolor red}
   else {write-host $VLoad}
   write-host "-------------------------------------------`n"
}
```

FIGURE 10.45
Better CPU load report

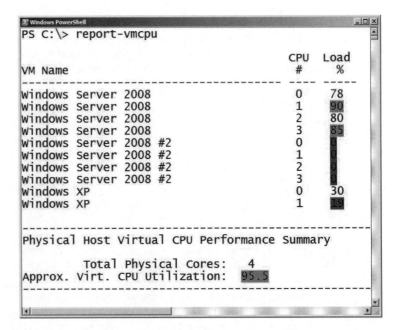

The code may not reflect the acme of Windows PowerShell or mathematics, but you can use the output to clearly show a high CPU load condition.

NOTE MSVM_Processor also includes LoadPercentageHistory, which is an array of recent measurements of LoadHistory.

Performance Monitoring and PowerGadgets

The previous code sample produces some usable and ugly output. SoftwareFX sells a great set of inexpensive graphical tools that connect right into PowerShell, called PowerGadgets. You can use PowerGadgets to quickly and easily create interactive tools using gauges, charts, graphs, and maps; you can then use these tools with Windows PowerShell to monitor and manage Hyper-V. Gadgets you create can even be added to the Vista Sidebar. You can download an evaluation copy of PowerGadgets from the SoftwareFX Website at http://www.softwarefx.com/.

Summary

The WMI provider combined with Windows PowerShell or another scripting language can help you automate virtually any Hyper-V administrative task. Building on the work and insight of others can save you time. The HyperV.PS1 library maintained in www.codeplex.com is a useful resource. Learning basic tricks in Windows PowerShell can magnify your capabilities and the value of your Hyper-V environment.

Chapter 11

Systems Center Virtual Machine Manager 2008

Virtualization brings new flexibilities to the IT landscape, such as rapid deployment of systems, server migration, and the ability to deploy systems without regard to the physical server environment.

These virtualization flexibilities have spawned a new area of software dedicated to managing the virtualization environment. *Virtualization management* software is geared completely toward managing the virtualization platform, adding capabilities to a very flexible virtualization environment.

System Center Virtual Machine Manager (SCVMM) 2008 focuses on bridging the gap between physical systems management, virtualization management, and application knowledge. The ability to bring application knowledge into the virtualization-management space marries the flexibility of virtualization with the applications running in the virtual machines.

In this chapter, we focus on equipping you with the necessary information to get an SCVMM 2008 deployment going. Although SCVMM 2008 manages various virtualization platforms, the focus of this chapter is specifically on the Hyper-V environment. Detailed technical information about using SCVMM 2008 to manage other virtualization platforms is covered in the Sybex book *Mastering Virtual Machine Manager 2008*.

In this chapter, we cover the following topics:

◆ System Center suite overview

◆ SCVMM 2008 architecture

◆ Planning an SCVMM 2008 deployment

◆ Installing SCVMM 2008

◆ Provisioning virtual machines

◆ Integrating Operations Manager 2007 and SCVMM 2008

System Center Suite Overview

The System Center suite is a cohesive suite of products, each targeting specific systems-management functionality, directed at the IT lifecycle management. It's important to place the SCVMM 2008 functionality in the context of the broader System Center suite (see Figure 11.1).

FIGURE 11.1
Functionality within the System Center product family

IT management with System Center

Microsoft System Center Data Protection Manager
- Live host-level virtual machine backup
- In guest consistency
- Rapid recovery

Microsoft System Center Virtual Machine Manager
- Virtual machine management
- Server consolidation and resource utilization optimization
- Conversions: P2V and V2V

Microsoft System Center Operations Manager 2007
- End-to-end service management
- Server and application health management and monitoring
- Performance reporting and analysis

Microsoft System Center Configuration Manager
- Patch management and deployment
- Operating system and application configuration management
- Software upgrades

Four main software components of the System Center family of products offer management capabilities to the physical and virtual infrastructure. As a virtualization professional, you need to understand the capabilities of each component and how each applies to managing Microsoft and non-Microsoft virtualization platforms.

Systems Center Virtual Machine Manager 2008

SCVMM lets you perform heterogeneous Hypervisor management by managing Virtual Server 2005 R2 SP1, Hyper V, and ESX hypervisors. The plan of record for SCVMM is to continue to expand to manage other popular virtualization platforms in future releases. SCVMM provides you all the functionality for managing virtualization hosts and guests as well as the framework for enhancing virtualization management with application-level knowledge.

You can integrate with Systems Center Operations Manager (SCOM) 2007 through the Performance and Resource Optimization (PRO) functionality. PRO is a feature of SCVMM 2008 that enables dynamic management of virtualized infrastructure. Additional functionality in SCVMM includes:

- V2V and P2V conversions
- Self-service portal that allows end users to perform VM creation and delegation
- Delegated administration
- Library functionality
- Deep PowerShell integration
- Quick migration and VMotion support
- Storage Area Network (SAN) and N_Port ID Virtualization (NPIV) integration
- Intelligent placement of virtual machines in the managed environment
- Host-capacity management

Systems Center Operations Manager 2007

SCOM provides a health/service model: a real-time alerting, infrastructure-monitoring, and reporting environment that lets you manage physical and virtual environments as well as Microsoft and non-Microsoft platforms. SCOM provides the following functionality:

End-to-end monitoring   SCOM lets you look at the health of all virtualization components. For example, the Microsoft virtualization environment comprises the following components: Hyper-V, Quick Migration clusters, SCVMM components, and Systems Center DPM (DPM) components for host and virtual machine (VM) recovery. All of these components are important to the health of a Microsoft virtualization infrastructure. SCOM provides management packs, health models, alerts, and reports for each of these components.

Comprehensive views of health states   SCOM includes a health model in the management pack for each managed component. Health models include monitors to report on the health of all the components of the system. For example, the SCVMM management pack includes a model that looks at the health of the SCVMM components including the SCVMM server, the SQL database, the self-service portal, and the SCVMM agent. When one component isn't healthy, it affects the health of the entire service.

Rapid response to events for managed systems   You can respond to error conditions detected by managed components, or you can set up automated actions/tasks in the management pack.

Application-specific management packs   Each management pack is specific to a managed application. The management pack provides specific knowledge about the errors and conditions that determine the health of the application. In addition, the management pack also includes tasks, and reports on an application-by-application basis.

Automated tasks per application   Each management pack includes tasks that are specific to an application. For instance, you can start or stop services specific to each application.

Comprehensive automated reporting infrastructure   The reporting infrastructure built on top of SQL Reporting Services provides the infrastructure for reporting. Each managed component comes with a set of reports in the management pack that reports on health, availability, and other related items specific to the service.

Consider the following example. Suppose you've developed a custom line-of-business applications. Specific error conditions, dependencies between application components, and actions to take to maintain application health are largely stored in your brain. A management pack captures your knowledge in a health model stored in the management pack. As a result, that knowledge can be added to the SCOM infrastructure, and the applications can be detected on servers running in the environment. After the applications are detected, they can be managed immediately with the knowledge captured in the management pack.

The end goal is to bridge application alerting and monitoring into the virtualization management framework. SCVMM and SCOM provide the PRO system connector to share information about managed VMs and applications. This enables VMs that have SCOM management packs and PRO packs installed to exchange information with SCVMM 2008.

System Center Data Protection Manager 2007 SP1

DPM is a comprehensive disk-to-disk and disk-to-tape data-protection solution. It adds backup, recovery, and disaster-recovery functionality for key applications: Hyper V, Virtual Server, Exchange, SQL Server, and SharePoint.

DPM uses the Volume Shadow Services (VSS) infrastructure in Windows Server and application-specific VSS writers to take continuous snapshots of data. DPM combined with Hyper-V protects VM and configuration data and, when combined with a DPM agent in the VM, gives you the ability to do granular data recovery for support applications. With DPM-to-DPM server replication of protected applications, you can add disaster recovery of protected VMs.

You now have the flexibility to configure a DPM server in data center A to protect VMs and to configure another DPM server in data center B. You can then use the DPM replication functionality, which you can schedule, throttle, and configure to work over specific network interfaces. You can replicate protected content between data centers so that in the event of data center failure, you can recover DPM-protected content on the server in the surviving data center. Chapter 13, "System Center Operations Manager," provides more information about how DPM works with Hyper-V.

DPM provides the following functionality:

Disk-based protection and recovery DPM protects data by using storage to provide multiple recovery points for critical applications. For instance, VMs can have multiple recovery points that represent different days, are stored on disk, and can be recovered at any time.

Command-line driven via PowerShell All DPM actions in the user interface can be driven by the DPM PowerShell with a set of cmdlets offering flexibility to create event-driven recovery actions.

Tape-based backup and archival solution Some industry-compliance laws require long-term storage of sensitive data. In such cases, DPM can integrate directly with hardware tape-backup solutions.

Encrypted tape backup While protecting sensitive data to tape, DPM can also provide protect the content by using encryption.

Integration with leading tape solutions Integration with tape hardware solutions lets you move DPM-protected data directly from disk to tape.

Bare-metal disaster recovery Using the VSS services and system-state backup, DPM can recover the system configuration and data of protected applications to a bare-metal server.

Business continuity and continuous data protection DPM allows backups at 15-minute intervals, providing continuous data protection. Combine that functionality with the ability to replicate protected DPM data from one DPM server to another, and you have the components needed to provide a business continuity solution. See Chapter 13 for details of this solution.

System Center Configuration Manager 2007

Systems Center Configuration Manager (SCCM) provides a comprehensive solution for change and configuration management. It functions not only as a delivery infrastructure for software updates of all types but also as a comprehensive reporting solution. SCCM 2007 with

SCVMM 2008 provides a solution for ensuring that VMs stored in the SCVMM library can be brought online, scanned for needed patches, and placed back in the library in a completely automated fashion. You can find the VM offline servicing solution at the following website: `http://www.microsoft.com/downloads/details.aspx?FamilyId=8408ECF5-7AFE-47EC-A697-EB433027DF73&displaylang=en`.

SCCM 2007 provides the following functionality:

Operating system deployment   SCCM provides the ability to deploy the operating system to bare-metal machines without an operating system. This includes desktop and server operating systems.

Software application deployment   You can deploy custom business applications and off-the-shelf applications to targeted systems in the enterprise.

Deployment of software security updates   SCCM provides the infrastructure for reporting and targeting specific security updates to SCCM-managed systems. This includes reporting on systems that are missing updates and systems that have specific updates.

Assessment of variations from desired configuration   SCCM provides a desired-configuration management tool, which lets you base-line systems and report on configuration changes from the base configuration.

Hardware and software inventory   How often would you like to know the hardware configuration and applications deployed throughout the enterprise? SCCM provides reports on specific configurations' hardware and software. In addition, SCCM can differentiate between virtual and physical machines so you can generate inventory reports by VM.

Offline VM update integration with SCVMM 2008   Offline VMs that are stored in the SCVMM library can be brought online, scanned, patched, and then put back into an offline state. Doing so gives you the peace of mind that even offline VMs are in an up-to-date patched state. You can find the tool at `http://technet.microsoft.com/en-us/library/cc501231.aspx`.

Application virtualization integration   In keeping with the SCCM software deployment role, SCCM can deploy sequenced application packages from Microsoft Application Virtualization. This lets you use the existing SCCM infrastructure to target specific systems for deployment of application virtualization packages.

SCVMM 2008 Architecture Overview

The architecture and components of SCVMM 2008 provide its functionality. In this section, we'll explore the various components of the SCVMM 2008 system.

SCVMM 2008 provides virtualization administration and centralized control of your virtualization environment. It lets you perform rapid provisioning, migrate physical servers, and migrate VMs from other virtualization platforms. One of the core enhancements in SCVMM 2008 is the ability to manage additional virtualization platforms: Microsoft Hyper-V and VMware ESX environments.

An SCVMM 2008 implementation consists of required core components. Other components aren't required but are useful for specific scenarios like creating a test-and-development virtualization environment. The SCVMM architecture and components appear in Figure 11.2.

FIGURE 11.2
SCVMM 2008
architecture

The ports and protocols used by the SCVMM components as outlined in the architecture diagram in Figure 11.2 are listed in Table 11.1.

TABLE 11.1   Ports and Protocols for SCVMM

DATA FLOW BETWEEN SCVMM COMPONENTS	COMM TYPE	PORT
SCVMM server to Windows host agent (control)	WinRM	80
SCVMM server to Windows host agent (data)	SMB	445
SCVMM server to remote Microsoft SQL Server database	TDS	1433
SCVMM server to P2V source agent	DCOM	135
Administrator console to SCVMM 2008 server	WCF	8100
Self-service portal Web server to SCVMM 2008 server	WCF	8100

TABLE 11.1   Ports and Protocols for SCVMM   *(CONTINUED)*

DATA FLOW BETWEEN SCVMM COMPONENTS	COMM TYPE	PORT
Self-service portal to SCVMM 2008 self-service web server	HTTPS	443
Library to hosts	BITS	443
Host-to-host file transfer	BITS	443
VMRC connection to virtual server host	VMRC	5900
VMConnect (RDP) to Hyper-V hosts	RDP	2179
Remote desktop to VMs	RDP	3389

The components central to each SCVMM 2008 installation are as follows:

◆ SCVMM 2008 server

◆ Default library server

◆ SCVMM 2008 database

◆ SCVMM 2008 administrator console

Each SCVMM 2008 component fulfills a specific purpose and adds core virtualization-management functionality. Let's look in more detail at the core and secondary components.

SCVMM Server

The SCVMM 2008 server is the central brain of an SCVMM 2008 implementation. Through it, all other components interact and communicate. Because all core and secondary components depend on the SCVMM server, it's the first component installed.

The SCVMM 2008 server runs as a service and is always active regardless of direct user interaction with the system through the supported interfaces. The server is responsible for running commands, transferring files, and controlling communications with other SCVMM 2008 components and with all VM hosts and library servers.

The SCVMM 2008 server has a dependency on the SCVMM database server, as shown in Figure 11.2. The architecture of SCVMM 2008 is stateless with the exception of the SQL database, where all configuration information and short-term performance information is stored. This stateless architecture design adds recoverability of the SCVMM system.

By default, the SCVMM 2008 server is also the default library server. You can use the SCVMM 2008 library to store file-based resources such as virtual hard disks (unless attached to a stored VM), templates, ISO images, PowerShell scripts, answer files, and VMs. You can set up additional SCVMM 2008 library servers, which is recommended, when you'll be managing a large number of hosts.

SCVMM 2008 Library Server

The SCVMM library provides an inventory of resources to provision various types of VMs (see Figure 11.3). The library can store the following types of resources:

◆ Virtual hard disks: .vhd and .vmdk

◆ PowerShell Scripts and answer files: .ps1, .inf, .xml

◆ ISO Image files: .iso

◆ Virtual floppy disks: .vfd, .flp

◆ VMware templates: .vmtx

FIGURE 11.3
SCVMM library
server view

TIP SCVMM 2008 doesn't synchronize library server contents between library servers. If you need to keep library server content synchronized across many library servers, you can use file replication tools like Robocopy and Doubletake. SCVMM doesn't support Distributed File System Replication (DFSR) replication.

In each SCVMM server installation, the server is the default library server. After you install the SCVMM 2008 server, you can add other computers as library servers. You should take into account the amount of storage needed to store library objects and plan the storage to match.

NOTE You can't delete or move the default library server and library share installed on the SCVMM server. So, be very careful about the amount of content you store in the initial library. Take it as a best practice to create a second library server on at least one managed host right after installation of your first SCVMM server.

SCVMM Database

The SCVMM 2008 database stores all SCVMM 2008 configuration information. You interact with the database attributes by using the SCVMM administrator console.

The SCVMM database requires one of the following supported version of Microsoft SQL Server:

◆ SQL Server 2005 SP2

◆ SQL Server 2008

◆ SQL Server Express 2005 SP2

The database can be local to the SCVMM server, or you can use a remote database server. Because the state of the system is stored in the database, it's a best practice for large installations to either cluster the database or install the SCVMM database instance on a cluster.

NOTE   If you decide to install the SCVMM database on a new cluster, the Enterprise edition of SQL Server is required.

SCVMM Administrator Console

The SCVMM administrator console is one of three methods for interacting with the SCVMM server. You can also use the self-service portal or the PowerShell interface.

The administrator console is built on top of the SCVMM PowerShell interface, so all commands available in the console are available from PowerShell. This means PowerShell must be installed on each computer on which you plan to install the administrator console.

You can install the administrator console on the following systems:

◆ Windows Server 2008

◆ Windows Server 2003 and Windows Server 2003 R2

◆ Vista (all editions)

◆ Windows XP SP2 and SP3

All aspects of managing SCVMM 2008 are available from the administrator console (see Figure 11.4). The common actions that you as an administrator will perform include the following:

◆ Creating VMs

◆ Interacting with PRO tips

◆ Managing global configuration settings

◆ Managing hosts and host groups

◆ Implementing intelligent placement settings

We'll cover some of these tasks later in the chapter.

FIGURE 11.4
SCVMM adminis-
trator console

Virtual Machine Host

A *virtual machine host* is a physical computer that can run an SCVMM-supported virtualization platform. When you add a host to be managed by SCVMM (see Figure 11.5) and the virtualization platform hasn't been installed or enabled, you must take the actions outlined in Table 11.2.

TABLE 11.2   SCVMM Add-Host Actions by Server Operating System

SERVER OPERATING SYSTEM	VIRTUALIZATION SOFTWARE INSTALLED	SCVMM ACTION
Windows Server 2003 X86 and X64	No	Install latest version of Virtual Server 2005 R2 SP1.
Windows Server 2008 X86	No	Install latest version of Virtual Server 2005 R2 SP1.
Windows Server 2008 X64	No	Enable Hyper-V role.
Windows Server 2003 X86 and X64	Yes	Add an SCVMM 2008 agent, and add a host.
Windows Server 2008 X86	Yes	Add an SCVMM 2008 agent, and add a host.
Windows Server 2008 X64	Yes	Add an SCVMM 2008 agent, and add a host.
VMware ESX Server	N/A	Add a host, provided VirtualCenter (VC) server was already configured (see Figure 11.5).

FIGURE 11.5
Adding a Virtual-
Center host

SCVMM supports the following types of hosts (see Figure 11.6):

◆ Windows Server hosts located in an Active Directory (AD) domain that doesn't have two-way trust with the SCVMM 2008 server's AD domain

◆ Windows Server–based hosts located in a demilitarized zone (DMZ)

◆ Windows Server–based hosts that are in a disjointed namespace, where the host's fully qualified domain name (FQDN) resolved from the domain name service (DNS) isn't the same as the name obtained from AD

◆ VMware ESX Server hosts located anywhere in your environment

FIGURE 11.6
VM Add Hosts
Wizard; machine
manager adminis-
trator console

SCVMM Additional Components

Some components of the SCVMM environment are optional and map to specific environments and use cases. These optional components include the following:

- VM self-service portal
- PRO

SCVMM SELF-SERVICE WEB PORTAL

The SCVMM 2008 self-service portal is an optional, web-based component that you can install and configure to let users create and manage their own VMs within a controlled environment on a limited group of VM hosts (see Figure 11.7). You create self-service user roles that determine the scope of the users' actions on their own VMs.

FIGURE 11.7
SCVMM self-service web portal

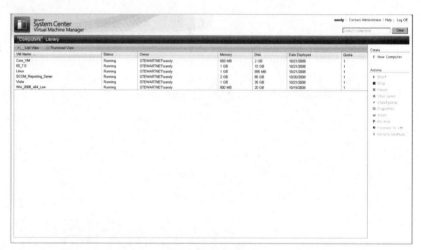

You determine the host groups where self-service users can create VMs. When a self-service user creates a VM, the VM is automatically placed in the most suitable host in the host group based on host ratings. You can set a VM quota in a self-service user role and assign quota points to VM templates to limit the number of VMs that a user or group can deploy.

PERFORMANCE AND RESOURCE OPTIMIZATION (PRO)

PRO supports workload- and application-aware resource optimization in a virtualized environment (see Figure 11.8). Based on performance and health data provided by PRO-enabled management packs in SCOM 2007, PRO can automatically or manually implement recommendations for minimizing downtime and accelerating time to resolution.

FIGURE 11.8

PRO view

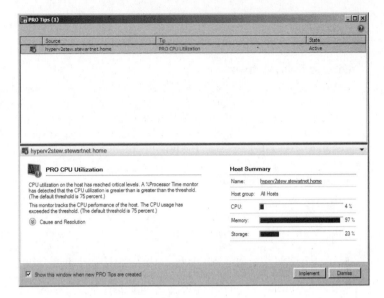

Planning an SCVMM 2008 Deployment

You should now have a solid understanding of the various SCVMM 2008 components: what they do and how they work as a part of the larger system. Next, let's turn our attention to some important planning aspects you should consider before you deploy your first SCVMM server.

One of the driving factors that affects SCVMM design discussions is the overall scalability of a single SCVMM deployment. Scalability is important because any SCVMM server you add is considered a separate and distinct installation. No common state or configuration information is shared between SCVMM installations. This raises several design considerations:

- How do you divide managed hosts between separate SCVMM installations? This can play out across a single data center, multiple data centers, and branch office environments.

- What management model do you need to manage multiple SCVMM instances, given that there is no common view between multiple SCVMM instances?

You can have a maximum of 400 supported and tested managed hosts and 8,000 VMs.

NOTE   Although you may be able to exceed the 400 hosts and 8,000 VMs on a single SCVMM instance, you'll be in uncharted, untested territory and your results will be unpredictable.

The type of SCVMM deployment you undertake depends a lot on the requirements of the deployment. Some of the most common deployment scenarios are as follows:

- Single data center

- Multiple data centers

- Branch office

Each scenario has specific requirements to consider during the planning phase of the SCVMM deployment. Let's look at each scenario and the considerations and best practices for each.

Single Data Center

In the single–data center scenario, all SCVMM resources, as well as managed host resources, are located in the same data center. This is a common design scenario for customers with a single data center. Depending on the number of managed resources, managed hosts, and VMs, you may have multiple VM manager servers or a single VM manager server. Whether to install additional instances depends largely on the number of managed hosts and VMs.

SINGLE DATA CENTER, MULTIPLE INSTANCES SCENARIO

In this scenario, all SCVMM resources are in the same data center, but the number of managed hosts requires additional SCVMM instances. This entails creating another SCVMM instance along with a separate database server and separate self-service portal instances.

TIP Deciding how to divide virtualization hosts between SCVMM instances requires a chart or algorithm to key off. Some installations use the virtualization hostname as a trigger; others use internal business logic or a server role/boundary; or, in the case of branch-office deployments, branch offices may be divided between SCVMM instances.

Multiple Data Centers

In the multiple–data center scenario, all managed hosts, VMs, and SCVMM installations are spread over multiple physical data centers. Each data center is actively hosting virtual workloads; this isn't considered a disaster-recovery scenario, where servers are configured in a warm or hot standby solution and aren't actively hosting workloads.

This scenario has the same challenges as the single–data center/multiple-instances scenario. The hosts must be divided among SCVMM instances, and you have to manage multiple views for managed servers. This scenario is most common in large enterprises where the number of servers is spread between different data centers for redundancy and data center cost purposes.

Branch Office and Remote Locations

If your environment extends beyond a central data center to include branch offices or other remote sites where you want to create, run, and manage VMs, you must consider additional topology factors for implementing SCVMM.

CENTRALIZED SCVMM 2008 IMPLEMENTATION

The primary advantage of having a single, centralized SCVMM 2008 implementation is the ability to manage your primary data center and all remote locations with only one SCVMM 2008 implementation. Another advantage is that you need to maintain only a single SCVMM 2008 database, which contains data about your entire virtual environment.

The files you use to create VMs are large. Therefore, if you choose to have a centralized SCVMM 2008 server and database, it's a best practice not to have a centralized SCVMM 2008 library, but instead to deploy a library server and one or more hosts at each remote site. Users in those locations can then create VMs by using resources from a local library server instead of copying multigigabyte files from a centralized library server over a wide area network (WAN). This ability to use resources from a local library server can also help ensure the availability of files during WAN outages or server failures.

DECENTRALIZED SCVMM 2008 IMPLEMENTATION

The primary advantages of having separate SCVMM 2008 implementations at each location are as follows:

◆ Each location can configure and manage its SCVMM 2008 implementation in a way that best meets the needs of its environment.

◆ Virtual operations at remote locations aren't disrupted if a centralized SCVMM 2008 implementation becomes unavailable because of a WAN outage or server failure.

HOST AND LIBRARY SERVER CONFIGURATION

In either scenario, if you're using a local area network (LAN) instead of a SAN to perform VM transfers, it's a best practice to locate your hosts as close as possible to the library servers that the hosts will use to create VMs, and to have them as highly connected as possible. It's also a best practice to connect all computers in an SCVMM 2008 configuration with at least a 100MB Ethernet connection. You may want to consider isolating the library server and the hosts that use it on their own subnet.

As noted earlier, you shouldn't have a centralized SCVMM 2008 library if you choose to have a centralized SCVMM 2008 implementation. In either case, you might consider installing a host and a library server on the same computer. This configuration is well-suited when you have 150 or fewer images (templates, ISOs, virtual hard disks [VHDs]) stored on the library server.

The primary advantage of having a host and a library server on the same computer is rapid VM deployment. The files for building VMs aren't transferred across the network, reducing equipment costs because you use one computer rather than two.

The primary disadvantage of having a host and a library server on the same computer is that it can require more overall hard disk space to maintain multiple copies of the same files, rather than use a single, central library server at each location.

Installing SCVMM 2008

Now that you've learned about the SCVMM 2008 components and you're familiar with the planning and design considerations, you need to install SCVMM to manage the Hyper-V environment.

You can install SCVMM components on a single server (which is acceptable for small installations), but in this chapter we'll focus on multiple-server installations with various VM components on separate servers.

Installing the SCVMM 2008 Database

SCVMM is essentially a stateless system; the state and configuration information kept by SCVMM is stored in a SQL Server database. This makes the SQL Server database installation and configuration a critical decision. Although you can rapidly recover a stand-alone SQL database configuration several ways, during the recovery time the database instance is offline, meaning that your SCVMM instance is offline as well.

If you decide to go with a stand-alone configuration, a good option for rapid recovery that uses the VSS infrastructure and the SQL VSS writer is DPM 2007 SP1. It can provide continuous protection of SQL instances and a rapid-recovery option to protect SCVMM 2008 databases and availability.

If you decide to provide a highly available database configuration (such as Microsoft Failover Services) for your SCVMM database, you must set up a Windows Server 2003 Enterprise Edition or Data Center Edition or Windows Server 2008 Enterprise Edition or Data Center Edition failover cluster with SQL Server Enterprise installed. Only the Enterprise and Data Center Server editions and SQL Enterprise Edition support creating a highly available database configuration.

NOTE The following link provides detailed information about installing a SQL cluster on Windows Server 2008: http://msdn.microsoft.com/en-us/library/ms179530.aspx.

After you have the SQL cluster up and you've configured a SQL database instance on the cluster, you can move on to installing the SCVMM server.

The first step is to specify the name, as shown in Figure 11.9. This concludes the database setup portion of the SCVMM server setup.

FIGURE 11.9
SCVMM clustered
SQL setup

Installing the SCVMM 2008 Server Role

One of the first things you should do before you install any SCVMM roles on a server is use the Virtual Machine Manager Configuration Analyzer (VMMCA). This diagnostic tool can spot configuration issues and absent prerequisites before you discover them during the actual installation, thereby saving you time during installations. The VMMCA tool includes a model that checks for predetermined problems and assists in providing best-practice configuration guidance.

You can access the VMMCA tool directly from the SCVMM 2008 setup screen (see Figure 11.10). The link takes you directly to a website where you can download the tool, an approach that allows the tool to be revised with new best practices and updates without affecting the SCVMM 2008 setup program.

FIGURE 11.10
VMMCA link in the SCVMM 2008 installation

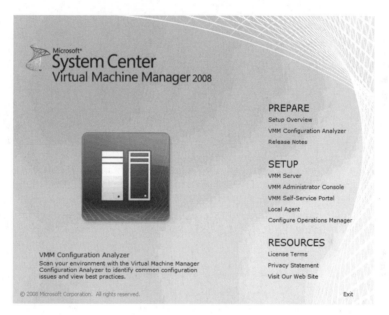

After installing the tool, you can run it directly on the server where you plan to install SCVMM roles or against a remote server. The VMMCA tool checks the server for the following SCVMM server roles (see Figure 11.11):

- SCVMM server
- SCVMM administrator console
- SCVMM self-service portal

FIGURE 11.11
VMMCA tool

When you've worked out any alerts sent from the VMMCA tool (see Figure 11.12), you're ready to start the SCVMM server installation. To start the installation, launch the SCVMM setup program, and select the SCVMM server install under the Setup heading. Some of the most important decisions during the setup are the database configuration (covered earlier in "Installing the SCVMM 2008 Database") and the default library configuration, as shown in Figure 11.13.

FIGURE 11.12
VMMCA tool
report output

NOTE The SCVMM server role can be installed only in Windows Server 2008 x64 editions. Other roles, like the self-service portal and the administrator console, can be installed on x86 and x64 Windows Server 2003 and Windows Server 2008 editions.

FIGURE 11.13
Default library
installation

You can accept the default library configuration, which completes a share automatically or uses an existing share. It's important that you specify a disk location that has available storage, because the default library share can't be removed or relocated to another disk location. You can create additional library servers from the SCVMM administrator console at any time.

TIP   We usually pre-create a share on a location that has enough disk resources and is separate from any database disk locations. We call the share vmlib, which is easily identified as the share for the library. You should make it a point to add a library server on the first set of managed hosts that you add.

Installing the SCVMM 2008 Administrator Console

On any computer where you plan to administer an SCVMM instance, you can install the SCVMM administrator console. Because the administrator console is built on top of the SCVMM PowerShell interface, PowerShell and the .NET Framework version 2.0 are prerequisites. You can install the administrator console on both client and server operating systems from:

◆   Windows XP Service Pack 2-3 x86/x64 editions

◆   Windows Vista Service Pack 1 x86/x64 editions

◆   Windows Server 2003 x86/x64 editions

◆   Windows Server 2008 x86/x64 editions

Installing the SCVMM 2008 Self-Service Portal

The self-service portal is an excellent tool especially for creating self-service test and development environments. This allows you to target development environments for individual developers or entire development groups. The self-service portal lets you set policies and granular access that provides self-service flexibility while giving you control over scarce virtualization capacity. If that doesn't excite you, it uses AD to authenticate and authorize users on the portal. The requirements for the self-service portal are a Windows-based Internet Information Services server (IIS) and an existing SCVMM installation.

You can scale out a self-service environment by using a hardware load balancer like F5 or Cisco SS. Those load balancers allow you to create a virtual IP (this IP will be used to direct requests to the real web servers) that front various real web servers that all point to the same instance of an SCVMM server.

NOTE A self-service portal installation must point to an SCVMM instance. This can cause trouble in SCVMM environments with multiple SCVMM instances. You have to know what SCVMM instance a user is storing VMs on and make sure users are routed to that instance.

After you've configured and installed the self-service portal on a web server, you're ready to move to the next configuration steps.

CREATING A SELF-SERVICE USER POLICY

In order for users to leverage the self-service portal to control and create virtual machines, a self-service user policy must be created. The self-service user policy is used to shape the actions that an end user can perform when using the self-service portal. Consider the self-service polict as the blueprint that shapes the self-service environment for an end user. Let's walk through the steps to creating a self-service policy:

1. Open the SCVMM administrator console, and select the Administration tab.

2. Select the User role, right-click Profile Type, and select the New User role.

3. Assign a user-role name, and select User Role Profile: Self Server User.

4. Add user-role users or groups from AD.

5. Select the scope of hosts that this self-service user profile can use. The scope of hosts maps back to the host-group layout that you as an administrator create. Each host group contains specific managed hosts. You can use host groups to segment managed hosts by location or purpose (for example, dev and test) or for purposes of migration like a Quick Migration cluster.

6. Assign the granular actions that users can perform when logged into the console. Figure 11.14 shows the self-service policy rights you can assign to users.

7. Decide whether you'll allow users to create VMs from the portal, and assign a template to the user or group for provisioning VMs.

8. Decide whether users can store VMs in an SCVMM library server, and assign the self-service policy to a specific set of one library server.

9. Create a self-service policy.

10. Log on to the portal by going to http://*nameofwebserver*:assigned port as configured in Figure 11.15.

FIGURE 11.14
Granular rights assignment for self-service

USING POWERSHELL TO CREATE A SELF-SERVICE POLICY

You can use a PowerShell script to create a self-service policy that gives user test1 on the stewartnet domain access to the self-service portal:

```
$VMPermission = 511
$AddScope = Host group
$AddMember = @("STEWARTNET\test1")
Set-VMMUserRole -VMPermission $VMPermission -QuotaPoint 0 -AddScope $AddScope
-VMMServer 192.168.2.101 -JobGroup 2c0c9c4e-ce57-49f2-b98d-727ff8516823
-AddMember $AddMember
New-VMMUserRole -Name "New_User" -Description "" -UserRoleProfile SelfServiceUser
-JobGroup 2c0c9c4e-ce57-49f2-b98d-727ff8516823
```

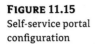

FIGURE 11.15
Self-service portal
configuration

Integrating SCOM 2007 and SCVMM 2008

One of the most compelling features of SCVMM 2008 is the connector established between SCOM 2007 SP1 and SCVMM. This PRO functionality highlights the ability to perform virtualization actions that map to specific applications. The ability to handle performance and application issues directly from the virtualization console is a compelling scenario that does require you to use several management consoles to find out information about the applications running in the virtual machine. You can perform not only normal virtualization actions but also implement rich application actions.

This turns our attention from the VM to the applications running in the VM; we're bridging the two worlds into a cohesive management approach. PRO provides the infrastructure for alerts triggered by applications running in VMs. You need certain components: an SCOM agent in the VM, and management and PRO packs for the applications running in the VM. The PRO infrastructure is built such that software vendors and line-of-business application developers can create PRO packs, thus expanding the infrastructure to support any application.

NOTE   You can find information about authoring PRO packs for applications at `http://go.microsoft.com/fwlink/?LinkId=68949`.

The out-of-the-box PRO components include the ability to trigger VM workload balancing based on the resource-consumption triggers. The initial management packs include the following elements:

SCVMM PRO VMware Host Performance   The VMware Host Performance pack provides monitors and rules for monitoring the performance of VMware ESX hosts managed by SCVMM 2008 to support PRO in SCVMM.

SCVMM PRO Virtual Machine Right-Sizing   The Virtual Machine Right-Sizing management pack provides monitors and rules for monitoring the performance of VMs managed by SCVMM 2008 to support PRO in SCVMM.

SCVMM PRO Library   The Library management pack provides the base class and group definitions that are used by PRO in SCVMM 2008.

SCVMM PRO Host Performance   The Host Performance management pack provides monitors and rules for monitoring the performance of Microsoft Hyper-V and virtual server hosts managed by SCVMM 2008 to support PRO in SCVMM.

The PRO functionality requires an existing SCOM 2007 SP1 environment (see Chapter 13 for planning guidance). PRO ties the SCVMM environment to an SCOM 2007 environment to form a two-way information flow in the form of PRO *Tips*. These consist of information and actions detected by SCOM 2007 SP1 and triggered by a condition on a managed virtualization host or VMs with an SCOM 2007 agent. This information is forward into the SCVMM console with the condition and action that you can use to clear the condition. See Figure 11.8 for a PRO Tip view.

Let's dive into the steps required to enable the PRO functionality. We'll assume you have an existing SCOM 2007 SP1 infrastructure:

1. Install an SCVMM server, and install the SCVMM administrator console on the server.

2. Install the SCOM console on the existing SCVMM server.

3. Import the following management packs into SCOM:

    ◆ Microsoft SQL Server 2000/2005 management pack:

    ◆ Microsoft SQL Server Library

    ◆ Microsoft SQL Server 2005 Monitoring (recommended)

    ◆ Microsoft SQL Server 2005 Discovery (recommended)

    ◆ Microsoft Windows Server 2000/2003 Internet Information Services (IIS) management pack:

        ◆ Microsoft Windows Internet Information Services Common Library

        ◆ Microsoft Windows Internet Information Services 2003

4. Run the Configure Operation Manager option from the SCVMM setup screen on the SCOM root management server.

5. Add the default action account to the SCVMM server as an administrator user role.

6. Enable remote running of PowerShell scripts on all servers running the VM administrator console. Start the PowerShell console, and select A for Always Trust Remote Signed Scripts.

7. On the SCVMM Server, configure the Operations Manager Server name on the Administration tab, as shown in Figure 11.16.

FIGURE 11.16
Configuring the
operation manager
in SCVMM

8. Test the integration by clicking the diagram view in the SCVMM administrator console, as shown in Figure 11.17.

FIGURE 11.17
Successful SCOM
integration

You can also verify that PRO has been configured in SCOM by ensuring that the SCVMM and SCOM connectors are configured. To do this, open the SCOM console, click the Administration option, and then click Product Connectors (see Figure 11.18). You should see several SCVMM connectors in the format *SCVMMConnector-SCVMM ServerName-Connecter number* (see Figure 11.19). You have several connectors to divide the workload of forwarding alerts in the form of PRO Tips to SCVMM servers.

FIGURE 11.18

SCVMM PRO connectors in SCOM

FIGURE 11.19

SCVMM PRO connector properties

CUSTOMIZING THE BASE PRO MONITORS

Now that you have the out-of-box PRO functionality configured, you'll want to customize the base PRO monitors. Customizing the PRO alerts comes down to configuring overrides on management-pack monitors in SCOM. Remember that the PRO infrastructure uses the SCOM infrastructure and adds management packs to SCOM. Those management packs contain the knowledge, triggers, and alerts that drive PRO. Let's dive into customizing some of the PRO management packs.

One of the scenarios you may want to customize is the host CPU utilization threshold, because by default, the plan is to run virtualization hosts with high rates of CPU usage. The threshold is set to provide a critical alert at 75% CPU usage. You should to customize it to 80% for your Hyper-V environment.

NOTE   Remember that SCVMM manages Hyper-V, Virtual Server, and ESX environments and provides PRO packs for each environment. This gives you granular PRO capability so you can set thresholds for each environment selectively.

1. Open the SCOM console with a user account that has author rights.

2. Select the Author tab and click Management Pack Objects, and then click Monitors.

3. Scroll down to find each PRO-related monitor, and click through each one to find the CPU monitor under Performance (see Figure 11.20). Or, use the Look For option in the monitor UI to find the CPU monitors.

FIGURE 11.20
PRO CPU monitors by host type

4. Under PRO Hyper-V Host Target, select PRO CPU Utilization, right-click, select Overrides, select Override The Monitor, and then select For All Objects Of Type: PRO Hyper-V Host Target (see Figure 11.21).

FIGURE 11.21
Selecting an
override for the
Hyper-V CPU
host target

5. In the CPU override properties screen, select Threshold, and type in the new CPU threshold (see Figure 11.22). You may also want to change Alert Severity, which is set to Critical, by selecting Alert Severity.

FIGURE 11.22
Changing the PRO
CPU threshold for
Hyper-V hosts

You can use the same process to configure memory thresholds as well; of course, the target will be PRO memory counters. It's also important to note that if you want a threshold to apply to all virtualization managed host types, you must perform an override for each type.

Provisioning Virtual Machines

One of the most important functions that makes virtualization attractive is the ability to rapidly provision new VMs. This is a core part of SCVMM functionality. The task of provisioning a new VM will be one of the most frequent tasks that you as a virtualization administrator will perform. It's important that you understand how to use SCVMM to do this.

As a virtualization administrator, you'll be called on to decide what VMs are placed on what virtualization host. You can use performance counters, the number of VMs on each host, or your gut feeling to make the decision.

VM Host Placement

Because VM host placement is critical to the health of the virtual environment, SCVMM provides functionality to aid you. The Intelligent Placement functionality helps you by looking across all the virtualization hosts or specific host groups and using capacity-planning algorithms to place the VM on the most appropriate host.

Intelligent Placement uses the following elements to decide on VM placement on a host:

◆ CPU utilization

◆ Free memory

◆ Disk I/O

◆ Network utilization

You can tweak this Intelligent Placement algorithm by choosing which virtualization host resources are prioritized during placement. To configure Intelligent Placement properties, follow these steps:

1. In the SCVMM administrator console, select the Administration tab, select the General option, and then highlight Placement Settings (see Figure 11.23).

2. Change the sliding bar of each resource you want to change; the range isn't important.

FIGURE 11.23
Configuring Intelligent Placement options

Doing so prioritizes the selected resources during the VM placement process. Also, remember that Intelligent Placement happens not only during new VM provisioning but also during migration of VMs from host to host using Quick Migration or over-the-network movement. This ensures the best host is always selected for a specific VMs resource requirement.

It's important to understand how to use SCVMM templates to provision VMs. You can use templates to create new VMs repeatedly with standardized hardware and software settings. A VM template is an SCVMM library resource consisting of the following parts:

Hardware profile   To define a standard set of hardware settings, you can create a hardware profile and associate it with a template. When you create a new template or create a VM from a template, you can specify the virtual hardware settings or reuse an existing hardware profile from the library.

Virtual hard disk   You can use a generalized VHD from the library or create a VHD from an existing VM. If the source VM for your template has multiple VHDs, select the disk that contains the operating system.

Guest operating-system profile   To use the same product key, administrator password, time zone, and so on, in a set of templates, you can create a guest operating-system profile and store it in the library. When you create a new template or create a VM from a template, you can specify the settings manually or use an operating-system profile associated with your answer files.

CREATING A NEW TEMPLATE FROM AN EXISTING HARD DISK

To create a new template from an existing hard disk, you can use the default blank hard disks created by the SCVMM installation in the default library or another VHD stored in any SCVMM library server. Follow these steps:

1. In the SCVMM administrator console, select the Library tab.

2. In the library, choose a VHD object that you want to use to create a template. Right-click the object, and select the New Template option.

3. Add Active Directory Identity, User or Group owner to template from active directory, and add a description of the template.

4. Configure a new hardware profile, or select an existing hardware profile for the VM.

5. Configure a new operating-system profile, or select No Customization Needed. The options you can fill in are Machine Netbios Name, Admin Password, Product Key, Time Zone, Operating System, and Domain/Workgroup.

You can now use the new template stored in the SCVMM library server to create VMs.

NOTE   Always use the No Customization Needed option for templates that provision Linux VMs, because the operating-system profile options apply to Windows systems only.

Let's move on to the provisioning process. We'll explore the different types of provisioning capabilities in SCVMM.

PROVISIONING VMS WITH BLANK OR EXISTING VHDS

One method of provisioning allows you to provision a virtual machine with a blank or existing hard drive. In the blank hard drive approach you can provision and install a operating systems at a later time. In the case of leveraging an already existing virtual machine hard drive file, you can use this virtual hard drive to create new virtual machines. Let's explore the steps:

1. Open the SCVMM administrator console.

2. Select New Virtual Machine to start the New Virtual Machine Wizard.

3. Select Source For New Virtual machine. Create the new machine with a blank hard drive.

4. Select the name of the VM, the owner of the VM (AD user or group), and enter a description of the VM.

5. You can now set up the VM's hardware profile (see Figure 11.24), including the VHD, processor count, network adapters, and either IDE or SCSI adapters.

FIGURE 11.24
Hardware properties for a new VM

6. Select a destination. You can either deploy directly to an existing host or store the VM on an SCVMM library server.

7. Intelligent Placement determines the best host for the workload using the star rating system (see Figure 11.25). The host with the most stars represents the best host for placement of this VM (driven by the Intelligent Placement settings shown in Figure 11.23).

8. Click Create The Virtual Machine, and verify that the VM is created on the selected host.

FIGURE 11.25
Intelligent Placement in action

PROVISIONING FROM TEMPLATES, VHDS, AND VMS IN THE LIBRARY

Provisioning Virtual machines from templates is one of the most used methods for provisioning virtual machines. The template provides a blueprint for creating virtual machines that has populated virtual machine properties for example the number of virtual processors assigned to a virtual machine and the size a type of virtual hard drive dynamic or fixed.

1. Open the SCVMM administrator console.

2. Select New Virtual Machine to start the New Virtual Machine Wizard.

3. Select the source for the new VM. Choose Use Existing Virtual Machine, Template Or Virtual Hard Disk.

4. You have the option to select a template, a existing VHD, or a VM stored in the SCVMM library (see Figure 11.26).

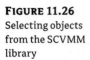

FIGURE 11.26
Selecting objects from the SCVMM library

5. Select the name of the VM, select the owner of the VM (AD user or group), and enter a description of the VM.

6. Depending on your selection, you can configure various parts of the hardware properties. If you use a template, those options are predefined. If you select a VHD, you can configure all options except the VHD for the VM.

7. Select the destination. You can either deploy directly to an existing host or store the VM on an SCVMM library server.

8. Intelligent Placement determines the best host for the workload using the star rating system. The host with the most stars represents the best host for placement of this VM (driven by the Intelligent Placement settings shown in Figure 11.23).

9. Click Create The Virtual Machine, and verify that the VM is created on the selected host.

Provisioning Systems via P2V Functionality

One of the great capabilities of the virtualization environment is the ability to take a physical system running on physical hardware and capture that configuration to make the physical system a VM. This action is called physical to virtual (P2V). As the name implies, the process converts a physical system to a VM. This process is very popular for several reasons:

Server consolidation Server consolidation is by far the most popular use of P2V technology. In this case, underutilized physical systems are converted to VMs. This saves power, cooling, and data center footprint.

Disaster recovery   The P2V process captures an exact copy of the physical system as a VM that can be started and run at any time. Think of a disaster scenario where the physical system or the data center where the server is located goes down. If you have a P2V of the physical system, all you need to do is start that VM. The services will be up and running in a short time.

SCVMM P2V functionality provides two options for doing a P2V: online or offline. Offline P2V uses the Windows Pre-installation Environment (Windows PE) to capture an exact copy of the physical system. This process deploys an SCVMM agent to the source machine and restarts the source machine into Windows PE to capture the image. The following operating systems without the VSS infrastructure have to use offline P2V:

◆ Windows 2000 Server SP4

◆ Windows 2000 Advanced Server SP4

NOTE   If you need to perform a P2V of a Linux physical system, you have to use a third-party solution like Novell Platespin.

The online functionality uses the VSS infrastructure to take a disk snapshot of the source machine. The VSS infrastructure allows the P2V process to perform the disk capture without any system downtime. While online, P2V is ideal because it doesn't cause user or service interruption. It works only for Windows operating systems that have the VSS infrastructure:

◆ Windows Server 2008 (32-bit)

◆ Windows Server 2008 (64-bit)

◆ Windows Server 2003 (32-bit) SP1 or later

◆ Windows Server 2003 (64-bit) SP1 or later

◆ Windows XP Professional (32-bit) SP2 or later

◆ Windows XP Professional (64-bit) SP2 or later

◆ Windows Vista Service Pack 1 (32-bit)

◆ Windows Vista SP1 or later (64-bit)

After you've identified the server for which you want to perform a P2V, you need to understand what type of P2V you'll be performing—offline or online—because offline affects system availability and may have to be performed in off hours. Now you're ready to start the P2V process.

Performing an Online P2V

An online P2V leverages the VSS infrastructure in Windows machines to capture the physical system data for inclusion in the new virtual machine. The VSS infrastructure provides you the ability to take a backup of the actual virtual machine as well a the applications running in the system provided each application had a VSS writer.

1. From the SCVMM administrator console, select the Convert Physical Server option.

2. Provide the IP address or machine name of the source machine, and provide administrator credentials for the source machine.

3. SCVMM scans the system. During this process, an SCVMM agent is deployed to the machine to gather systems information.

4. On the Volume Configuration page, review the lists of volumes and determine whether you want to make any changes.

5. Select volumes to copy. Initially, all volumes appear in the results pane and are selected for duplication to the new VM. The new VM must contain the system volume and the boot volume from the source machine.

6. Adjust volume settings. You can change the VHD Size (MB) field to adjust the size of any volume (NTFS volumes are automatically expanded to the size indicated), the VHD Type field to adjust the type (Dynamic or Fixed) of any volume, and the Channel field to adjust the channel (for both IDE devices and SCSI adapters) of any selected volume.

7. Select the number of processors and amount of memory for the new VM.

8. Intelligent Placement provides the best host to host the machine. Select the host.

9. Choose the path for the VM to be stored on the virtualization.

10. Attach to a network on the virtual host, or select Not Connected (you can connect the VM to a network later).

11. Review any issues reported by the wizard; the P2V won't process with any reported issues. Click Create to start the P2V process.

PERFORMING AN OFFLINE P2V

Follow the same process as in the previous section for online P2V, but select conversion options and select Offline P2V. You need to provide configuration information for the Windows PE environment. To do so, on the Offline Conversion Options page, select one of the following methods to provide an IP address to the boot environment on the host:

◆ Obtain an IP address automatically via DHCP.

◆ Use the following IPv6 address specify a IPv6 address, subnet prefix length, and default gateway of the host.

◆ Use the following IPv4 address specify the IPv6 address, subnet mask, and default gateway of the host.

TIP If you perform a P2V of an AD Domain Controller, you get a warning to perform an offline P2V if you select an online conversion (see Figure 11.27). To avoid AD Update Sequence Number issues, always perform an offline conversion.

FIGURE 11.27
Offline P2V net-
work options

Creating Highly Available Virtual Machines

Last but not least, one of the most important provisioning options is the ability to make a VM highly available. Doing so provides availability in the event that the virtualization host experiences planned or unplanned downtime. Planned downtime can occur when you perform maintenance on a host; unplanned downtime can occur when a virtualization host goes down completely for any reason.

In the event of planned downtime, the VM state is saved and migrated to another virtualization host in a Hyper-V Quick Migration cluster. If a virtualization host crashes that is a part of a Quick Migration cluster, the VM and associated resources are restarted on another Hyper-V host in the Quick Migration cluster.

To provision highly available VMs, you first must have set up a Quick Migration cluster (see Chapter 8, "High Availability"). Then, you're almost ready to use SCVMM to create highly available VMs. You have to make SCVMM aware of the host cluster the same way you add any host to SCVMM for management. Let's walk through the steps for making a VM highly available:

1. Add the Quick Migration cluster to SCVMM via the SCVMM administrator console using the Add Host option. SCVMM detects that you're adding a node to the Quick Migration cluster and adds SCVMM agents to each host in the cluster. A cluster object is created and available in the SCVMM console. See Figure 11.28 for a view of the new cluster object.

FIGURE 11.28
SCVMM Quick
Migration cluster
object

2. You're ready to configure a highly available VM. Open the SCVMM administrator console.

3. Select New Virtual Machine to start the New Virtual Machine Wizard.

4. Select the source for the new VM. Create the new machine with a blank hard drive.

5. Select the name of the VM, the owner of the VM (AD user or group), and enter a description of the VM.

6. Set up the hardware profile of the VM, including the VHD, the processor count, the network adapters, and either IDE or SCSI adapters.

7. The most important step is to scroll down to the Availability option and select the check box to make this VM highly available (see Figure 11.29).

FIGURE 11.29
Making the VM
highly available

8. Select the destination. You can either deploy directly to an existing host or store the VM on an SCVMM library server.

9. Intelligent Placement determines the best host for the workload using the star rating system. The host with the most stars represents the best host for placement of this VM (driven by the Intelligent Placement settings shown in Figure 11.23).

10. Select a VM path that is in the Quick Migration cluster and a SAN volume.

11. Click Create The Virtual Machine, and verify that the VM is created on the selected cluster node.

12. Verify the high-availability configuration for the VM by right-clicking the VM and performing a migration of the VM to another node in the Quick Migration cluster.

Summary

In this chapter, we provided the knowledge you need to begin using SCVMM 2008 with Hyper-V deployments. Any Hyper-V deployment without SCVMM 2008 doesn't truly exercise the flexibility that the virtualization environment provides.

Virtualization management will continue to evolve and add new capabilities; the first glimpse of the future is the PRO functionality included in SCVMM 2008. Look for the virtualization-management mind-set to change from provisioning individual VMs to provisioning entire applications and services as a unit/model.

In addition, as the underlying virtualization platform evolves with new capabilities (like including live migration functionality in Hyper-V in Windows Server 2008 R2). Virtual Machine Manager will continue to evolve functionality to take advantage of new Hyper-V and managed Hypervisor capabilities. Remember the formula for successful virtualization deployments: virtualization platform capabilities + functionality rich management software = a flexible, dynamic virtualization deployment.

Chapter 12

Protecting Virtualized Environments with System Center Data Protection Manager

There's a motto that says, "If you're going to put all of your eggs in one basket, you better have a good basket." Certainly this applies to virtualization: If you're going to put multiple servers, all of which you rely on, within a virtualization host, then you need a reliable way to protect that host. Within the Microsoft portfolio of virtualization technologies, Hyper-V is only one component (albeit a big one). The Microsoft virtualization portfolio obviously includes System Center Virtual Machine Manager (SCVMM), but the rest of System Center is equally applicable for managing a virtual infrastructure.

System Center Data Protection Manager (DPM) is the component of the Microsoft management family responsible for protecting all the assets in a Windows infrastructure, including virtualization hosts and guests. This chapter will explore how you can use it to protect virtualization hosts, guests, and the configuration between them.

In this chapter, we'll cover the following topics:

♦ Technical overview of Data Protection Manager

♦ Protecting your Hyper-V environment

♦ Configuring the protection of Hyper-V hosts

♦ Considerations when protecting virtualized environments

♦ Restoring your virtual environment with DPM

♦ Disaster recovery using DPM with SCVMM

Technical Overview of Data Protection Manager

Data Protection Manager (DPM) is intended to be *the* backup and recovery solution of choice for all core Microsoft production workloads, including Hyper-V. DPM was designed around three core premises:

♦ Provide an optimized backup and recovery solution from Microsoft, for Microsoft that ensures supportability, reliability, and customer satisfaction with the core operating system or application. In part, DPM is intended to ensure that customers are confident in their Hyper-V (or other Microsoft server platform) deployment because they're assured of reliable protection and recovery.

◆ Use only approved backup and recovery mechanisms within the production workloads, such that each application is backed up only as intended by the application designers. This means DPM uses only those constructs provided by Hyper-V in order to protect Hyper-V.

◆ Demonstrate additional value by choosing a comprehensive Microsoft portfolio, instead of using one Microsoft operating system or application server and then choosing non-Microsoft add-on components. In this case, DPM, like the other System Center components, is intended to offer "best for Windows" capabilities: It was designed by Microsoft with Microsoft applications as its top priority, and it incorporates lessons learned and feedback from the platform teams. Specifically for Hyper-V, DPM is intended to be "the best protection for Windows virtualization."

DPM 2007 is a native disk-to-disk-to-tape (D2D2T) solution, meaning that DPM replicates from the primary server disk to the DPM disk (referred to as the *replica*) to DPM tape. This gives you fast recovery (from disk) as well as long-term retention (from tape). Because DPM can replicate from one DPM server to another DPM server, you can technically have D2D2D2T—or what Microsoft refers to as DPM 2 DPM 4 DR (disaster recovery). Figure 12.1 presents the complete DPM solution for Microsoft backup and recovery for Microsoft workloads, with integrated disk, tape, and disaster-recovery replication.

FIGURE 12.1
Solution diagram for DPM 2007 SP1

In the case of Hyper-V, this means the virtual hard disks (VHDs) from the production host are held on the premises of the DPM disk replica, can be replicated to an offsite DPM replica, and can eventually be backed up to long-term tape. To do this, DPM installs a single agent technology on each production platform to be protected, including not only Hyper-V hosts but also SQL Server, Exchange Server, SharePoint products and technologies, Windows file servers, and Windows desktops. The agent, using a filter driver, monitors the physical blocks that are being updated on the production disk volumes. As production workloads—in this case, the Windows hypervisor—write to disk blocks within the VHDs, the DPM agent tracks which blocks have been updated. On a predefined schedule that we'll discuss later, DPM captures just those changed blocks as reported by the filter and propagates those blocks to the DPM replica.

Backup Alternatives

The advocated method for protecting virtualized guests from a Microsoft virtualization host is to use the Hyper-V Volume Shadow Copy Services (VSS) writer. By using the APIs provided by VSS and delivered through a VSS writer from the Hyper-V development team, you can do backups and recoveries of your virtual infrastructure in an application-consistent and supported way.

Remember that not all backup solutions use VSS writers, which can mean potential supportability issues, possible data corruption in the guest operating systems and the physical VHDs, and backups that may not be restorable. With those heady considerations in mind, you may ask, "Why would any backup solution not use VSS?"

Often, third-party tape technologies use a generic architecture in their agent/server model that allows them to back up anything and everything from a laptop to a mainframe computer. This flexibility gives them a broad reach in their marketplace. However, it also often precludes them from using API sets or other original application-provided methods for data backup and recovery (such as VSS). In fairness, an application's VSS writer may not provide every desirable backup and restore scenario. Sometimes, third-party tape backup vendors ignore VSS in order to create additional capabilities not provided by the native writer. Although this may satisfy some customer desires, it results in the same concerns about supportability and potential data corruption.

DPM, as a Microsoft product, is committed to using only approved backup and recovery methods (such as VSS) from Microsoft application teams (like the Hyper-V development team). This ensures the most reliable and supportable backup and recovery solution.

Understanding DPM Storage

The DPM server or appliance usually starts with one defined NTFS volume for the bootable operating system, as well as the DPM application and its supporting SQL Server database. In addition, the DPM server or appliance should have a significant amount of unallocated storage and possible a tape drive or library. The additional disk storage can be locally direct-attached storage (DAS) or a Storage Area Network (SAN) attached via fibre channel or Internet SCSI (iSCSI); but it must appear as *locally mounted* via the Windows Disk Administrator. Removable disk media such as USB hard drives aren't directly supported because DPM presumes that any disk medium is always connected. In addition, DPM uses VSS, which isn't available for removable media types.

For each production data source being protected by DPM, the DPM server allocates two NTFS volumes out of its raw storage—one for the replica and the other for recovery points:

♦ The *DPM replica volume* is a real NTFS volume, usually defined to be equal in size to or slightly larger in size than the production NTFS volume that holds the virtualization VHDs. Within the replica, you can find the VHDs for a given virtual machine (VM).

♦ The *DPM recovery point* volume holds the block-level changes between one synchronization point and the one before it. Specifically, whenever DPM synchronizes the production volume against the DPM replica, the changed blocks that are overwritten within the replica are moved into the recovery-point volume.

Consider the following scenario:

1. Day one: The original VHD (or any other data object protected by DPM) contains eight blocks on disk (ABCDEFGH).

2. Upon initially protecting the VHD with DPM, two volumes are allocated for the replica and recovery points. Immediately after that, DPM does its initial baseline, which populates the replica volume with an exact copy of the production VHD (ABCDEFGH).

3. Day two: During the day, two blocks (*IJ*) are updated, resulting in AB*IJ*EFGH.

4. At the next scheduled synchronization, referred to by DPM as an *express full*, the two changed blocks (*IJ*) are identified and replicated from the production VHD to the DPM replica—resulting in the replica also having AB*IJ*EFGH. The two displaced blocks (CD) are then moved from the replica into the recovery-point volume.

5. Day three: After another day, three more blocks (B, J, G) are overwritten (*KLM*) and synchronized, resulting in A*KILEFMH*. Again, DPM replicates just the three changed blocks within the VHD to the DPM replica, and the displaced blocks are moved to the recovery-point volume.

This process can occur up to 512 times—based on a limit of 512 snapshots via VSS. This may equal 512 daily points in time equaling nearly 1.5 years—or, at 4 per day, 128 days (four months) of changes.

DPM DATA STORAGE

It's important to recognize the *full* or complete copy of the VHD happens only once and is always maintained. Previous points in time are held strictly as the changed blocks from one iteration to the next, which results in a very efficient form of storing past data without consuming inordinate amounts of space.

Another nuance of this behavior is that it's exactly the opposite of a traditional tape backup. In a traditional tape backup, you do a full that copies the entire data set. From that point on, the full ages, meaning that after a day, the full backup is one day old. Because of this, most environments do an incremental or a differential backup of simple changes since the full backup was completed. After another day, subsequent incrementals or differentials are also done. The result is that if you need to recover data after four days, you start by recovering the full and then layer over the top each of the subsequent daily backups to reconstitute the most current state of the production data set. DPM changes this paradigm completely:

♦ In the case of DPM, the full is the replica and is always current within one day (or synchronization window). Each daily synchronization refreshes the full and creates a differential between the current point in time and the backup before it. This means that after a catastrophic failure, you don't have to go back to an aged full and then layer one or more dailies over the top of it. Instead, to restore the complete server to the most recent backup, you need only restore the full (replica).

♦ To recover to a previous point in time, DPM still doesn't require any kind of layering between the full and the daily differentials. Instead, because DPM uses a native disk such that all the data is held as individual disk blocks, DPM simply selects the specific blocks from whichever point in time is requested by the DPM administrator.

In the earlier example, if you wish to recover to day two (step 3 in the scenario), DPM requests the eight blocks ABIJEFGH. Although some of those blocks still exist in the disk replica, other blocks are held in the recovery-point volume. Because both volumes are disks in the DPM storage pool, no additional disk I/O or layering is required. DPM simply selects the appropriate eight blocks. Thus, the recovery-point volume is not only extremely efficient for storing previous points in time but also enables a very rapid restore based on how the previous points in time are retained.

DPM Storage and Hyper-V Protection

To put all of this together, the DPM disk is your first line of defense (or recovery) for recovering VMs that are lost due to, for example, a hardware failure on a Hyper-V host. DPM gives you a calendar- and time-based view to select a point in time to which to recover the VHD(s). DPM then selects the blocks from both the replica and recovery-point volumes that constitute those VHD(s) to that particular point in time.

Beyond the disk-based protection of a DPM server, DPM can replicate the replica to another DPM server for offsite disaster recovery. Microsoft commonly refers to this as *DPM 2 DPM 4 DR*. Pragmatically speaking, the secondary DPM server treats the primary DPM server as a protectable workload. On a less frequent schedule, it replicates those changed blocks in the primary DPM replica as if it were the production VHD volume. On a separate schedule, the secondary/offsite DPM server retains an additional replica and points in time. This may result in the primary DPM server protecting the production VHD 4 times per day for 2 weeks, while the secondary DPM server protects the primary perhaps nightly for 60 days.

In addition to disk-based protection, DPM offers native, tape-based backup. To do this, you configure a traditional tape-backup retention system on the DPM server, which backs up the DPM replica to tape. This means Microsoft customers don't require third-party tape-backup software in order to protect their Windows hypervisors (or any other workload protectable by DPM). As a general rule of thumb, any tape drive, library, medium changer, or virtual tape library (VTL) that is visible from the Windows Device Manager can be used with DPM. There are of course exceptions, and you can find a list of tested tape devices at www.microsoft.com/DPM. The ever-growing list of tape devices for DPM isn't exclusive; it just includes devices whose original manufacturers have chosen to run the DPM-provided test utility on their tape device(s) and report the results to Microsoft. Many other devices whose manufacturers haven't chosen to run the test utility may also work. Because of the transparency that DPM provides by using most devices that are visible from the Windows Device Manager, you may find that even de-duplication appliances that present themselves as VTLs may be usable for long-term retention.

Protecting Your Hyper-V Environment

Deploying DPM 2007 SP1 to protect a virtualized environment involves three primary phases:

- Setting up your first DPM server, including software installation as well adding disk and/or tape media

- Deploying DPM agents to the production servers, meaning the Hyper-V hosts and/or inside the virtual machines

- Configuring one or more Protection Groups, which define what is to be protected and how

Setting Up Your First DPM Server

DPM 2007 installs onto a dedicated platform running Windows Server 2003, Windows Server 2003 R2, or Windows Server 2008. As an alternative, you can acquire a *Data Protection Appliance*, which is usually a Windows Storage Server (OEM-version of Windows Server) that is preinstalled on server hardware and includes a pre-installation of DPM.

As mentioned earlier, your DPM platform should have one production disk with the operating system and capacity/performance for the DPM application and related SQL Server. After you insert the DPM installation DVD, DPM performs a minimum requirements check, or *preflight inspection*. Assuming you have adequate hardware as defined in the hardware requirements (shown in Table 12.1, which is abridged from `http://technet.microsoft.com/library/bb808832.aspx`), the installation will guide you through a four-step wizard.

TABLE 12.1 DPM 2007 Server Hardware Requirements and Recommendations

COMPONENT	MINIMUM REQUIREMENTS	RECOMMENDATION
Processor	1GHz or faster	2.33GHz quad-core CPUs
Memory	2GB RAM	4GB RAM
Disk space for DPM installation	Program hard drive: 410MB Database files drive: 900MB System drive 2650 MB	2–3GB of free space on the program files volume
Disk space for storage pool	1.5 times the size of the protected data	2–3 times the size of the protected data

NOTE   Here's a recommendation that isn't documented. Although you can run DPM 2007 on a 32-bit platform, a 64-bit DPM server will scale much higher—so you can protect significantly more servers and much more production data (VHDs and other data).

After you enter your name and company on the first screen, you select where the DPM application will go as well as whether to use the included SQL Server or an existing SQL Server (see Figure 12.2):

- DPM 2007 includes SQL Server 2005 standard edition on the DPM DVD or downloadable installation software, which you can install on the DPM server. This is the default choice and doesn't require a separate SQL Server license; nor is there a SQL client-access license (CAL) requirement, because the End User License Agreement (EULA) and software enforce only using this included instance of SQL Server by DPM.

- Alternatively, you can use an external SQL Server 2005 database, with the proper permissions. For most scenarios, the included SQL Server instance is adequate; however, for high I/O environments or deployments with multiple DPM servers, an external and centralized SQL Server may be desirable.

FIGURE 12.2

DPM server installation—choosing which SQL Server to use

The third screen varies (based on whether you chose the internal SQL Server or an external database) and requests authentication information for SQL Server and/or its reporting services.

The last installation screen (Figure 12.3) walks through all the components to be installed from this point forward, including Internet Information Services and Single Instance Storage (prompting for your Windows Server installation i386 directory, if it isn't already installed), Windows PowerShell, SQL Server 2005 with SP2, and finally System Center DPM 2007.

FIGURE 12.3

DPM server installation—components

Essentially, you answer a few key questions up front, and if the prerequisites are met, you'll watch a status bar for about 45 minutes—with the only interruptions being a possible request early on for your Windows Server installation media for some initial components. After installation completes and you reboot, you have a DPM 2007 server.

NOTE Upon completing the installation of DPM (and rebooting), you'll need to install Service Pack 1 for DPM 2007 (http://technet.microsoft.com/en-us/dpm/dd296757.aspx). This is important because the original DPM 2007 didn't natively protect Hyper-V. In addition to the DPM installation, some DPM-protected workloads require updates to their VSS writers. If Hyper-V, KB959962 (from Hyper-V), or its future successor is necessary, you need to enable online backups of VMs.

After preparing your new data-protection server, you'll need to allocate one or more disks for the DPM storage pool. As mentioned earlier, this can consist of any internal/external, locally attached disks (DAS), fibre channel, or iSCSI storage solutions. It can't include removable disk media (such as USB hard drives) or remotely mounted volumes (such as shares from Network Attached Storage (NAS) or other filer-type appliances. Optionally, you can attach tape-based storage to the DPM server as well. After you confirm that the tape device is visible from the Windows Device Manager, the DPM server should be able to "find" it and use it. You perform these media configuration tasks from the DPM Administrator Console's Management tab, discussed in the next section.

That's it! You now have a data-protection server with disk and probably tape—and you're ready to protect your production environment, including physical servers, virtualization hosts, and guests.

Introducing the DPM Administrator Console

When you first power up the DPM Administrator Console, you should intuitively understand the core functionality based on previous Microsoft Management Console (MMC) snap-ins and similar System Center interfaces.

Across the top of the DPM console is the *ribbon*, which divides the five areas of DPM 2007 administration:

◆ *Monitoring* presents the active and previous jobs as well as status/completion/failure information that may be necessary during troubleshooting.

◆ *Protection* (shown in Figure 12.4) configures what is protected and how.

◆ *Recovery* (shown in Figure 12.12) is used for data restoration and is discussed later in this chapter.

◆ *Reporting* utilizes SQL Server reporting services to provide information about tape and disk usage, job status, protection compliance, and so on.

◆ *Management* is used for managing the DPM server, including three subtabs for agents (discussed next), disk storage, and tape devices/media.

FIGURE 12.4

The DPM 2007 Administrator Console— Protection tab

Deploying Agents and Application Workload Prerequisites

At this point, you're ready to deploy agents on the production servers (the Hyper-V hosts and/or the guests).

DPM AGENT LICENSES

Every production server that is to be individually protected, physical and/or virtual, requires its own DPM agent. DPM uses a single agent to protect all of its workloads so that Microsoft customers don't require different agents and installations for protecting Hyper-V than they would need for protecting Exchange Server, SQL Server, or components of a SharePoint farm.

There are three different purchasable agents for the production servers' DPM licenses, referred to as Data Protection Management Licenses (DPMLs):

◆ *Client DPML*—For protecting files on Windows XP and Windows Vista

◆ *Standard DPML*—For protecting files on Windows Server 2003 and 2008

◆ *Enterprise DPML*—For protecting files as well as application workloads, including SQL Server databases, Exchange storage groups, SharePoint farms, and virtualization hosts and guests

DPM agents can be pushed from the DPM Administrator Console or from any automated software-deployment mechanism, including System Center Configuration Manager, group policy in Active Directory (AD), or preinstallation in a Windows operating system base image.

DEPLOYING DPM AGENTS THROUGH THE DPM ADMINISTRATOR CONSOLE

While there are different DPML agent price tiers and capabilities, you install only one agent package, which has variants for x86 and x64 systems. For this first installation, you push agents from the DPM console—although, as discussed earlier, you can also deploy them en masse from your favorite software distribution solution. The agent communicates with the DPM server as well as with whatever VSS writers are on each production server (Hyper-V host or virtual guests, in this case). Follow these steps:

1. In the DPM Administrator Console, click the Management button on the ribbon and then select the Agents tab. Click Install Agent in the right task pane to start a wizard that will push the agent to multiple production servers at the same time.

2. On the first screen after the opening welcome (Figure 12.5), you can see the list of production servers in the same AD domain as the DPM server. By clicking servers in the left pane and moving them to the right pane, you select the servers to be protected by this particular DPM server.

FIGURE 12.5
Agents: selecting which production servers to protect

3. On the second screen, you're asked for an administrator-level username and password, to allow you to install the DPM agent on the production machines.

4. Choose whether the production machines will be automatically rebooted after their agent is installed. Because the DPM agent uses a filter technology, the agent is initialized after a reboot; however, this reboot can be done later during off-hours. The screen offers no default choice so you can't accidentally click Next ➤ Next ➤ Finish and reboot your production server farm. Here are the options:

   ◆ Selecting Automatic enables each production server to independently reboot when its agent installation is complete. This is often done after hours or in large deployments where you don't have direct access to the production server(s).

♦ Selecting Manual deploys the agent to all the production server(s), but you must intentionally and individually reboot each server.

The wizard completes by showing you a list of servers currently under installation, with a percentage complete next to each one.

FIGURE 12.6
Installing agents: status

TIP You can close the installation status window (Figure 12.6) with a good level of confidence if all the agents show greater than 6% complete, which indicates that the DPM server has been able to connect with the production server, isn't hindered by most firewalls, and appears to be authorized to install software on the server. Of course, you can also wait until 100% to be sure—or you can refer back to the Monitoring tab of the Administrator Console to see what didn't complete.

DEPLOYING DPM AGENTS MANUALLY

For larger and more automated deployments, you can deploy the DPM agents using traditional software-deployment vehicles such as System Center Configuration Manager 2007, group policy in AD, or preinstalled in a base operating system image.

The primary difference between installing the agent manually versus using the DPM user interface (UI) is the attachment of the production server with the DPM agent to a particular DPM server. When you use the DPM UI, that attachment is done automatically; but for agents that are manually installed, you must use a simple Windows PowerShell script.

From the DPM Management Shell (PowerShell), shown in Figure 12.7, run the `Attach-Production.ps1` script (provided in the BIN directory in which the DPM agent was installed and which is automatically usable from the Management Shell). It prompts you for five variables, which you can also include in the command line:

♦ DPMserver—The DPM server that will protect the Hyper-V production server(s)

♦ PSname—The name of the production server (for example, HYPERV is the name of our host)

◆ `Username`—The username (without domain) that has administrator-level privileges on both the DPM server and the production server

◆ `Password`—Hidden by asterisks

◆ `Domain`—The domain for the user entered earlier

FIGURE 12.7

Installing agents: manually connecting an agent via PowerShell

ADDRESSING FIREWALLS ON THE PRODUCTION SERVER

From the DPM Administrator Console, go to the Management tab and the Agents subtab. There, you should see a list of the production servers that have the agent successfully installed. If one or more of the server(s) shows that their agent(s) are installed but not connected, this is often due to the firewall on the production server.

DPM 2007 provides a utility that automatically configures the firewall with the appropriate permissions for the DPM agent. From `c:\Program Files\Microsoft Data Protection Manager\DPM\bin` (installed agent directory), run SetDPMserver.exe. This has only one command-line variable: the name of the DPM server that the agent should be allowed to talk to. The complete command-line is as follows:

```
SetDPMserver.exe -DPMserverName DPM
```

(The last *DPM* is the name of your DPM server.)

APPLICATION VSS UPDATES OR HOTFIXES

With the DPM agent(s) installed and the appropriate updates or hot fixes from the application (e.g. Hyper-V) applied, your production environment, including your Hyper-V hosts, is ready to be protected.

NOTE Individual hotfixes may be required for each application being protected by DPM. In this case, Hyper-V VSS hotfix KB959962, or an update that supersedes it, is required in order to allow online backups using the Hyper-V VSS writer.

Configuring Protection of Hyper-V Hosts

DPM 2007 was designed with several wizards and managed workflows in mind. One of the most common wizards that you'll become familiar with in DPM creates a protection group. A *protection group* is a policy defining what you want to protect and how you want to protect it.

What Do You Want to Protect?

On the first screen of the Create New Protection Group Wizard, the left pane shows a list of the production servers that are currently running the DPM agent. By expanding any server, you see some common data object types and some data sources that are specific to the workloads running on that machine. On all production servers protected by DPM, you can select the following elements:

◆ *Volumes*—A traditional view of a production server, whereby you can select individual directories for protection in a Windows Explorer–like view.

◆ *Shares*—Typically for file servers but available on all protected machines. This view lists all the file shares on a production server. Selecting an individual share for file-server protection makes DPM identify where the directory is in the production server and protect from that directory down within the volume file system. As an interesting side note, if you select multiple shares that reside on the same physical volume, DPM is intelligent enough to protect that volume only once but discern only those directories as appropriate from the shares that are selected.

◆ *System State*—Protects the Registry, metadata, and other operating system–specific information necessary to re-create the configuration of the production server. Again, because DPM is intended to use only those mechanisms that are supported for protecting its various workloads, DPM protection as system state uses the built-in backup utility provided by the operating system. This built-in backup utility (NTBackup or WSBackup) provides a native capability to back up the system state on the local machine. DPM automates this process by presenting system state as a logical workload or data source within the production server to be protected. Behind the scenes, when protecting system state, DPM invokes the native utility, which first protects system state to a local file on the production server. Then, DPM replicates the captured or *dumped* system state to the DPM server so that its information can be secured along with the other data objects from that machine. This also gives you confidence that you can restore the system state locally using the native utility for minor recovery scenarios, or restore the system state along with the other server data after larger calamities.

In addition to these three common protectable object types, the DPM agent exposes any additional application workloads that are protectable by DPM—for this book, the virtualization workloads provided by Virtual Server 2005 R2 and Hyper-V.

When expanding a virtualization host, the DPM UI presents one option host–specific information as well as a single item for each VM currently defined on that host. These have different names as exposed from the Hyper-V VSS writer, but their function is similar.

When protecting VMs from the host, note that you can't select any granularity other than each entire VM. In addition, the DPM UI selects the VMs for protection with a few qualifiers, as shown in Figure 12.8:

◆ For *Virtual Server 2005 R2*, the VMs are defined as protectable by an offline or an online backup, when you've selected them in the left pane and they're visible in the right pane.

◆ For *Hyper-V*, the VMs in the left pane are noted as being backed up using either saved state or a child partition.

FIGURE 12.8
Configuring protection: data-source selection

These concepts are nearly parallel but will be discussed later in the chapter—see the section "Protecting Virtual Machines from the Host." Although this book is written for Hyper-V, the functional parallels include Virtual Server references to show continuity and functional comparatives between the Microsoft virtualization platforms.

Notice that the entire process for selecting what you want to protect occurs on one screen. You can choose one or more VMs, along with any other directories or shares on the virtualization host, the host configuration, and data from any other protectable workload visible by DPM—all on one screen.

How Do You Want to Protect It?

For the next four to six screens, you choose how to protect the data you selected, by configuring the following:

◆ Disk-based protection

◆ Tape-based protection

◆ Initial synchronization

Configuring Disk-Based Protection

Disk-to-disk protection in DPM can be as simple as two business-driven questions:

◆ How long would you like to keep the data on disk (for fast recovery)?

◆ How often would you like to synchronize the data to disk?

For the retention window (Figure 12.9), typical values are between 5 and 14 days but may often be 30, 45, or even 60. This is the number of days you can restore from DPM disk. By selecting 30, you'll be able to restore to any previously synchronized point in time for a complete month backward, with no need for tape-based restore.

FIGURE 12.9
Configuring protection: disk-based replication

If you've selected additional workloads for protection besides virtualization hosts, you may see a second question about synchronization frequency, presented as a pull-down list with selectable options from 15 minutes to 24 hours. However, this pull-down list is generic to DPM and the protection group—it isn't entirely applicable to virtualized environments. If your protection group includes only virtualization hosts, then this selection is predefined as Immediately Before An Express Full or perhaps isn't visible in the UI. If your protection group includes not only virtualization hosts but also transactional applications like SQL Server, 15 minutes is the default and most common answer (although it won't apply to the protection of the virtualization hosts themselves).

UNDERSTANDING DPM DISK-BASED PROTECTION

DPM uses two different processes to protect Windows data sources:

◆ For all workloads protected by DPM, you can do an *express full*. This is a block-level resynchronization at predetermined points in time, usually between one and six times per day. The mechanics of how an express full identifies, replicates, and applies the changed blocks were covered earlier in this chapter in the section "Understanding DPM Storage."

◆ For transactional applications that are protectable by DPM, such as SQL Server and Exchange Server, DPM can synchronize the backup of transactional logs in between express fulls—up to every 15 minutes. The configuration for these transactional applications is what is referred to by the second question on the disk-to-disk protection screen.

Unfortunately, VHDs don't have transactional logs and therefore can't be protected every 15 minutes. Instead, to configure the schedule for VHD protection, you should configure one or more express fulls per day. The frequency for VHD protection is determined in part by whether the VMs can be protected while online or offline:

If all the VMs selected for protection can be protected while online (no downtime), then it may be reasonable to select one to six express fulls per day, which would allow you to recover a VM to multiple previous points in time without interrupting production users during the backups.

If one or more VMs selected for protection can't be protected online, perhaps because of running Linux or an older Windows operating system, then these VMs will be taken offline during the backup (saved state and later resumed). In this case, you would normally configure a single express full to be run during non-production hours.

Later in the chapter, we'll discuss more about what enables a machine to be protected without interruption (online). For now, and for your first protection group, schedule one express full for after-production hours. Later, by right-clicking the protection group and selecting Modify Protection Group, you can change this or any other setting for protection.

ALLOCATING DISK-BASED STORAGE

On the second disk-based protection screen (Figure 12.10), you select the disk allocation for protecting your data sources (the VMs). As discussed earlier, for each data source protected by DPM, two NTFS volumes are allocated out of the DPM storage pool. On this screen, you define how large each of those volumes (per data source) will be—specifically, the replica volumes and the recovery-point volumes:

Replica volumes should be at least as large as the production data file set (not the production volume), but with some room for expansion. For example, if one VM currently has 3GB of VHDs on a 10GB volume, it isn't necessary to define 10GB for the DPM replica. If the VHDs are fixed size, the replica need be only slightly larger to allow for the natural expansion as blocks are overwritten. However, if the VHDs are dynamic, the replica should be appreciably larger.

Recovery-point volumes should be sized based on the number of days you would like to retain previous point in time. This may take more experimentation to better define, because daily growth depends directly on the data-change rate. DPM retains all the previous points in time if either one of two conditions is met. When DPM reaches the maximum number of days as defined in the protection-group policy (for example, 30 days), then on the thirty-first day, the block-level changes between day 30 and day 31 are discarded from the recovery-point volume. Or, when the recovery-point volume is full, the block-level changes consisting of the oldest day are retained or discarded as a whole. This means that if the recovery-point volume is undersized, DPM may be able to hold only 24 or 16 days of data regardless of the policy (because of lack of capacity).

FIGURE 12.10
Configuring
protection: disk
allocation

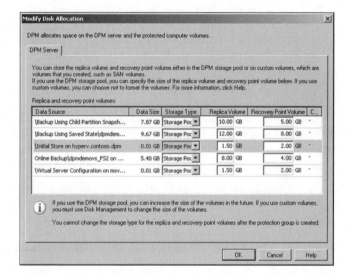

NOTE   Typically, DPM volumes can be expanded later—but they usually can't be reduced, so over-allocation of disk space isn't often recommended.

Configuring Tape-Based Protection

The previous two screens define the DPM disk-to-disk protection by essentially asking

◆   How long should the data reside on disk?

◆   How frequently (and on what schedule) should the data be synchronized?

◆   How should the medium be configured for retention?

Tape-based protection with DPM asks the same three questions (see Figure 12.11):

How long should the data reside on tape?   The default is three months, but you can easily configure this setting by choosing a number in the first field and pulling down a menu for Weeks, Months, or Years. Often, this question is best answered from the corporate retention policy that is defined by either your senior management or perhaps in an industry regulation such as Sarbanes Oxley (SOX), HIPAA, or CO-OP/DOD 5015.2.

How frequently should tape backup occur? The default value and often the best choice is Weekly. Other choices include Daily, Biweekly, Monthly, and Annually. However, because most of your recoveries will now come from disk, tape backups (and recoveries) will be far less frequent and can be done less often. A best practice here is to ensure that at least two tape backups occur during your disk-retention window. This ensures that you have at least two different tapes (in case of tape media failure) to restore data from, above and beyond your disk storage pool.

On what schedule should tape backups occur? As shown in Figure 12.11, after you select the maximum retention time as well as the frequency of tape backups, DPM automatically configures a traditional *grandfather, father, son* tape-rotation system that typically comprises weekly, monthly, and annual tapes. You can configure exactly when the tape backups occur for each of the three tiers or define a custom schedule based on business practices that may be less typical.

Which tape device(s) should be used? Similar to allocating storage in the disk-protection screens, you need to define which tape device(s) will be used for this backup. If your tape library has multiple drives, you may choose how many of those tape drives should be allocated for this particular protection group. This allows you to create some load balancing: in a four-drive library, this protection group may be allowed to use two of the drives, whereas a different protection group protecting SQL or Exchange servers uses the other two drives.

Additionally, you may wish to create copies of some tapes so that one tape resides in the tape library (onsite) and a copy is created for offsite courier services or vaulting. Additional options include the ability to encrypt the tapes, compress the tapes, or neither.

FIGURE 12.11
Configuring
Protection—tape
backup

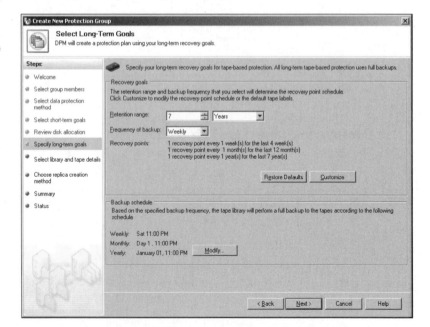

Setting Up the Initial Baseline

Because DPM is natively a disk-to-disk solution, all of its protection capabilities are based on the requirement that the DPM replica has a complete copy of the production data set. The last screen in the Create New Protection Group Wizard determines how the initial synchronization or *baseline* occurs:

Now is the most common choice, particularly in cases where the VMs can be protected while they remain online. Within the data center and without significant production load, it may be reasonable to immediately start popping the data from the production virtualization host(s) to the DPM server.

Later provides for the ability to schedule the data synchronization to occur after hours. This allows you to configure the data-protection group during your typical day, without affecting the production user base. Instead, you can schedule the baseline to occur after hours and finish before the next business day. Selecting this choice enables simple calendar and time-based selection choices.

Manually provides for branch-office scenarios and other circumstances where pulling the production data may not be appealing. Instead, as in a remote office with a significant amount of data, you can do an offline backup of the branch office server (using tape, USB hard drive, or other portable media) and ship the media from the branch to the DPM server location. Then, you can restore the offline backup into the DPM replica partition.

By selecting Manually, you notify the DPM server that the data already resides in or has been manually copied to the DPM replica. In turn, DPM performs an immediate consistency check, which does a block-level comparison of what is on the remote production server and what is in the DPM replica. This allows the DPM server to replicate those block-level changes that have occurred over the past few days since the initial backup was taken—making it ideal for the initial setup of branch-office or remote servers with large amounts of data.

After a confirmation screen that summarizes the choices you've made, DPM allocates the appropriate storage for the replica and recovery-point volumes, defines the protection group, configures the protection schedule(s), and initiates the baseline copy or consistency check.

During a consistency check, each data source initially appears as a green OK and then later turns to a yellow Warning while the block-level comparison happens. For the baseline copy, the object appears with a white Informational for notifications until the baseline is complete. After either case, the data source changes back to a green OK and begins synchronizing on the schedule you've defined.

You've now protected your virtualization environment.

Considerations When Protecting Virtualized Environments

Just because you can protect your virtual infrastructure from the host perspective doesn't necessarily mean that you'll always want to. There are reasons to protect VMs from the outside (host-based agent). Similarly, there are reasons to protect your VMs using the same methodology you use to protect physical machines from the inside (guest-based agent).

Virtual Machines, Hosts, and Guests

If your VMs are all running Windows Server 2003 or Windows Server 2008, you might consider ignoring this entire chapter—other than backing up the hypervisor's host configuration. You can protect the VMs as if they were physical—by running a DPM agent inside each virtualized production server. Fundamentally, there is no difference between protecting a virtualized Windows Server running an application such as SQL Server and protecting a physical server with the same operating system and application. And there are reasons you may choose to do this—most notably, granular data selection during backups and recovery.

Assume for a moment that you have five virtualization hosts, and each happens to be running approximately 10 virtualized Windows Server and SQL Server application platforms. If they're all generic database platforms, then protecting their entire machine set may have you protecting 50 copies of essentially the same Windows Server operating system and 50 copies of the SQL Server application, when all you really want is the 50 database sets. In this scenario, in the case of a crisis, you may consider restoring only a select subset of those databases onto a few consolidated SQL servers for recovery purposes. Or, if complex applications are installed on each of those 50 database servers, then perhaps the best resolution method is to protect the machine sets and bring all 50 virtualized application platforms back online.

CHOOSING WHAT TO PROTECT AND HOW TO RECOVER

The previous scenario illustrates the primary question for which you need a clear answer when you're deciding whether to protect your virtual infrastructure from a guest perspective or from a host perspective: what are you trying to restore?

If your primary requirement is protecting the data, meaning specific SQL Server databases, Exchange storage groups, SharePoint farms, or Windows file-server home directories, then the appropriate choice may be to run DPM agents in each guest and protect strictly those data objects.

But it isn't quite that simple. What is your recovery goal?

If you're primarily protecting application data sets with the anticipation of being able to roll back to previous points in time in anticipation of user error, hardware calamity, or ad hoc point-in-time requests, then you'll be predominantly restoring individual data objects and therefore should protect those individual data objects (from within the guest).

If you're primarily protecting application servers in anticipation of whole server failure or as part of your disaster recovery or business continuity preparedness plan (or you have other requirements for being able to restore an entire servers application set in a very short time frame), then you should protect the entire virtualized server (from the host).

The two choices aren't mutually exclusive, and we'll discuss a hybrid approach later in the section.

If you do choose to protect each virtualized server as if it were physical, then you should plan not only for how the virtual data will be protected but also for the aggregate impact to the host and overall I/O. For example, although protecting transactional applications like Exchange Server or SQL Server may be fairly transparent and non-impacting during the production day, it's not zero impact. Plan for some amount, albeit minor, of network/disk/performance impact during the backup windows themselves. Also, recognize that if you have 10 virtualized SQL Servers on the same host and you've configured them to be in the same DPM protection group, then your host will see a significant increase in network traffic every 15 minutes (or as often as you're set up to synchronize)—the aggregate of the backup traffic that might normally be seen on 10 separate physical servers. Consider dedicated network segments (physical and virtual in those cases—or stagger the replication with multiple protection groups on different schedules).

Protecting Virtual Machines from the Host

When the VMs' operating system is Windows Server 2003 or Windows Server 2008 and they're running Microsoft application server platforms, then you may have the choice of protecting from the host or guest.

The opposite corollary is also true. If the VMs aren't running a Windows operating system, DPM isn't a choice for protecting them within the guest(s) and therefore makes a compelling argument for protecting from the host. At that point, DPM provides a crash-consistent backup of the VM, regardless of the operating system. As a twist on this idea, for secure environments as well as outsourcing situations, this enables you to back up entire VMs from the host without any visibility of the contents or data inside.

GUEST OPERATING SYSTEMS AND APPLICATIONS

Similarly (but not exactly), if the VMs are running a Windows operating system but the applications aren't currently protectable by DPM 2007, there is merit in protecting each VMs from the host-based perspective. Of course, to make the decision slightly more blurry, some Windows applications, which may not be explicitly defined as protectable by DPM, may have known recipes to be protected by DPM 2007 using its pre-/post-backup scripting method. In this case, it still comes back to "What do you want to protect?" and "How do you need to restore?"

Aside from the VMs' applications and operating systems, there are other considerations when choosing whether to protect from the host or the guest.

STORAGE CONFIGURATION OF GUESTS

If the guest operating system isn't using VHDs for its data volumes but instead is using the Hyper-V capability for passthrough disks, then the Hyper-V VSS writer doesn't have access to those data volumes and can't protect those volumes using a host-based backup.

Similarly, if the guest operating system is using an iSCSI initiator or a virtualized Host-Bus Adapter (HBA) to use storage not visible from the hypervisor host, then a host-based backup of those volumes isn't viable.

Interestingly, some administrators consider this an ideal scenario—the operating system and application volume are in a VHD that can be protected from the host, but the data sets are conveniently missing. Instead, many administrators choose to protect the data volumes by protecting the actual data objects using a guest-based DPM agent. This provides the best of both worlds, where you can protect and recover the whole machine (operating system and applications) as a single VHD while still providing granular data restoration from within the data volumes.

Choosing Guest or Host or Both

Let's summarize the decision points we've presented so far:

◆ VMs running VSS-capable Windows operating systems and applications have the choice of being protected from the host or the guest (in general).

◆ VMs *not* running a VSS-capable operating system or application should generally be protected from the host. This scenario is most commonly seen in DPM environments where a significant majority of production physical and virtual servers are protectable by DPM 2007; however, the business requirements mandate a minority of non-Microsoft platforms to be backed up as well. By virtualizing those platforms, you enjoy the benefits of DPM for the majority of your servers while getting at least a crash-consistent external backup of your few non-Windows machines, to maintain a single backup and recovery solution for their entire environment.

◆ Storage architectures that preclude the Hyper-V VSS writer from having direct access to the VHD enclosed data may not be protectable from the host.

Often, the ability to restore a *complete (virtual) machine*, similar to the desire to do a *bare-metal recovery* of physical servers, is the primary reason to protect and recover from the host.

The other primary reason for protecting from the host is cost. DPM is often positioned as one of the most cost-effective backup and recovery solutions for Windows environments, or for providing enterprise-type backup capabilities (such as D2D2T and DR) without enterprise prices. However, because virtualization tends to encourage a significant proliferation of small, standalone (virtual) servers, you may be hesitant to acquire, deploy, and manage an ever-growing number of guest DPMLs.

From a licensing viewpoint, the street price for an Enterprise DPML capable of protecting SQL Server, Exchange, SharePoint, or a hypervisor host is approximately $425 in the United States. If you had to acquire E-DPMLs for 20 virtualized application servers, you might pay more than $8,000 (interestingly, the cost of some other replication or backup technology agents for the host alone).

As a different cost consideration, although DPM 2007 is designed around ease of use, protecting 20 servers (virtual or physical) has some incremental operational costs for deployment and monitoring (but not nearly 20 times the cost). So, although protecting one host, with its related guests' VHDs, may be appear operationally easier, it's usually outweighed by other considerations such as data granularity (discussed earlier).

SYSTEM CENTER SERVER MANAGEMENT SUITE ENTERPRISE (SMSE)

As discussed earlier, DPM is one component of the System Center family of management products. As an acquisition vehicle, System Center provides a suite for the production servers' agents. Specifically, the enterprise suite contains the management licenses (MLs) for each of the four components of System Center:

An E-DPML for Data Protection Manager

An E-OML for Operations Manager

An E-CML for Configuration Manager

A VMML for Virtual Machine Manager

Because this is a licensing bundle, there are cost benefits strictly on the basis that if you're currently using or need more than one of the System Center components, the SMSE becomes cost-effective. In addition, one of the benefits of acquiring DPMLs as part of SMSEs is free-use rights for the guest operating systems when using an SMSE on your virtualization host. This means that by deploying an E-DPML from an SMSE on your Hyper-V host, you can protect any/all of the VMs from the host perspective and also deploy DPMLs within the appropriate VMs at no additional cost.

Restoring Your Virtual Environment with DPM

And now for the fun part.

After all, no one intentionally purchases *backup* software—you purchase *recovery* software, where backup is simply a preparation task. That twist on words isn't entirely meant as a joke, but it's intended to demonstrate that DPM is designed as recovery software and not backup software. Often, backup software is just that: software intended to conduct backups and typically used only for whole server recoveries or as a proof point to confirm that backups are occurring for compliance or retention purposes. DPM really is *recovery* software.

Overview of the DPM Restore UI

Similar to the wizards for protecting data, DPM uses restoration wizards to provide recovery with the same ease-of-use goals.

1. In the DPM Administrator Console, select Recovery from the ribbon. Here (see Figure 12.12), the left pane provides a tree-based view of all the production servers that have been protected by this DPM server.

FIGURE 12.12
Restoring data: the DPM 2007 console Recovery screen

When you expand each of the servers, you see the same kinds of data objects that you can select for a protection group, such as volumes, system state, and application workloads.

2. Expand the Hyper-V host, and you can see the virtualization workload being protected, including the host configuration as well as each of the VMs.

3. Click a protected data object to refresh the calendar and detail panes on the right side.

The calendar presents a typical monthly view. The dates in bold have recovery points available for restoration.

4. Select any bold date on the calendar, and a pull-down menu to the right presents any points in time from that day that are available for restore.

5. Click a desired time, and the details pane in the lower-right corner displays the VM for restoration.

6. Right-click the VM, and select Restore.

Literally, you can select any data object for recovery to any point in time in as few as four mouse clicks:

1. Select the data objects from the left pane.

2. Select the date you wish to recover to.

3. Pull down the time you wish to recover to.

4. Right-click the data object in the right pane, and choose Recover.

Restoring a Virtual Machine from the DPM UI

Following the previously described steps, you can select the VM to restore from the DPM UI. Doing so invokes a Recovery Wizard (see Figure 12.13) that walks you through the remaining steps. After the introduction screen, you see several different recovery choices, some of which are specific to the workload being restored (in this case, a VM) and other of which are generic to all DPM recovery scenarios.

The last two recovery options are generic for all DPM data sources:

Recover To A File Location The Recover To A File Location option restores the files that make up your data source to any file share or directory that is accessible from the DPM server. The intent is to provide the files in such a way that an application owner can then manually act on them. In the case of SQL Server or Exchange Server, you may choose to manually mount the database for some particular recovery scenario.

In the case of a VM, you can create a directory that will receive the VHDs. You can then choose to manually create a new VM, or perhaps use SCVMM to automate that VM creation.

Recover To Tape Note that the Recover To Tape option isn't misspelled as *recover from tape*. With the Recover To Tape option, the files of the selected data source are *restored* from the DPM repository onto their own tape. This approach is normally used for IT environments that must periodically ship data offsite to an auditor, a vault, or an e-discovery judicial proceeding. A typical (and non-optimal) method has been to copy an existing backup tape from the nightly library, which includes not only the requested data but also other, unnecessary information.

Instead, this DPM capability lets you select only the data object you desire at the specific point in time that it's required, and *restore* the data to its own individual tape. This tape can then be sent off to the auditor, vault, or attorney.

The other restore option(s) are specific to the type of data being recovered. For applications such as SQL Server, Exchange, and SharePoint, you may see multiple choices for restoring the data back to the original location, alternate locations, and additional options based on the granularity of the data being restored. In the case of Hyper-V (see Figure 12.13), the choice is to restore the VM back to its original hypervisor.

FIGURE 12.13

Restoring data: VM restoration options

By selecting Recover To Original Instance, you restore the VM to the original Hyper-V host server. To restore to an alternate Hyper-V host, you can choose Copy To A Network Folder and then select a folder on the Hyper-V host. From there, you'll need to mount the VHDs by creating a new VM on that host (or automate the process via batch file or SCVMM PowerShell script).

Assuming that you choose to restore to the original Hyper-V host, the second wizard screen presents some standard DPM restoration options:

◆ *Network Bandwidth Throttling* ensures that the restoration activity doesn't overwhelm limited bandwidth segments between the DPM server and the restoration target. For this, DPM provides Kbps and Mbps settings, including variations for time of day, so you may use partial wide area network (WAN) bandwidth during the production day and all available bandwidth during non-production hours.

◆ *SAN Recovery* uses a SAN that is shared between the DPM server and the Hyper-V host. This invokes a SAN-specific script that instructs the SAN to make a mirror of the DPM replica volume within the shared disk array and then remount the mirror on the host. This can be a powerful feature if the production server(s) and the DPM server are on the same SAN, because terabytes of data can be restored in a matter of seconds.

◆ *Notification* uses a Simple Mail Transfer Protocol (SMTP) mail server and notifies the appropriate systems administrators when the restoration process is complete.

On the third of three Recovery Wizard screens, you see the summary of what will be restored (see Figure 12.14). Note that on this screen, the VM is made up of three VHDs for an application server that runs Windows Server and SQL Server on one virtual disk, with separate virtual disks for its databases and logs. Here you see each of the VHDs (and where they will restore to) as well as the VM definition information (noted by the GUID).

FIGURE 12.14
Restoring data:
VM restored
components

Restoring a Virtual Machine from the DPM PowerShell Command Line

DPM provides two PowerShell commandlets that work together for restoring data objects—encompassing not only the options seen in the Restore Wizard but also accommodating all of the workload-specific restore tasks. It would take too much space to explain all of the options and scenarios that are enabled by these two commandlets, but they are listed here for reference. After each commandlet name, you will notice several, mostly optional command-line switches—each prefaced by a hyphen. For each option switch that requires supplemental information, an additional descriptor follows the switch. Both the switch and its information descriptor are encapsulated by [block-parenthesis] for readability in this text, but are not required during execution.

The first commandlet, New-RecoveryOption, sets most of the generic restore options that should be recognizable if you have already tried any restores from the DPM administrator console and its restore wizard—such as whether to recover to tape or alternate file location, whether to use SAN recovery, etc.

```
New-RecoveryOption -PrimaryDpmServer -RecoverToReplicaFromTape [-DPMLibrary
<Library> ] [-RecoveryLocation <RecoveryLocation> ]  [-SANRecovery]
[-TargetServer <String> ] [ <CommonParameters> ]
```

The second commandlet, Recover-RecoverableItem, is the main restoring command. In fact, this commandlet receives its additional options from the first commandlet mentioned earlier— almost as if you had written one really, really long command-line.

```
Recover-RecoverableItem [-RecoverableItem] <RecoverableObject> [-RecoveryOption]
<RecoveryOption> [-JobStateChangedEventHandler <JobStateChangedEventHandler> ]
[-RecoveryNotification <Notification> ] [-RecoveryPointLocation
<RecoverySourceLocation> ] [ <CommonParameters> ]
```

The two commands work together to define what type of object is being restored (like a Virtual Machine), where and how to restore it, how to provide status information on the recovery, etc.

Between the two commandlets and their several optional switches, you get a very flexible recovery capability that can be executed via command line, batch file, or even as a task within System Center Operations Manager or some other management platform. For more information on the DPM commandlets, including their switches and options—check out http://technet .microsoft.com/en-us/library/bb842063.aspx.

As an alternative, if the VM is performing correctly, and you want to add the VM from a certain point in time to a VHD library or bring a previous iteration of the VM back online, you can restore the VHD(s) to an alternate location (file share or directory). You can then manually add the VHD to an SCVMM library or mount it in a different VM. To accomplish this, you only need to change the -RecoveryLocation variable in the cmdlet from the original Hyper-V host to an alternative directory someplace else on the network, such as a different Hyper-V host or SCVMM library share.

Disaster Recovery Using DPM with SCVMM

Thus far, we've discussed data protection and virtualization within the context of protecting a virtualized environment. When speaking with a backup administrator, virtualization hosts are sometimes considered "just another kind of application platform to be protected." In other environments, virtualization hosts may be considered "troublesome" either because the backup solution must be specific and is often complex or because they encourage the proliferation of new servers that must then be individually backed up. We hope you've seen that DPM 2007 addresses both of these concerns and provides a reliable and scalable virtualization protection solution that you can also use across the rest of your Windows infrastructure.

However, there is another way to put these same elements together and enable a completely different solution:

♦ *Backup* tends to be a tactical requirement for network administrators that frequently consumes an inordinate amount of operational costs and causes a nightly burden.

♦ *Disaster recovery*, on the other hand, is usually regarded as a strategic initiative by executives and managers that may sometimes seem cost-prohibitive or unattainable.

In this section, we'll explore how DPM and virtualization can address the larger goals of disaster recovery.

Challenges with Traditional Disaster Recovery

Two traditional methods are typically used for disaster recovery of a computing infrastructure:

Offsite tape couriers   For large companies that have either a regulatory requirement or a common business practice of retaining key documents at an offsite location, it's common to engage courier services to ship copies of nightly tape backups off premises. Although this satisfies offsite goals, frequently you can't meet today's requirements for fast recovery when you can't begin the recovery exercise until those tapes or offsite media have been returned to your facility.

Replicated data center   Many companies of all sizes send backup media to alternate data centers at remote locations for the purposes of disaster recovery. In smaller environments, two regional offices may mirror each other. For larger corporations, completely redundant and isolated data centers may be built. In almost all cases, this solution requires redundant servers with their associated storage, power, space, cooling, and management costs.

Virtualization and Disaster Recovery Staging

But, as a reader of a book about Hyper-V, you understand that there is a better way to address underutilized servers and eliminate many of the space, power, cooling, and management costs associated with server infrastructure: virtualization. The trick becomes how to get your data and server configurations from a physical production environment into a virtualized disaster-recovery site. Again, because you've read this chapter, you know that DPM can replicate the data offsite—and reliably restore it.

Protecting Your Physical Machines

Fundamentally, three types of information should be protected for disaster preparedness, as shown in Figure 12.15:

♦ The operating systems and applications of the production server farm—for use at the disaster-recovery location

♦ The operating systems and applications of the production server farm—for the purposes of recovering the original physical servers after the crisis has been resolved

♦ The data

Using SCVMM to Protect the Operating System and Applications

SCVMM provides a utility for migrating physical production servers into virtual environments. This physical to virtual (P2V) utility is usually run once per physical production server, with the result being a VHD on a Windows hypervisor. Usually, you can execute the P2V utility safely without interrupting the production server. Then, at an appropriate time, you typically power down the physical server while you bring the virtualized copy online as an easy migration scenario.

FIGURE 12.15
Disaster recovery from DPM + SCVMM

You can run this same process routinely to capture a physical operating-system and application set to a VHD, which you can then replicate from the production facility to the disaster-recovery site. Instead of being used for migration purposes, these VHDs are left dormant until a disaster is declared.

Because SCVMM is scriptable with Windows PowerShell, you can automate this process weekly or perhaps execute it ad hoc after server maintenance or configuration changes. This dramatically reduces the amount of redundant server hardware at the disaster-recovery site. Instead of racks of underutilized physical servers, companies can deploy a few dedicated virtualization hosts—while retaining complete and autonomous instances of the entire production physical server farm.

Using DPM to Protect Data

As discussed in the beginning of this chapter, DPM isn't simply for protecting virtual environments. Unlike the backup mechanisms provided by other virtualization vendors, Microsoft DPM provides backups not only for Microsoft virtualization hosts and guests but also for physical production servers running Windows Server, including SQL Server, Exchange Server, and SharePoint.

Some environments completely embrace virtualization and migrate all their production physical servers, but many other environments run a mixture.

For physical production servers, DPM can natively protect the data to a local primary DPM server for fast recovery, which can then be replicated to an offsite DPM server for disaster preparedness. Alternatively, DPM can also protect from the physical production servers (without a local DPM replica) directly to an offsite DPM server for disaster recovery.

For virtual production servers, all of the previous guidance on protecting from the guest versus the host applies. This is typically a great example of running protection from the host and guest. You might protect the virtualized production server from within the guest to the on-premises DPM server for fast recovery of the individual data objects, while protecting the entire VM from the host to the disaster recovery site in preparation for whole-server recovery.

In either case, you can use DPM to protect production data, including replication to the disaster recovery facility. In addition, DPM can protect the system state of the production servers. In the more common scenario where you don't lose the entire production facility, but just a single server, you can use the system state to restore an individual server configuration back to similar hardware, if needed.

Planning for Long-Term Server Restoration

In the event of a true site calamity, where the entire production server farm is critically affected, you may be operating within the virtualized environment for a while. Your initial disaster-recovery execution may include a plan whereby all your production physical servers are replicated, but the virtualization host environment can't sustain all of them running simultaneously. It's perfectly reasonable, based on a Business Impact Analysis (BIA), to predetermine that only a percentage of production servers can be brought online immediately after averting a crisis. Based on your future outlook, you may then plan to expedite additional virtualization hosts to bring the remaining virtualized servers online.

At some point, however, you'll need to enact your long-term server-restoration plan:

- Some companies, after confirming that the virtualized servers are performing adequately, use this crisis as the forcing function toward an all-virtual infrastructure and remain in production from the virtualized machines.

- Other companies wish to rebuild their physical production server farm. Currently, the SCVMM P2V utility doesn't provide a virtual to physical (V2P) mechanism, meaning that the virtualized server can't be used to reconstruct the original physical server. But because DPM can protect the physical servers' system state along with the production data, the system state can be used to reconstitute the production server farm.

Restoring Your Infrastructure within Hyper-V

Assuming that you've been routinely capturing your physical server configurations using SCVMM P2V, as well as continually protecting your data with DPM, let's now look at the recovery procedure after a disaster. The highest priorities of a disaster recovery plan include ensuring the safety of personnel and enacting the larger disaster-recovery plan as defined by your executive leadership. That being understood, most disaster-recovery efforts succeed or fail based on your ability to access your corporate information. Said another way, without your data, the rest of your plan may not work.

Using SCVMM to Bring Servers Online

The first task is to bring the virtualized production servers online. Fortunately, SCVMM provides a PowerShell cmdlet (Start-VM) for this purpose:

```
Start-VM  -VMMServer localhost  -VM "WebServices14" -RunAsynchronously
```

Bringing 20 VMs online can literally be done as a 20-line batch file. Alternatively, by using the smart-placement technology in SCVMM 2008, you can be more selective or judicious about which virtualization hosts bring up which virtualized guests.

USING DPM TO RESTORE DATA

After the VMs are brought online, most will have only the C: partition (operating system and applications) in their first VHD. You can use SCVMM to add storage to each VM, as if a production server had lost one or more hard drives and new one(s) were installed.

Similar to SCVMM, DPM can be controlled using PowerShell. The cmdlet isn't as universal because the options vary based on the data type being restored. However, because these scripts are defined before a disaster occurs, you're encouraged to explore the Microsoft TechNet center on DPM PowerShell scripting: Look at the `Recover-RecoverableItem` and `New-RecoveryOption` cmdlets at `http://technet.microsoft.com/en-us/library/bb842063.aspx`.

With the VMs online and the data restored, the company can now begin to resume IT operations.

MAKING THE PROCESS EVEN BETTER

With the basics understood, you can do several things to optimize this recovery process:

Script per server instead of per phase. Consider creating individual scripts that include all of the SCVMM and DPM PowerShell commands per server. This provides a few benefits including these:

◆ You may choose to stagger the server booting process, such that critical servers can be completely brought online first while less essential servers are deferred, if necessary.

◆ In the case where the entire production site hasn't failed entirely, but one or more physical servers have been individually critically affected, you can choose to selectively bring just those virtualized servers online.

Use SCOM to monitor the production environment and provide intelligent information about the scope of the disaster. In addition, by embedding the SCVMM/DPM recovery scripts as tasks in SCOM, the recovery tasks can be invoked by the same operator who determined the scale of the crisis. By first defining rigorous diagnostic criteria, you may choose to automate the entire disaster-recovery process, to be invoked when the appropriate conditions are met in SCOM. You should do this with care, however, to avoid a false positive where the disaster-recovery environment is enabled when a site crisis hasn't actually occurred.

Automate the network resolution for remote clients. For remote users outside of the primary production facility, consider using either a dynamic/round-robin DNS configuration or an Internet gateway so that remote clients can be transparently switched from accessing the primary production facility and the disaster-recovery site.

Collectively, you can use virtualization along with data protection to address your disaster-recovery goals with products and technologies that you're already familiar with—and thus deliver capabilities that may otherwise be cost-prohibitive.

Summary

Microsoft System Center DPM 2007 with Service Pack 1 is designed, in part, to complement Hyper-V in the larger scope of the Microsoft virtualization portfolio. Referring back to the beginning of this chapter, if you're going to put all of your eggs in one basket, it better be a good basket. DPM helps ensure that Hyper-V is a "good basket" for your virtual infrastructure:

◆ In contrast to the backup capabilities provided by other virtualization vendors, DPM doesn't require a SAN or third-party tape backup software to protect its VMs.

◆ In contrast to third-party tape-backup software for Hyper-V, DPM provides an all-Microsoft backup and recovery solution that is wholly supportable and uses only protection and restoration methods that are directly supported by the Hyper-V development team and customer service organization.

◆ In contrast to a third-party replication technology for Hyper-V, DPM provides onsite and offsite protection of VMs and the host configuration, and does so at a fraction of the cost for most replication software and in a more supportable way.

Chapter 13

System Center Operations Manager 2007

In this chapter, we'll cover System Center Operations Manager (SCOM) 2007 and the role it plays in the Microsoft virtualization infrastructure for managing both physical and virtual systems. The scope of this chapter will be how you can use SCOM 2007 to manage a Microsoft virtualization infrastructure. This is a narrow focus for SCOM 2007 because SCOM is designed to handle all aspects of IT operations. Note that this chapter isn't designed to be an install or design guide for SCOM 2007—several very good guides are available for installing core SCOM 2007 functionality.

SCOM is a feature-rich platform for IT management, with functionality that maps to specific operational areas defined in the Information Technology Infrastructure Library and the Microsoft Operations Framework. It's important for you to spend time getting up to speed on all aspects of SCOM 2007 that aren't covered in this chapter. We recommend that you read the book *Mastering Microsoft System Center Operations Manager 2007* from Sybex. In addition, the SCOM 2007 white papers located at `http://technet.microsoft.com/en-us/opsmgr/bb498235.aspx` should be considered required reading.

This chapter covers the following topics:

◆ SCOM technical overview

◆ Using SCOM for your virtualization environment

◆ Monitoring and reporting

System Center Operations Manager 2007

SCOM provides the health/service model, real-time alerting, monitoring infrastructure, and reporting environment that let you manage physical and virtual environments as well as Microsoft and non-Microsoft platforms. SCOM provides the following functionality:

◆ End-to-end monitoring

◆ Comprehensive views of health states

◆ Rapid response to events for managed systems

◆ Application-specific management packs

◆ Automated tasks per application

◆ A comprehensive automated reporting infrastructure

An SCOM management pack provides application-level knowledge and custom tasks tailored to the specifics of an application. The end-state goal is to bridge application alerting and monitoring into the virtualization management framework. System Center Virtual Machine Manager (SCVMM) and SCOM provide a system connector to share information about managed virtual machines (VMs) and applications. The functionality providing deep integration between SCOM and SCVMM is called Performance Resource Optimization (PRO) and is described in detail in Chapter 11, "System Center Virtual Machine Manager 2008." This enables VMs that have SCOM management packs and PRO packs installed to exchange information with SCVMM 2008.

SCOM Technical Overview

In this section, we'll introduce the key concepts that all virtualization administrators should be familiar with before deploying SCOM. SCOM 2007 forms the backbone of monitoring, reporting, and alerting services in the Microsoft virtualization infrastructure. SCOM 2007 integration with SCVMM provides 360-degree monitoring, real-time triggers, and alerting of not only the physical systems but VMs and the applications running in VMs.

All hardware, software, services, and other logical components that you want SCOM to be aware of are described in a model. A *model* is a consumable representation of software or hardware components that captures the nature of the components and the relationships between them. For example, monitoring Microsoft virtualization services involves monitoring a variety of components such as Hyper-V hosts, quick migration clusters, operating-system components, disk subsystems, and SCVMM components. The diagram view shown in SCVMM is an example of how all the Microsoft virtualization components in a model are monitored and displayed in a single view. Some would call this service-level monitoring, and that's accurate; but all service management begins from a model. To fully monitor Microsoft virtualization services, you must discover and monitor the interaction and interdependencies between these systems, such as whether PRO Tips and alerts are flowing through the system. In SCOM 2007, a health model for the service can alert you when one component of the service is unhealthy and change the state of the overall service until all components are functioning correctly.

SCOM uses management packs to model and monitor software and hardware components. In SCOM, management packs contain the models required for the software to interpret the structure of an application and determine the health of the application. This knowledge is expressed as an XML document and uses a predefined XML scheme understood by SCOM.

The model-based design uses this standard specification language to tell SCOM about important elements of your application or component. Objects in your model can represent hardware components, such as whether a physical switch that connects into a virtual switch is running; or they can represent software, such as whether a particular application in a VM or service is running. By combining different objects and relationships, you can create a distributed application model that spans different components, applications, and hardware. Understanding models helps you make the best use of SCOM 2007.

Core Components of SCOM

The following SCOM components make up the SCOM functionality that provide alerting, reporting, monitoring, and service-modeling capabilities.

SCOM Database

The SCOM database is the first component to be installed in all management groups. It must be installed on a Microsoft SQL Server 2005 with SP2. This database holds all the configuration data for the management group, and it stores all the monitoring data that the agents collect and process.

To optimize performance of SCOM, you must optimize performance of the SCOM database. You do so by controlling the size of the database: Testing has shown that 50GB is a good upper limit. To control the database size, SCOM 2007 automatically grooms out older, unnecessary data according to parameters you set.

Because there can be only one SCOM database in a management group, it must be functional in order for the management group to work. To mitigate the single instance of the SCOM database from being a single point of failure, you can place it in a Microsoft Cluster Service (MSCS) failover cluster.

Root Management Server

The root management server (RMS) is a specialized type of management server in a management group, and it's the first management server installed in a management group. There can be only one active RMS per management group. In brief, management servers are the focal point for administering the management group configuration, administering and communicating with agents, and communicating with the SCOM database and other databases in the management group.

The RMS performs all these functions plus some additional ones. It serves as the target for the operations console and the preferred target for the Web console.

In addition, the RMS hosts the SCOM SDK service and the SCOM Config service. These services run only on the RMS. The SDK service provides a communication layer between the SCOM database and the rest of the management group. The Config service calculates the configuration of all agents, which management packs they should receive, and the overall configuration of the management group.

Like the SCOM database, you can install the RMS role into an MSCS failover cluster to make it highly available. In addition, you can manually promote other management servers in the management group (if you have them) to the role of RMS.

Operations Console

The operations console provides a single, unified user interface (UI) for interacting with SCOM 2007. The operations console provides access to monitoring data, management-pack authoring tools, SCOM reports, all the controls and tools necessary for administering SCOM, and a customizable workspace.

For a user to access the operations console, you must assign the user's Active Directory (AD) user account to an SCOM 2007 role. A *role* is the combination of a scope of devices to which access is granted and a profile that defines what the role can do within its defined scope. For example, you can use a role to define a virtualization administrator for a specific set of Hyper-V hosts. Role-based security is enforced in the operations console so you can define what any given user can see in the console and what actions the user can take on those items.

AGENT

An SCOM 2007 *agent* is a service that you deploy on a computer that you want to monitor. Once a machine is managed by SCOM, the the SCOM health service is listed. Every agent is owned by a management server in the management group, and this server is referred to as the agent's *primary* management server. Agents watch data sources on the monitored device and collect information according to the configuration sent from its management server. This data is used to calculate the health state of the monitored object. When the health state of a monitored object changes or other criteria are met, an alert can be generated, which lets you know that something has gone awry and requires attention.

Agents can also take many types of actions to help you diagnose or correct issues. It's most important to note that agents feed a constant stream of data back to the management server about the monitored device so that an up-to-date picture of the health of the device and all the applications that it supports is always available.

It's possible to monitor devices in an agentless fashion. In this case, an agent on a management server performs the monitoring remotely.

MANAGEMENT PACKS

Management packs contain the definition of an application's health as defined by the application developers. When you import management packs into SCOM, the agent can then monitor the health of an application, generate alerts when something of significance goes wrong in the application, and take actions in the application and its supporting infrastructure to further diagnose the application or restore it to a healthy state. Without an application-, operating system–, or device-specific management pack, SCOM 2007 is unaware of those entities and is unable to monitor them.

Optional Server Roles and Components

These additional server roles extend the functionality of a management group. Most of these components are installed separately from the required core components, but you can install some at the same time as the core components

MANAGEMENT SERVER

A management server isn't the first one installed into a management group; it's automatically configured as a regular management server and doesn't perform any of the special functions of the RMS. You can promote this type of management server to the RMS role if the RMS fails, as long as the server was present in the management group prior to the RMS failure.

You can install multiple management servers in a management group to provide extra capacity for agent management. In addition to providing scalability, introducing additional management servers into a management group allows agents to fail over and start reporting their data to another management server if they lose communication with their primary management server.

Management servers that aren't in the RMS role are used primarily for agent administration. One additional role for a management server is to host the Audit Collection Service (ACS) Collector role. The ACS Collector can be installed only on a management server.

GATEWAY SERVER

An SCOM 2007 gateway server can drastically reduce the administrative overhead required to maintain communication between agents and management servers that are separated by a trust boundary.

SCOM 2007 requires that agents and management servers authenticate each other and establish an encrypted communication channel before they exchange information. Kerberos is the authentication protocol used for the agent-to-server and server-to-agent authentication. When the agent and the management server are in the same AD domain or in domains that share a two-way trust relationship, mutual authentication occurs automatically. This is because Kerberos is the default authentication protocol in AD.

WEB CONSOLE SERVER

The web console server provides an administrative interface to the management group that is accessible via a web browser. It doesn't have the full functionality of the operations console, however. The web console provides access to all the monitoring data and tasks that are actions that can be run against monitored computers from the operations console. It also exposes the operator's personalized My Workspace. Access to data in the web console has the same restrictions as access to content in the operations console.

REPORTING DATA WAREHOUSE

The Reporting Data Warehouse stores monitoring and alerting data for historical purposes. The management servers write their data to the Reporting Data Warehouse at the same time it's written to the SCOM database, so the reports generated always contain the most up-to-date data. The Reporting Data Warehouse automatically aggregates performance data on an hourly and daily basis. This lets you run long-term trending reports much more quickly than would be possible otherwise, and far less data needs to be retained to support long-term trend reporting.

The Reporting Data Warehouse can receive data from multiple management groups, thereby allowing for an aggregated view of data in your reports.

REPORTING SERVER

The reporting server is an important part of the managed virtualization infrastructure because it provides reports for virtualization functionality like Virtualization Candidate reports. SCVMM 2008 uses the reporting server functionality to report on critical SCVMM services. The SCOM reporting server is installed into an instance of Microsoft SQL 2005 Reporting Services with SP1 or SP2. It builds and presents the reports using data queried from the Reporting Data Warehouse. All reports can be accessed from the SCOM operations console; and when SCVMM is integrated with SCOM 2007, you can view the reports directly from the SCVMM administration console. This is great because you don't need to move out of the same console you use to manage VMs.

AUDIT COLLECTION SERVICES (ACS)

ACS is a high-performance, secure solution that collects and stores events from the security event log on monitored computers. Events are stored in a separate ACS database (discussed later in this chapter) in Microsoft SQL Server 2005. ACS collects all events written to the security event log on computers for which you've enabled ACS Forwarder. Events are forwarded from monitored computers to the ACS Collector, which runs on a management server and which processes them and writes them to the ACS database. Forwarders transmit events in an encrypted, near-real-time fashion to the collector. A separate component, ACS Reporting, is then used to generate reports from the stored ACS data.

Proxy Agent

SCOM 2007 can monitor network devices via Simple Network Management Protocol (SNMP) v2, computers that aren't running a Windows operating system, and computers without agents. In these cases, another computer that has an agent installed is performing the monitoring remotely. The computer that performs the remote monitoring is called a *proxy agent*. The agent that acts as a proxy for monitoring other devices is a standard SCOM agent: You merely configure it differently by selecting the Allow This Agent To Act As A Proxy And Discover Managed Objects And Other Computers option in the Agent Properties. Then, you configure the agentless managed device to designate the proxy agent it's to use.

SCOM 2007 Command Shell

The SCOM 2007 command shell interface includes an interactive prompt and a scripting environment that you can use independently or in combination. The command shell is a grouping of 203 individual cmdlets that have been specifically developed for automating SCOM administrative tasks. You can install the command shell on any computer that will have the operations console installed, which ensures that the prerequisites for the command shell are loaded on the system. You can query the cmdlets on any system in the command shell installed by typing **get-OperationsManagerCommand**; this gives you a list of the cmdlets. Each cmdlet comes with detailed help information.

We've gone through a lot of concepts, but each SCOM component fulfills specific roles with needed functionality. It's important to understand the roles each component plays in providing rich management functionality. Now that you have the SCOM 2007 core concepts under your belt, it's time to concentrate on enabling SCOM to manage the Microsoft virtualization infrastructure.

Using SCOM for Your Virtualization Environment

Either you're deploying a Microsoft virtualization environment or you're far along in the planning of the environment, and it's time to consider how the virtualization environment will work with SCOM. Consider the two most common deployment scenarios for SCOM 2007 for managing virtual environments, each with various levels of effort associated to integrate SCOM 2007:

Scenario 1 You're deploying a new SCOM 2007 environment to manage existing servers/applications and new or existing virtualization components. This scenario requires you to deploy an SCOM 2007 infrastructure for physical and virtual systems, and you must go through the SCOM 2007 architecture design, scalability, and topology process. By following this process, you'll design an infrastructure that not only meets the existing systems' management needs but can also scale to new requirements for managed systems.

Scenario 2 An SCOM 2007 environment is already deployed in the enterprise for monitoring existing systems. In this case, you're adding any management packs for applications that you'll run in VMs. The next step is to configure SCVMM PRO functionality that uses SCOM 2007, which will add additional management packs and reports for the virtualization environment.

TIP In most large enterprises, a separation exists between the virtualization engineering function and the system management team. So, any discussion to deploy a new management platform is a joint exercise between groups. This can become a long process, full of engineering rigor and integration of the new management platform into existing IT processes. Don't plan for it to be quick.

NOTE The assumption is that you are deploying not only Hyper-V or Virtual Server 2005 R2 SP1 but SCVMM as well. Deploying SCVMM is a critical component in managing a Microsoft virtual environment and generally is the first management software deployed unless you have an existing SCOM environment.

Before we walk through the processes associated with these scenarios, let's identify the critical virtualization components that SCOM 2007 will manage and the components needed to manage them effectively. SCOM needs a management pack that has knowledge, rules, tasks, and reports associated with the managed component.

It's important that as a virtualization administrator, you separate the management packs needed to manage the Microsoft virtualization environment from additional application and operating system management packs. You can download the base operating system management packs as well as management packs for Microsoft Server applications here: `http://technet` `.microsoft.com/en-us/opsmgr/cc539535.aspx`.

The management packs needed for the Microsoft virtual environment are shipped with SCVMM. The process of configuring the PRO functionality to work with SCOM 2007, covered in Chapter 12, adds those management packs to the SCOM 2007 infrastructure automatically. See Table 13.1 for all managed components and associated SCOM management packs that must be added to SCOM to manage the components.

TABLE 13.1 MANAGED MICROSOFT VIRTUALIZATION COMPONENTS

MANAGED COMPONENTS	SCOM MANAGEMENT PACK (NEEDED)	ADDITIONAL COMPONENT DETAILS
Hyper-V hosts	Hardware-specific management packs from server vendors (Dell, HP)	Management pack for monitoring physical hardware attributes.
Windows Server 2008	2008 operating system management pack	Management pack for the core operating system and base performance rules and thresholds.

TABLE 13.1 MANAGED MICROSOFT VIRTUALIZATION COMPONENTS *(CONTINUED)*

MANAGED COMPONENTS	SCOM MANAGEMENT PACK (NEEDED)	ADDITIONAL COMPONENT DETAILS
SCVMM 2008	SCVMM 2008 management pack and Reports pack	Management pack includes all SCVMM components: database server, self-service portal, SCVMM server, library servers, and rules and thresholds for all managed virtual platforms. This also includes the virtualization reports that are available in the SCVMM administration console.
Quick Migration clusters	2008 cluster management pack	Specific to failover clusters, not Quick Migration directly.
VM application workloads	Various application management packs, Exchange, SQL, SharePoint	Deployed management packs depend on applications running in the VMs. These include any PRO packs made for specific applications.

Scenario 1: Deploying a New SCOM Environment

When you deploy a new Microsoft virtualization infrastructure and a new SCOM 2007 infrastructure to manage that environment, you must consider the planning and design aspects. Certain tools are available to facilitate the planning process, such as System Center Capacity Planner 2007, which can help you determine the physical server's needs for a new SCOM 2007 environment. In addition, you can use tools like the Microsoft Assessment and Planning toolkit to discover physical servers and VMs that will be managed by SCOM 2007. Determining the number of servers to manage is critical to determining needed SCOM 2007 capacity, because each managed machine, physical or virtual, needs an SCOM agent.

System Center Capacity Planner 2007 can help you model a new SCOM 2007 infrastructure that matches the needed management capacity for all SCOM server roles. It includes a capacity planning model for SCOM 2007 that allows you to take into account multiple datacenters in the final architecture deployment model. You can download System Center Capacity Planner 2007 from www.microsoft.com/systemcenter/en/us/capacity-planner.aspx.

You're deploying a new SCOM 2007 environment to manage existing servers/applications and new or existing virtualization components. You need to determine the number of hosts for which you need management capacity, including virtual and physical systems. Strictly from an SCOM perspective, it doesn't matter if the managed host is physical or virtual. If the needed management packs are imported into the SCOM infrastructure and an SCOM agent is deployed to the endpoint, all systems are considered under management.

Determine the number of Hyper-V hosts and VMs to be managed by SCOM 2007. This is an important step because this number may drive the deployment of additional SCOM servers. Although this step is important for SCOM, planning it is usually tackled during normal virtualization deployment planning.

Tools are available to help you determine what existing systems you have in your environment and which systems are good virtualization candidates. Those same tools can help you with VM density planning as well. An example of a tool on the market that offers this capability for Microsoft virtualization environments is Novell PowerRecon.

TIP An excellent tool to use is the free Microsoft Assessment and Planning (MAP) toolkit V3.2. The MAP tool inventories existing systems via an agentless discovery mechanism and makes recommendations about the number of physical Hyper-V hosts and VM density. You can also use MAP to determine the number of virtual hosts and VMs you'll need to account for in SCOM deployments. You can find MAP at http://technet.microsoft.com/en-us/library/bb977556.aspx.

Using System Center Capacity Planner

Now that you have some idea of the number of systems you'll need to manage with SCOM, it's time to design an infrastructure to provide those management services. This can be a very time-consuming, intimidating process—even more so because as a virtualization administrator, you may be new to SCOM. A tool is available to simply the process, thanks to the systems-management gods. System Center Capacity Manager 2007 includes a model for SCOM 2007 and a design wizard that steps you through design decisions. Let's walk through the steps you can take using System Center Capacity Planner 2007 to determine the SCOM 2007 infrastructure for managing your new virtualization deployment:

NOTE The System Center Capacity Planning Wizard is as accurate as the data you provide for the number of managed hosts. It's a good idea to not just depend on automated collection tools but also query and survey application-development leads for large application projects that will affect the number of servers deployed.

1. Download and install System Center Capacity Planner 2007. Launch the application, and the initial screen will appear, as shown in Figure 13.1:

FIGURE 13.1
Initial System Center Capacity Planner view

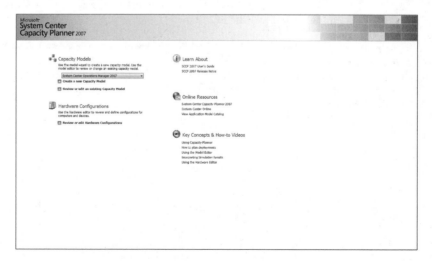

2. Under Capacity Models, select System Center Operations Model from the drop-down menu, and then click the Create A New Capacity Model link in the same section.

3. The wizard for the modeling phase opens (see Figure 13.2).

FIGURE 13.2

Add a new management group

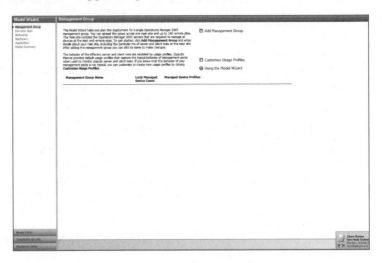

4. Click the green arrow next to Add Management Group. On the next screen, the New Management Group section appears.

5. In the New Management Group section, name your model and begin to enter the number of managed devices (see Figure 13.3). This number should include the number of physical Hyper-V hosts as well as VMs that will have an SCOM 2007 agent deployed. Also, choose whether you'll use SAN storage for the SCOM 2007 Server roles and if you plan to manage client operating systems (not outside the realm of possibility with VDI deployments in the virtual world).

FIGURE 13.3

Select New Management Group settings and the number of managed devices

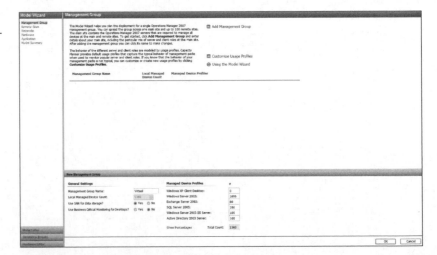

6. After you enter the required number of hosts and name the management group, you must add any additional sites, such as another datacenter where you'll have Hyper-V hosts and VMs (see Figure 13.4). Add the additional site, the required number of hosts, and the site name, and click Next.

FIGURE 13.4
Remote site information

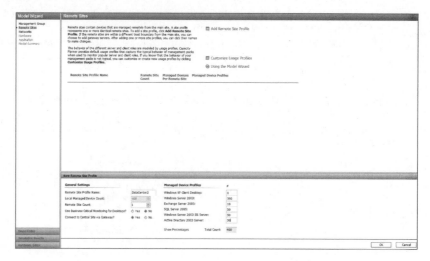

7. In the Networks section, choose how sites are connected, and specify the available bandwidth. You can select either a dedicated site-to-site link or a shared WAN (see Figure 13.5).

FIGURE 13.5
Add network information

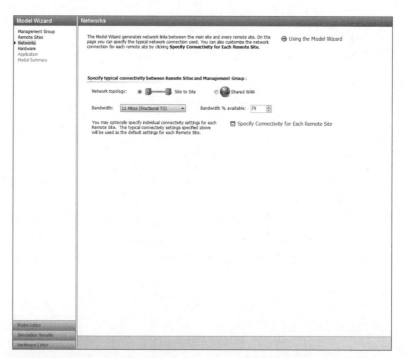

8. Under Hardware, choose the specific hardware configuration for the various SCOM 2007 server roles: management servers, database server, and disks types for storage configuration (see Figure 13.6).

You may already have hardware standards for configuring specific servers—especially database servers. You should check with those service owners to understand the base hardware configurations in use so you can use this knowledge in the SCOM design. In addition, most of those service owners control configuration of those services, so in some cases all you have to provide is the size of the database, the storage needed, and a growth factor all for this Capacity Planner assists you with.

FIGURE 13.6
Hardware configuration by SCOM server role

TIP Understanding the SAN storage layout and disk types in use requires you to have a talk with your company's storage engineering group to get this information. This may be a good time to introduce the project to them and give them a heads-up about storage needs for your SCOM 2007 servers.

Let's move on to the Application section in the model, where you'll determine the items that will drive additional SCOM 2007 management server counts (see Figure 13.7). Let's examine those items in detail.

FIGURE 13.7
Application
configurations

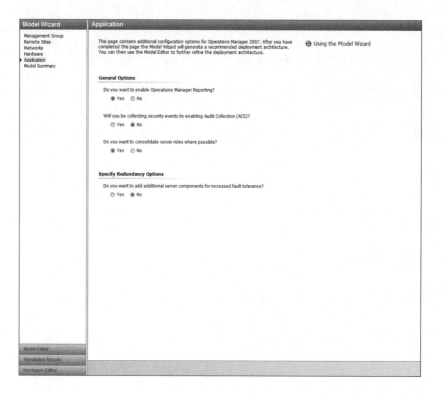

In the General Options section are the following items:

Do you want to enable Operations Manager Reporting?   Choose this option to deliver scheduled reports of managed machine health and status. Most management packs come with predefined reports.

Will you be collecting security events by enabling Audit Collection (ACS)?   If you plan to collect security events from managed machines for analysis by a security team, then you should consider the use of this feature.

Do you want to consolidate server roles where possible?   Running multiple SCOM 2007 roles on a single server reduces the needed number of servers. This approach complicates SCOM recovery in case of failure. Instead of a single role being down, like a reporting server, a physical server with several roles affects multiple roles when planned or unplanned down-time happens. Therefore, this option isn't recommended for enterprise deployments.

NOTE   System Center Capacity Manager 2007 makes best-practice recommendations to ensure the Reporting Server role and the Management Server role aren't on the same server.

Specify Redundancy Options   In order to provide fault tolerance, you can have additional servers functioning as management servers and provide a cluster for the SCOM 2007 database back-ends. Doing so provides failover support in event of hardware failure.

After you finish the Application section, you're presented with your model summary, which includes the number of sites, managed machines, and SCOM servers needed to provide capacity to manage the required number of devices (see Figure 13.8).

FIGURE 13.8

Model summary

You can now run a simulation that shows you potential performance bottlenecks in the model you outlined (see Figure 13.9). You can change the performance settings by clicking the Update Settings link under the Thresholds section.

FIGURE 13.9
Simulation results

The last step in the process is to look at the global topology (see Figure 13.10) as well as the site topology (see Figure 13.11) and save the architectural model. This is your actual layout of your SCOM 2007 topology. You can refine the model as your SCOM infrastructure grows and requirements change. You now have a plan that includes the number of servers as well as the actual configuration of each by SCOM 2007 role.

FIGURE 13.10
Global Topology

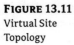

FIGURE 13.11
Virtual Site
Topology

1. Install and configure SCOM 2007 servers and roles based on the plan from Capacity Planner 2007. We won't cover the detailed SCOM installation process in this chapter, but you can find detailed instructions at `http://technet.microsoft.com/en-us/library/bb381350.aspx`.

2. Import management packs into the new SCOM 2007 infrastructure. This is a critical step: You want to make sure you have the latest reports and health models for applications you plan to run and manage in your environment. Use Table 13.1 as a guide, but remember that the SCVMM management packs are loaded automatically when you configure the integration between SCVMM and SCOM.

3. Determine the SCOM agent deployment process for new physical and virtual machines. Because you're doing a new deployment and there is no existing process for installing SCOM agents, you should consider the SCOM agent as base software that is installed on each server (physical or virtual) in your environment. Agents can use the current process you have for installing antivirus and backup software. Those software agents are typically integrated directly into the build process and ecosystem.

Even if you install the SCOM agent manually, you still need to run the discovery process before you add the managed endpoint to the management group. For automated agent installation from the SCOM console, we recommend that you use the automated discovery process provided by SCOM.

4. The Computer And Device Management Wizard lets you choose between two options: scan an entire domain for all systems, or use advanced discovery options that let you specify types of systems to look for (servers or clients; see Figure 13.12).

5. The last part of the process is specifying an account to use to install the SCOM agent: either the default actions account or another domain account with administrative privileges on the endpoint to be managed.

FIGURE 13.12
Computer And
Device Manage-
ment Wizard scan
options

FIGURE 13.12
Computer And
Device Manage-
ment Wizard scan
options

For VMs, because we're talking about an existing SCOM 2007 deployment, an agent deployment process is already in place. Either you're using the standard domain-discovery process, or you're installing the SCOM agent as part of a standardized build process.

The VM build process offers some additional flexibilities. Typical VMs are built from a Syspreped VHD file that's already created. In this instance, you can stage the SCOM agent on the VHD file and silently install it after the mini Sysprep wizard runs. After the agent is installed on the system, manual and automated SCOM discovery can discover the system and add it to the relevant computer group.

You can configure SCVMM PRO functionality to work with the existing SCOM 2007 deployment. Determine whether PRO packs are available for applications you'll run in VMs, and deploy the PRO packs into the SCVMM and SCOM 2007 environment. (See Chapter 11 for detailed instructions for setting up SCOM and SCVMM PRO functionality.)

Scenario 2: SCOM Already Deployed

Now, let's dive into the deployment process for SCOM 2007 for a Microsoft virtual environment. If you already have an SCOM environment deployed into your infrastructure, you'll be interested in the components you can deploy into your environment for additional or new capabilities. SCOM can be used as the single console solution for doing enterprise management or as the driven, task-oriented component that can forward rich alerts into an existing enterprise management solution.

To deploy SCOM, you must work with your systems management counterparts to deploy the necessary components. If you're deploying a new SCOM 2007 environment, then you may require more detailed collaboration between groups. If you work in a small to medium enterprise, you may be in charge of not only the virtualization deployment but the operational management tools as well.

We'll drill into this scenario to make sure we cover all bases. You've decided to deploy virtualization in your environment because of all the great things it provides: better server-asset utilization, workload migration, and deployment flexibility. You're going to deploy Hyper-V and SCVMM to manage the Hyper-V environment, and you want to use your existing SCOM 2007 environment. Let's walk through the process of connecting SCOM and your virtualization deployment.

You must determine the number of Hyper-V hosts and VMs that will be managed by SCOM 2007. This is an important step because this number may drive the deployment of additional SCOM servers. Although this step is important for SCOM, planning it is usually tackled during normal virtualization deployment planning.

Tools are available to help you determine what existing systems you have in your environment and which systems are good virtualization candidates. Those tools can help you with VM density planning as well. An example of a tool on the market that offers this capability for Microsoft virtualization environments is Novell PowerRecon.

TIP   An excellent tool to use is the free MAP toolkit V3.2. The MAP tool inventories existing systems via an agentless discovery mechanism and makes recommendations about the number of physical Hyper-V hosts and VM density. You can also use MAP to determine the number of virtual hosts and VMs you'll need to account for in SCOM deployments. You can find MAP at http://technet.microsoft.com/en-us/library/bb977556.aspx.

In this scenario, you already have SCOM 2007 deployed, so you can use the Virtualization Candidates report to find under-utilized servers that are being managed by SCOM 2007. To use the Virtualization Candidates report, follow these steps:

1. If you don't already have Reporting Services installed in SCOM, you'll have to install it before you can use the Virtualization Candidates report. You can find detailed Reporting Services installation instructions at http://technet.microsoft.com/en-us/library/bb381267.aspx.

2. Download and install the SCVMM 2008 Reports management pack.

3. Import the SCVMM 2008 Reports management pack into SCOM (see Figure 13.13).

FIGURE 13.13
Importing the Reports management pack

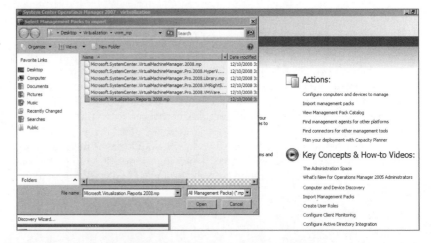

4. You're ready to run the report either from the SCOM console under the Reports section or from the SCVMM administration console. Running reports from the SCVMM administration console requires that you've configured the Reporting option in SCVMM (see Figure 13.14).

5. Select the Virtualization Candidates report, and fill in the parameters (CPU, Memory, DISK, and Network) for what you consider an underutilized physical machine (see Figure 13.15).

FIGURE 13.14
Virtualization reports

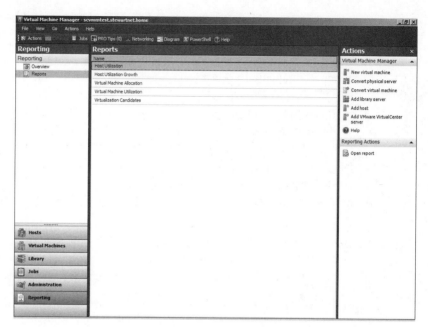

FIGURE 13.15
Virtualization Candidates report

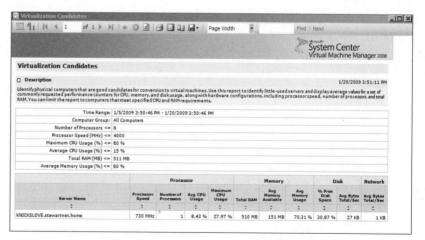

You can use the Virtualization Candidates report to determine the number of physical systems you'll virtualize. In addition, to giving you an idea of the number of potential VMs, you can use this report to generate P2V lists.

6. Create a list of additional management packs that need to be deployed into an existing SCOM environment to support the virtualization components. This process comes down to understanding the types of server applications you do or will run in the virtualized environment.

In this scenario, because you have an SCOM 2007 environment running, you already have management packs imported in the environment and managing server applications. The only additional management packs you need are any for new server applications and SCVMM management packs for managing the virtual environment. VM management packs are added automatically when you configure the PRO functionality. (See Chapter 11 for the steps involved in configuring PRO.)

7. Coordinate with the SCOM 2007 administrators to review the additional number of systems identified that need SCOM 2007 agents. Either the needed capacity fits into the existing SCOM environment, or you add existing management servers to meet the additional demand.

Consider the agent-deployment process for VMs. Because we're talking about an existing SCOM 2007 deployment, an agent deployment is already in place. Either you're using the standard domain-discovery process or you're installing the SCOM agent as part of a standardized build process.

The VM build process offers some additional flexibilities. Typical VMs are built from a Syspreped VHD file that's already created. In this instance, you can stage the SCOM agent on the VHD file and silently install it after the mini Sysprep wizard runs. After the agent is installed on the system, manual and automated SCOM discovery can discover the system and add it to the relevant computer group.

You can configure SCVMM PRO functionality to work with the existing SCOM 2007 deployment. Determine whether PRO packs are available for applications you'll run in VMs, and deploy the PRO packs into the SCVMM and SCOM 2007 environment. (See Chapter 11 for detailed instructions for setting up SCOM and SCVMM PRO functionality.)

Monitoring and Reporting

Now that you've deployed agents to all the physical and virtual machines, all machines with an agent are being managed by SCOM. What does it mean to be *managed*? All the talk about models and management packs starts to come to life now. The knowledge from the management packs is deployed to the managed systems.

Take, for instance, a managed SQL Server. The rules and health model from the imported SQL management pack are deployed to the system, and all SQL events and services are monitored for health. If one of the SQL components isn't functioning correctly, the SQL service shows up as unhealthy until the condition is corrected.

Let's explore managed systems and the systems' health. Now that you have managed systems, you can look at the initial state of the managed machines by going to the Administration tab on the SCOM console and selecting Agent Managed (see Figure 13.16).

FIGURE 13.16
Managed
system state

You can also get a quick overview of the systems' state by selecting the Monitoring tab (see Figure 13.17). This view shows you alerts, the state of the managed systems, and specific types of managed services and applications.

FIGURE 13.17
Monitoring view

We've been discussing the idea of a health model; but how do you drill into the health model of a managed endpoint? You can do so by using the Health Explorer in SCOM (see Figure 13.18), which you access from the Action menu. It lets you drill into the monitors for the managed systems and determine health. You can see the exact monitors that run and determine which monitor specifically is failing if the service or system is listed as unhealthy.

FIGURE 13.18
Health Explorer

FIGURE 13.18
Health Explorer

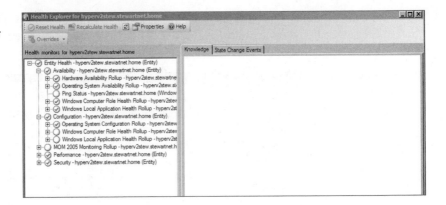

SCOM also allows you to run tasks on all managed systems. If you're alerted to a problem on a system, you can perform some tasks directly from the SCOM console to discern and pinpoint issues. You can even use the remote-desktop functionality directly from the SCOM console Task menu to troubleshoot an alert generated in SCOM. You access the tasks from the Action menu (see Figure 13.19 and Figure 13.20).

FIGURE 13.19
Tasks for managed systems

FIGURE 13.20
Completed
SCOM task

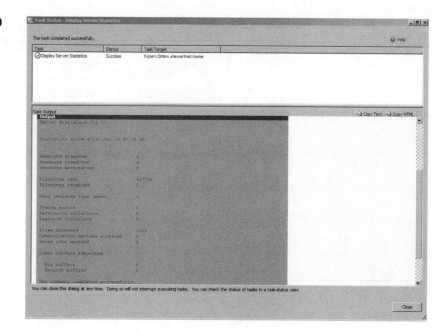

The SCOM reporting infrastructure provides rich reports for managed endpoints. It's important to understand that these structured reports come from the management packs for specific applications and services. Most, if not all, management packs provide reports with the health models and service-application knowledge. When the reporting infrastructure is in place, each time you import a management pack with reports, those reports are available to be run from within the SCOM console on the Reporting tab.

For this section, we'll concentrate on reports for the managed virtualization environment. System Center Virtual Manager provides the Reports management pack that is imported into the SCOM environment. This management pack isn't imported automatically during the configuration of SCOM SCVMM integration like the PRO management packs; virtualization reports must be downloaded and imported separately.

After you import the reports into the SCOM infrastructure, they're available to run. You can run them from within SCOM console; or, with the integration between SCOM and SCVMM, you can run them directly from the SCVMM administration console. Before you can run the reports from the SCVMM console, you must configure the SCOM server, enable reporting, and add the reporting server URL (see Figure 13.21).

After you add the reports, they're listed on the Reporting tab in the SCVMM administration console (see Figure 13.22).

FIGURE 13.21
Configuring reporting in SCVMM

FIGURE 13.22
Reports in SCVMM

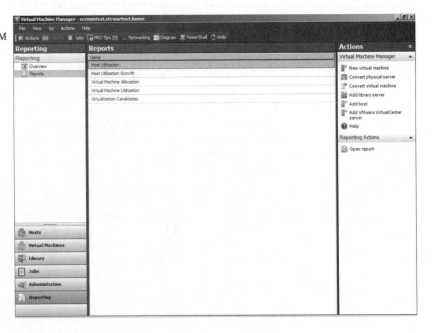

The following virtualization reports are available:

◆ Host Utilization (see Figure 13.23)

◆ Host Utilization Growth (see Figure 13.24)

◆ Virtual Machine Allocation (see Figure 13.25)

◆ Virtual Machine Utilization (see Figure 13.26)

◆ Virtualization Candidates

FIGURE 13.23
Host Utilization
report

FIGURE 13.24
Host Utilization
Growth report

FIGURE 13.25
Virtual Machine
Allocation report

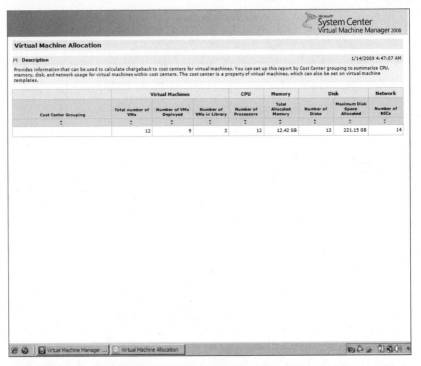

FIGURE 13.26
Virtual Machine
Utilization report

You can use all of these reports to make proactive decisions about the capacity needed or used in your Microsoft virtualization environment. You can even use the Virtual Machine Allocation report to create a chargeback report that you can use to report and charge virtualization capacity usage by cost center. On the Host Utilization report, you can drill into the performance charts and VMs running on a host.

Summary

SCOM 2007 brings critical functionality to managing the Microsoft virtualization environment, such as real-time alerting, reporting, and application knowledge. As you can see from this chapter, planning the SCOM 2007 environment with your virtualization deployment in mind will help ensure that you have the needed management capacity. SCOM 2007 in combination with SCVMM and the PRO functionality provides a rich 360-degree view of your VMs and other critical virtualization components.

Index

Note to the Reader: Throughout this index **boldfaced** page numbers indicate primary discussions of a topic. *Italicized* page numbers indicate illustrations.